RETRIEVING THE
American Past

A CUSTOMIZED U.S. HISTORY READER

Primary Readings
HIS 101
Chesapeake College

Pearson Learning Solutions

New York   Boston   San Francisco
London   Toronto   Sydney   Tokyo   Singapore   Madrid
Mexico City   Munich   Paris   Cape Town   Hong Kong   Montreal

Senior Vice President, Editorial and Marketing: Patrick F. Boles
Senior Sponsoring Editor: Natalie Danner
Development Editor: Mary Kate Paris
Editorial Assistant: Jill Johnson
Marketing Manager: Nathan Wilbur
Operations Manager: Eric M. Kenney
Production Manager: Jennifer Berry
Rights Manager: Jillian Santos
Art Director and Cover Designer: Renée Sartell

Cover Art: Courtesy of Library of Congress and the Chicago History Museum.

Please visit our websites at *www.pearsoncustom.com*.

Attention bookstores: For permission to return any unsold stock, contact us at *pe-uscustomreturns@pearson.com*.

Pearson Learning Solutions, 501 Boylston Street, Suite 900, Boston, MA 02116
A Pearson Education Company
www.pearsoned.com

ISBN 10: 0-536-87684-3
ISBN 13: 978-0-536-87684-3

CONTRIBUTORS

Senior Editor
Mitch Lerner

Managing Editor
David Staley

Copy Editor
Ann Heiss

Assistant Managing Editor
William Sturkey

Contributing Editors

Tyler Anbinder
Kenneth J. Andrien
Jean Harvey Baker
Michael Les Benedict
Mansel Blackford
Paul C. Bowers
Rowland Brucken
John D. Buenker
John C. Burnham
Joan E. Cashin
William R. Childs
Albert J. Churella
Steven Conn
Saul Cornell
Nick Cullather
Jeanette Davis
Merton L. Dillon
Daniel Feller
Charles Coleman Finlay
Emily Greenwald
Mark Grimsley
Bernard N. Grindel
Peter L. Hahn
James Hansen
Susan M. Hartmann
Mary Ann Heiss
Earl J. Hess
Michael J. Hogan
R. Douglas Hurt

Bruce Karhoff
Michael Kazin
Terence Kehoe
K. Austin Kerr
Frank Lambert
Valerie Mendoza
James McCaffrey
Allan R. Millett
Pamela J. Mills
Daniel Nelson
Margaret E. Newell
Josef Ostyn
Carla Gardina Pestana
Patrick D. Reagan
Randolph A. Roth
Hal K. Rothman
John A. M. Rothney
Leila J. Rupp
Richard D. Shiels
David Sicilia
C. Edward Skeen
Amy L. S. Staples
David L. Stebenne
David Steigerwald
Marshall F. Stevenson, Jr.
Warren R. Van Tine
Christopher Waldrep
J. Samuel Walker

Your *Retrieving the American Past* purchase includes access to online resources designed to complement your readings. This Companion Website is located at the following URL:

http://www.pearsoncustom.com/dbrtap/rtap/student

When prompted, enter the User Name: **rtapstudent** and Password: **rtaplearn**

(*Note:* The User Name and Password are case-sensitive, so be sure to use upper and lower case characters exactly as shown above.)

Once logged in, you will have access to the following resources:

- *Link Library.* A collection of vetted web links, organized by key terms and historical figures, which offer you background and context for many of the selections you'll be reading.

- *Documents.* Access (via links) to the full text of historical documents, which can furnish a backdrop to events that might have preceded, or followed, their drafting.

- *The Writing Process.* Advice that can aid you during the writing process. Included are guidelines and suggestions for each phase of writing, from start to finish.

- *Plagiarism.* Suggestions to help you maintain academic honesty, with illustrative examples.

- *Style Guide.* A brief guide to help you follow either MLA or Chicago Manual styles in citing your sources. The Modern Language Association style is widely used for papers in English composition, literature, and foreign languages. History, the fine arts, and some fields in the humanities (but not literature) use traditional footnotes or endnotes, which should conform to standards set by *The Chicago Manual of Style.*

We invite you to explore!

Contents

Chapter I

[THE SEPARATIST INTERPRETATION OF THE REFORMATION IN ENGLAND, 1550-1607]

It is well known unto the godly and judicious, how ever since the first breaking out of the light of the gospel in our honourable nation of England, (which was the first of nations whom the Lord adorned therewith after the gross darkness of popery which had covered and overspread the Christian world), what wars and oppositions ever since, Satan hath raised, maintained and continued against the Saints, from time to time, in one sort or other. Sometimes by bloody death and cruel torments; other whiles imprisonments, banishments and other hard usages; as being loath his kingdom should go down, the truth prevail and the churches of God revert to their ancient purity and recover their primitive order, liberty and beauty.

But when he could not prevail by these means against the main truths of the gospel, but that they began to take rooting in many places, being watered with the blood of the martyrs and blessed from Heaven with a gracious increase; he then began to take him to his ancient stratagems, used of old against the first Christians. That when by the bloody and barbarous persecutions of the heathen emperors he could not stop and subvert the course of the gospel, but that it speedily overspread, with a wonderful celerity, the then best known parts of the world; he then began to sow errours, heresies and wonderful dissensions amongst the professors themselves, working upon their pride and ambition, with other corrupt passions incident to all mortal men, yea to the saints themselves in some measure, by which woeful effects followed. As not only bitter contentions and heartburnings, schisms, with other horrible confusions; but Satan took occasion and advantage thereby to foist in a number of vile ceremonies, with many unprofitable canons and decrees, which have since been as snares to many poor and peaceable souls even to this day.

So as in the ancient times, the persecutions by the heathen and their emperors was not greater than of the Christians one against other:-the Arians and other their complices against the orthodox and true Christians. As witnesseth Socrates in his second book. His words are these:

The violence truly (saith he) was no less than that of old practiced towards the Christians when they were compelled and drawn to sacrifice to idols; for many endured sundry kinds of torment often rackings and dismembering of their joints, confiscating of their goods; some bereaved of their native soil, others departed this life under the hands of the tormentor, and some died in banishment and never saw their country again, etc.

The like method Satan hath seemed to hold in these later times, since the truth began to spring and spread after the great defection made by Antichrist, that man of sin.

For to let pass the infinite examples in sundry nations and several places of the world, and instance in our own, when as that old serpent could not prevail by those fiery flames and other his cruel tragedies, which he by his instruments put in ure everywhere in the days of Queen Mary and before, he then began another kind of war and went more closely to work; not only to oppugn but even to ruinate and destroy the kingdom of Christ by more secret and subtle means, by kindling the flames of contention and sowing the seeds of discord and bitter enmity amongst the professors and, seeming reformed, themselves. For when he could not prevail by the former means against the principal doctrines of faith, he bent his force against the holy discipline and outward regiment of the kingdom of Christ, by which those holy doctrines should be conserved, and true piety maintained amongst the saints and people of God.

Mr. Fox recordeth how that besides those worthy martyrs and confessors which were burned in Queen Mary's days and otherwise tormented, "Many (both students and others) fled out of the land to the number of 800, and became several congregations, at Wesel, Frankfort, Basel, Emden, Markpurge, Strasburg and Geneva, etc." Amongst whom (but especially those at Frankfort) began that bitter war of contention and persecution about the ceremonies and service book, and other popish and antichristian stuff, the plague of England to this day, which are like the high places in Israel which the prophets cried out against, and were their ruin. Which the better part sought, according to the purity of the gospel, to root out and utterly to abandon. And the other part (under veiled presences) for their own ends and advancements sought as stiffly to continue, maintain and defend. As appeareth by the discourse thereof published in print, anno 1575; a book that deserves better to be known and considered.

The one side laboured to have the right worship of God and discipline of Christ established in the-church, according to the simplicity of the gospel, without the mixture of men's inventions; and to have and to be ruled by the laws of God's Word, dispensed in those offices, and by those officers of Pastors, Teachers and Elders, etc. according to the Scriptures. The other party, though under many colours and presences, endeavoured to have the episcopal dignity (after the popish manner) with their large power and jurisdiction still retained; with all those courts, canons and ceremonies, together with all such livings, revenues and subordinate officers, with other such means as formerly upheld their antichristian greatness and enabled them with lordly and tyrannous power to persecute the poor servants of God. This contention was so great, as neither the honour of God, the common persecution, nor the mediation of Mr. Calvin and other worthies of the Lord in those places, could prevail with those thus episcopally minded; but they proceeded by all means to disturb the peace of this poor persecuted church, even so far as to charge (very unjustly and ungodlily yet prelatelike) some of their chief opposers with rebellion and high treason against the Emperor, and other such crimes.

And this contention died not with Queen Mary, nor was left beyond the seas. But at her death these people returning into England under gracious Queen Elizabeth, many of them being preferred to bishoprics and other promotions according to their aims and desires, that inveterate hatred against the holy discipline of Christ in His church hath continued to this day. Insomuch that for fear it should prevail, all plots and devices have been used to keep it out incensing the Queen and State against it as dangerous for the commonwealth; and that it was most needful that the fundamental points of religion should be preached in those ignorant and superstitious times. And to win the weak and ignorant they might retain divers harmless ceremonies, and though it were to be wished that divers things were reformed, yet this was not a season for it. And many the like to stop the mouths of the more godly, to bring them on to yield to one ceremony after another, and one corruption after another; by these wiles beguiling some and corrupting others till at length they began to persecute all the zealous professors in the land (though they knew little what this discipline meant) both by word arid deed, if they would not submit to their ceremonies and become slaves to them and their popish trash, which have no ground in the Word of God, but are relics of that man of sin. And the more the light of the gospel grew, the more they urged their subscriptions to these corruptions. So as (notwithstanding all their former presences and fair colours) they whose eyes God had not justly blinded might easily see whereto these things tended. And to cast contempt the more upon the sincere servants of God, they opprobriously and most injuriously gave unto and imposed upon them that name of Puritans, which is said the Novatians out of pride did assume and take unto themselves. And lamentable it is to see the effects which have followed. Religion hath been disgraced, the godly grieved, afflicted, persecuted, and many exiled; sundry have lost their lives in prisons and other ways. On the other hand, sin hath been countenanced; ignorance, profaneness and atheism increased, and the papists encouraged to hope again for a day.

This made that holy man Mr. Perkins cry out in his exhortation to repentance, upon Zephaniah ii:

Religion (saith he) hath been amongst us this thirty-five years; but the more it is published, the more it is contemned and reproached of many, etc. Thus not profaneness nor wickedness but religion itself is a byword, a mockingstock, and a matter of reproach; so that in England at this day the man or woman that begins to profess religion and to serve God, must resolve with himself to sustain mocks and injuries even as though he lived amongst the enemies of religion.

And this, common experience hath confirmed and made too apparent. But that I may come more near my intendment.

When as by the travail and diligence of some godly and zealous preachers, and God's blessing on their labours, as in other places of the land, so in the North parts, many became enlightened by the Word of God and had their ignorance and sins discovered unto them, and began by His grace to reform their lives and make conscience of their was, the work of God was no sooner manifest in them but presently they were both scoffed and scorned by the profane multitude; and the ministers urged with the yoke of subscription, or else must be silenced. And the poor people were so vexed with apparitors and pursuivants and the commissary courts, as truly their affliction was not small. Which, notwithstanding, they bore sundry years with much patience, till they were occasioned by the continuance and increase of these troubles, and other means which the Lord raised up in those days, to see further into things by the light of the Word of God. How not only these base and beggarly ceremonies were unlawful, but also that the lordly and tyrannous power of the prelates ought not to be submitted unto; which thus, contrary to the freedom of the gospel, would load and burden men's consciences and by their compulsive power make a profane mixture of persons and things in the worship of God. And that their offices and callings, courts and canons, etc. were unlawful and antichristian: being such as have no warrant in the Word of God, but the same that were used in popery and still retained. Of which a famous author thus writeth in his Dutch commentaries, at the coming of King James into England:

The new king (saith he) found there established the reformed religion according to the reformed religion of King Edward VI, retaining or keeping still the spiritual state of the bishops, etc. after the old manner, much varying and differing from the reformed churches in Scotland, France and the Netherlands, Ernden, Geneva, etc., whose reformation is cut, or shapen much nearer the first Christian churches, as it was used in the Apostles' time.

So many, therefore, of these professors as saw the evil of these things in these parts, and whose hearts the Lord had touched with heavenly zeal for His truth, they shook off this yoke of antichristian bondage, and as the Lord's free people joined themselves (by a covenant of the Lord) into a church estate, in the fellowship of the gospel, to walk in all His ways made known, or to be made known unto them, according to their best endeavours, whatsoever it should cost them, the Lord assisting them. And that it cost them something this ensuing history will declare.

These people became two distinct bodies or churches, and in regard of distance of place did congregate severally; for they were of sundry towns and villages, some in Nottinghamshire, some of Lincolnshire, and some of Yorkshire where they border nearest together. In one of these churches (besides others of note) was Mr. John Smith, a man of able gifts and a good preacher, who afterwards was chosen their pastor. But these afterwards falling into some errours in the Low Countries, there (for the most part) buried themselves and their names.

But in this other church (which must be the subject of our discourse) beside" other worthy men, was Mr. Richard Clyfton, a grave and reverend preacher, who by his pains and diligence had done much good, and under God had been a means of the conversion of many. And also that famous and worthy man Mr. John Robinson, who afterwards was their pastor for many years, till the Lord took him away by death. Also Mr. William Brewster a reverend man, who afterwards was chosen an elder of the church and lived with them till old age.

But after these things they could not bug continue in any peaceable condition, but were hunted and persecuted on every side, so as their former afflictions were but as fleabitings in comparison of these which now came upon them. For some were taken and clapped up in prison, others had their houses beset and watched night and day, and hardly escaped their hands; and the most were fain to flee and leave their houses and habitations, and the means of their livelihood.

Yet these and many other sharper things which afterward befell them, were no other than they looked for, and therefore were the better prepared to bear them by the assistance of God's grace and Spirit.

Yet seeing themselves thus molested, and that there was no hope of their continuance there, by a joint consent they resolved to go into the Low Countries, where they heard was freedom of religion for all men; as also how sundry from London and other parts of the land had been exiled and persecuted for the same cause, and were gone thither, and lived at Amsterdam and in other places of the land. So after they had continued together about a year, and kept their meetings every Sabbath in one place or other, exercising the worship of God amongst themselves, notwithstanding all the diligence and malice of their adversaries, they seeing they could no longer continue in that condition, they resolved to get over into Holland as they could. Which was in the year 1607 and 1608; of which more at large in the next chapter.

Chapter II

OF THEIR DEPARTURE INTO HOLLAND AND THEIR TROUBLES THEREABOUT,

WITH SOME OF THE MANY DIFFICULTIES THEY FOUND AND MET WITHAL. ANNO 1608

Being thus constrained to leave their native soil and country, their lands and livings, and all their friends and familiar acquaintance, it was much; and thought marvellous by many. But to go into a country they knew not but by hearsay, where they must learn a new language and get their livings they knew not how, it being a dear place and subject to the miseries of war, it was by many thought an adventure almost desperate; a case intolerable and a misery worse than death. Especially seeing they were not acquainted with trades nor traffic (by which that country cloth subsist) but had only been used to a plain country life and the innocent trade of husbandry. But these things did not dismay them, though they did sometimes trouble them; for their desires were set on the ways of God and to enjoy His ordinances; but they rested on His providence, and knew Whom they had believed. Yet this was not all, for though they could not stay, yet were they not suffered to go; but the ports and havens were shut against them, so as they were fain to seek secret means of conveyance, and to bribe and fee the mariners, and give extraordinary rates for their passages. And yet were they often times betrayed, many of them; and both they and their goods intercepted and surprised, and thereby put to great trouble and charge, of which I will give an instance or two and omit the rest.

There was a large company of them purposed to get passage at Boston in Lincolnshire, and for that end had hired a ship wholly to themselves and made agreement with the master to be ready at a certain day, and take them and their goods in at a convenient place, where they accordingly would all attend in readiness. So after long waiting and large expenses, though he kept not day with them, yet he came at length and took them in, in the night. But when he had them and their goods abroad, he betrayed them, having before hand complotted with the searchers and other officers to do; who took them, and put them into open boats, and there rifled and ransacked them, searching to their shirts for money, yea even the women further than became modesty; and then carried them back into the town and made them a spectacle and wonder to the multitude which came flocking on all sides to behold them. Being thus first, by these catchpoll officers rifled and stripped of their money; books and much other goods, they were presented to the magistrates, and messengers sent to inform the Lords of the Council of them; and so they were committed to ward. Indeed the magistrates used them courteously and showed them what favour they could; but could not deliver them till order came from the Council table. But the issue was that after a month's imprisonment the greatest part were dismissed and sent to the places from whence they came; but seven of the principal were still kept in prison and bound over to the assizes.

The next spring after, there was another attempt made by some of these and others to get over at another place. And it so fell out that they light of a Dutchman at Hull, having a ship of his own belonging to Zealand. They made agreement with him, and acquainted him with their condition, hoping to find more faithfulness in him than in the former of their own nation; he bade them not fear, for he would do well enough. He was by appointment to take them in between Grimsby and Hull, where was a large common a good way distant from any town. Now against the prefixed time, the women and children with the goods were sent to the place in a small bark which they had hired for that end; and the men were to meet them by land. But it so fell out that they were there a day before the ship came, and the sea being rough and the women very sick, prevailed with the seamen to put into a creek hard by where they lay on ground at low water. The next morning the ship came but they were fast and could not stir until about noon. In the meantime, the shipmaster, perceiving how the matter was, sent his boat to be getting the men aboard whom he saw ready, walking about the shore. But after the first boatful was got aboard and she was ready to go for more, the master espied a great company, both horse and foot, with bills and guns and other weapons, for the country was raised to take them. The Dutchman, seeing that, swore his country's oath sacremente, and having the wind fair, weighed his anchor, hoised sails, and away.

But the poor men which were got aboard were in great distress for their wives and children which they saw thus to be taken, and were left destitute of their helps; and themselves also, not having a cloth to shift them with, more than they had on their backs, and some scarce a penny about them, all they had being aboard the bark. It drew tears from their eyes, and anything they had they would have given to have been ashore again; but all in vain, there was no remedy, they must thus sadly part. And afterward endured a fearful storm at sea, being fourteen days or more before they arrived at their port; in seven whereof they neither saw sun, moon nor stars, and were driven near the coast of Norway; the mariners themselves often despairing of life, and once with shrieks and cries gave over all, as if the ship had been foundered in the sea and they sinking without recovery. But when man's hope and help wholly failed, the Lord's power and mercy appeared in their recovery; for the ship rose again and gave the mariners courage again to manage her. And if modesty would suffer me, I might declare with what fervent prayers they cried unto the Lord in this great distress (especially some of them) even without any great distraction. When the water ran into their mouths and ears and the mariners cried out, "We sink, we sink!" they cried (if not with miraculous, yet with a great height or degree of divine faith), "Yet Lord Thou canst save! Yet Lord Thou canst save!" with such other expressions as I will forbear. Upon which the ship did not only recover, but shortly after the violence of the storm began to abate, and the Lord filled their afflicted minds with such comforts as everyone cannot understand, and in the end brought them to their desired haven, where the people came flocking, admiring their deliverance; the storm having been so long and sore, in which much hurt had been done, as the master's friends related unto him in their congratulations.

But to return to the others where we left. The rest of the men that were in greatest danger made shift to escape away before the troop could surprise them, those only staying that best might be assistant unto the women. But pitiful it was to see the heavy case of these poor women in this distress; what weeping and crying on every side, some for their husbands 'lhat were carried away in the ship as is before related; others not knowing what should become of them and their little ones; others again melted in tears, seeing their poor little ones hanging about them, crying for fear and quaking with cold. Being thus apprehended, they were hurried from one place to another and from one justice to another, till in the end they knew not what to do with them; for to imprison so many women and innocent children for no other cause (many of them) but that they must go with their husbands, seemed to be unreasonable and all would cry out of them. And to send them home again was as difficult; for they alleged, as the truth was, they had no homes to go to, for they had either sold or otherwise disposed of their houses and livings. To be short, after they had been thus turmoiled a good while and conveyed from one constable to another, they were glad to be rid of them in the end upon any terms, for all were wearied and tired with them. Though in the meantime they (poor souls) endured misery enough; and thus in the end necessity forced a way for them.

But that I be not tedious in these things, I will omit the rest, though I might relate many other notable passages and troubles which they endured and underwent in these their wanderings and travels both at land and sea; but I haste to other things. Yet I may not omit the fruit that came hereby, for by these so public troubles in so many eminent places their cause became famous and occasioned many to look into the same, and their godly carriage and Christian behaviour was such as left a deep impression in the minds of many. And though some few shrunk at these first conflicts and sharp beginnings (as it was no marvel) yet many more came on with fresh courage and greatly animated others. And in the end, notwithstanding all these storms of opposition, they all get over at length, some at one time and some at another, and some in one place and some in another, and met together again according to their desires, with no small rejoicing.

Chapter IV

SHOWING THE REASONS AND CAUSES OF THEIR REMOVAL

After they had lived in this city about some eleven or twelve years (which is the more observable being the whole time of that famous truce between that state and the Spaniards) and sundry of them were taken away by death and many others began to be well stricken in years (the grave mistress of Experience having taught them many things), those prudent governors with sundry of the sagest members began both deeply to apprehend their present dangers and wisely to foresee the future and think of timely remedy. In the agitation of their thoughts, and much discourse of things hereabout, at length they began to incline to this conclusion of removal to some other place. Not out of any newfangledness or other such like giddy humor by which men are oftentimes transported to their great hurt and danger, but for sundry weighty and solid reasons, some of the chief of which I will here briefly touch.

And first, they saw and found by experience the hardness of the place and country to be such as few in comparison would come to them, and fewer that would bide it out and continue with them. For many that came to them, and many more that desired to be with them, could not endure that great labour and hard fare, with other inconveniences which they underwent and were contented with. But though they loved their persons, approved their cause and honoured their sufferings, yet they left them as it were weeping, as Orpah did her mother-in-law Naomi, or as those Romans did Cato in Utica who desired to be excused and borne with, though they could not all be Catos. For many, though they desired to enjoy the ordinances of God in their purity and the liberty of the gospel with them, yet (alas) they admitted of bondage with danger of conscience, rather than to endure these hardships. Yea, some preferred and chose the prisons in England rather than this liberty in Holland with these afflictions. But it was thought that if a better and easier place of living could be had, it would draw many and take away these discouragements. Yea, their pastor would often say that many of those who both wrote and preached now against them, if they were in a place where they might have liberty and live comfortably, they would then practice as they did.

Secondly. They saw that though the people generally bore all these difficulties very cheerfully and with a resolute courage, being in the best and strength of their years; yet old age began to steal on many of them; and their great and continual labours, with other crosses and sorrows, hastened it before the time. So as it was not only probably thought, but apparently seen, that within a few years more they would be in danger to scatter, by necessities pressing them, or sink under their burdens, or both. And therefore according to the divine proverb, that a wise man seeth the plague when it cometh, and hideth himself, Proverbs xxii.3, so they like skillful and beaten soldiers were fearful either to be entrapped or surrounded by their enemies so as they should neither be able to fight nor fly. And therefore thought it better to dislodge betimes to some place of better advantage and less danger, if any such could be found.

Thirdly. As necessity was a taskmaster over them so they were forced to be such, not only to their servants but in a sort to their dearest children, the which as it did not a little wound the tender hearts of many a loving father and mother, so it produced likewise sundry sad and sorrowful effects. For many of their children that were of best dispositions and gracious inclinations, having learned to bear the yoke in their youth and willing to bear part of their parents' burden, were oftentimes so oppressed with their heavy labours that though their minds were free and willing, yet their bodies bowed under the weight of the same, and became decrepit in their early youth, the vigour of nature being consumed in the very bud as it were. But that which was more lamentable, and of all sorrows most heavy to be borne, was that many of their children, by these occasions and the great licentiousness of youth in that country, and the manifold temptations of the place, were drawn away by evil examples into extravagant and dangerous courses, getting the reins off their necks and departing from their parents. Some became soldiers, others took upon them far voyages by sea, and others some worse courses tending to dissoluteness and the danger of their souls, to the great grief of their parents and dishonour of God. So that they saw their posterity would be in danger to degenerate and be corrupted.

Lastly (and which was not least), a great hope and inward zeal they had of laying some good foundation, or at least to make some way "hereunto, for the propagating and advancing the gospel of the kingdom of Christ in those remote parts of the world; yea, though they should be but even as stepping-stones unto others for the performing of so great a work.

These and some other like reasons moved them to undertake this resolution of their removal; the which they afterward prosecuted with so great difficulties, as by the sequel will appear.

The place they had thoughts on was some of those vast and unpeopled countries of America, which are fruitful and fit for habitation, being devoid of all civil inhabitants, where there are only savage and brutish men which range up and down, little otherwise than the wild beasts of the same. This proposition being made public and coming to the scanning of all, it raised many variable opinions amongst men and caused many fears and doubts amongst themselves. Some, from their reasons and hopes conceived, laboured to stir up and encourage the rest to undertake and prosecute the same; others again, out of their fears, objected against it and sought to divert from it; alleging many things, and those neither unreasonable nor unprobable; as that it was a great design and subject to many unconceivable perils and dangers; as, besides the casualties of the sea (which none can be freed from), the length of the voyage was such as the weak bodies of women and other persons worn out with age and travail (as many of them were) could never be able to endure And yet if they should, the miseries of the land which they should be exposed unto, would be too hard to be borne and likely, some or all of them together, to consume and utterly to ruinate them. For there they should be liable to famine and nakedness and the want, in a manner, of all things. The change of air, diet and drinking of water would infect their bodies with sore sicknesses and grievous diseases. And also those which should escape or overcome these difficulties should yet be in continual danger of the savage people, who are cruel, barbarous and most treacherous, being most furious in their rage and merciless where they overcome; not being content only to kill and take away life, but delight to torment men in the most bloody manner that may be; flaying some alive with the shells of fishes, cutting off the members and joints of others by piecemeal and broiling on the coals, eat the collops of their flesh in their sight whilst they live, with other cruelties horrible to be related.

And surely it could not be thought but the very hearing of these things could not but move the very bowels of men to grate within them and make the weak to quake and tremble. It was further objected that it would require greater sums of money to furnish such a voyage and to fit them with necessaries, than their consumed estates would amount to and yet they must as well look to be seconded with supplies as presently to be transported. Also many precedents of ill success and lamentable miseries befallen others in the like designs were easy to be found, and not forgotten to be alleged; besides their own experience, in their former troubles and hardships in their removal into Holland, and how hard a thing it was for them to live in that strange place, though it was a neighbour country and a civil and rich commonwealth.

It was answered that all great and honourable actions are accompanied with great difficulties and must be both enterprised and overcome with answerable courages. It was granted the dangers were great, but not desperate. The difficulties were many, but not invincible. For though there were many of them likely, yet they were not certain. It might be sundry of the things feared might never befall; others by provident care and the use of good means might in a great measure be prevented; and all of them, through the help of God, by fortitude and patience might either be borne or overcome. True it was that such attempts were not to he made and undertaken without good ground and reason, not rashly or lightly as many have done for curiosity or hope of gain, etc. But their condition was not ordinary, their ends were good and honourable, their calling lawful and urgent; and therefore they might expect the blessing of God in their proceeding. Yea, though they should lose their lives in this action, yet might they have comfort in the same and their endeavours would be honourable. They lived here but as men in exile and in a poor condition, and as great miseries might possibly befall them in this place; for the twelve years of truce were now out and there was nothing but beating of drums and preparing for war, the events whereof are always uncertain. The Spaniard might prove as cruel as the savages of America, and the famine and pestilence as sore here as there, and their liberty less to look out for remedy.

After many other particular things answered and alleged on both sides, it was fully concluded by the major part to put this design in execution and to prosecute it by the best means they could.

Chapter IX

OF THEIR VOYAGE, AND HOW THEY PASSED THE SEA; AND OF THEIR SAFE ARRIVAL AT CAPE COD

September 6. These troubles being blown over, and now all being compact together in one ship, they put to sea again with a prosperous wind, which continued divers days together, which was some encouragement unto them; yet, according to the usual manner, many were afflicted with seasickness. And I may not omit here a special work of God's providence. There was a proud and very profane young man, one of the seamen, of a lusty, able body, which made him the more haughty; he would alway be contemning the poor people in their sickness and cursing them daily with grievous execrations; and did not let to tell them that he hoped to help to cast half of them overboard before they came to their journey's end, and to make merry with what they had; and if he were by any gently reproved, he would curse and swear most bitterly. But it pleased God before they came half seas over, to smite this young man with a grievous disease, of which he died in a desperate manner, and so was himself the first that was thrown overboard. Thus his curses light on his own head, and it was an astonishment to all his fellows for they noted it to be the just hand of God upon him.

After they had enjoyed fair winds and weather for a season, they were encountered many times with cross winds and met with many fierce storms with which the ship was shroudly 1 shaken, and her upper works made very leaky; and one of the main beams in the midships was bowed and cracked, which put them in some fear that the ship could not be able to perform the voyage. So some of the chief of the company, perceiving the mariners to fear the sufficiency of the ship as appeared by their mutterings, they entered into serious consultation with the master and other officers of the ship, to consider in time of the danger, and rather to return than to cast themselves into a desperate and inevitable peril. And truly there was great distraction and difference of opinion amongst the mariners themselves; fain would they do what could be done for their wages' sake (being now near half the seas over) and on the other hand they were loath to hazard their lives too desperately. But in examining of all opinions, the master and others affirmed they knew the ship to be strong and firm under water; and for the buckling of the main beam, there was a great iron screw the passengers brought out of Holland, which would raise the beam into his place; the which being done, the carpenter and master affirmed that with a post put under it, set firm in the lower deck and otherways bound, he would make it sufficient. And as for the decks and upper works, they would caulk them as well as they could, and though with the working of the ship they would not long keep staunch, yet there would otherwise be no great danger, if they did not overpress her with sails. So they committed themselves to the will of God and resolved to proceed.

In sundry of these storms the winds were so fierce and the seas so high, as they could not bear a knot of sail, but were forced to hull 2 for divers days together. And in one of them, as they thus lay at hull in a mighty storm, a lusty young man called John Howland, coming upon some occasion above the gratings was, with a seele of the ship, thrown into sea; but it pleased God that he caught hold of the topsail halyards which hung overboard and ran out at length. Yet he held his hold (though he was sundry fathoms under water) till he was hauled up by the same rope to the brim of the water, and then with a boat hook and other means got into the ship again and his life saved. And though he was something ill with it, yet he lived many years after and became a profitable member both in church and commonwealth. In all this voyage there died but one of the passengers, which was William Butten, a youth, servant to Samuel Fuller, when they drew near the coast.

But to omit other things (that I may be brief) after long beating at sea they fell with that land which is called Cape Cod; the which being made and certainly known to be it, they were not a little joyful. After some deliberation had amongst themselves and with the master of the ship, they tacked about and resolved to stand for the southward (the wind and weather being fair) to find some place about Hudson's River for their habitation. But after they had sailed that course about half the day, they fell among dangerous shoals and roaring breakers, and they were so far entangled therewith as they conceived themselves in great danger; and the wind shrinking upon them withal, they resolved to bear up again for the Cape and thought themselves happy to get out of those dangers before night overtook them, as by God's good providence they did. And the next day they got into the Cape Harbors where they rid in safety.

A word or two by the way of this cape. It was thus first named by Captain Gosnold and his company, Anno 1602, and after by Captain Smith was called Cape James; but it retains the former name amongst seamen. Also, that point which first showed those dangerous shoals unto them they called Point Care, and Tucker's Terrour; but the French and Dutch to this day call it Malabar by reason of those perilous shoals and the losses they have suffered there.

Being thus arrived in a good harbor, and brought safe to land, they fell upon their knees and blessed the God of Heaven who had brought them over the vast and furious ocean, and delivered them from all the perils and miseries thereof, again to set their feet on the firm and stable earth, their proper element. And no marvel if they were thus joyful, seeing wise Seneca was so affected with sailing a few miles on the coast of his own Italy, as he affirmed, that he had rather remain twenty years on his way by land than pass by sea to any place in a short time, so tedious and dreadful was the same unto him.

But here I cannot but stay and make a pause, and stand half amazed at this poor people's present condition; and so I think will the reader, too, when he well considers the same. Being thus passed the vast ocean, and a sea of troubles before in their preparation (as may be remembered by that which went before), they had now no friends to welcome them nor inns to entertain or refresh their weatherbeaten bodies; no houses or much less town to repair to, to seek for succour. It is recorded in Scripture as a mercy to the Apostle and his shipwrecked company, that the barbarians showed them no small kindness in refreshing them, but these savage barbarians, when they met with them (as after will appear) were readier to fill their sides full of arrows than otherwise. And for the season it was winter, and they that know the winters of that country know them to be sharp and violent, and subject-to cruel and fierce storms, dangerous to travel to known places, much more to search an unknown coast. Besides, what could they see but a hideous and desolate wilderness, fall of wild beasts and wild men—and what multitudes there might be of them they knew not. Neither could they, as it were, go up to the top of Pisgah to view from this wilderness a more goodly country to feed their hopes; for which way soever they turned their eyes (save upward to the heavens) they could have little solace or content in respect of any outward objects. For summer being done, all things stand upon them with a weatherbeaten face, and the whole country, full of woods and thickets, represented a wild and savage hue. If they looked behind them, there was the mighty ocean which they had passed and was now as a main bar and gulf to separate them from all the civil parts of the world. If it be said they had a ship to succour them, it is true; but what heard they daily from the master and company? But that with speed they should look out a place (with their shallop) where they would be, at some near distance; for the season was such as he would not stir from thence till a safe harbor was discovered by them, where they would be, and he might go without danger; and that victuals consumed apace but he must and would keep sufficient for themselves and their return. Yea, it was muttered by some that if they got not a place in time, they would turn them and their goods ashore and leave them. Let it also be considered what weak hopes of supply and succour they left behind them, that might bear up their minds in this sad condition and trials they were under; and they could not but be very small. It is true, indeed, the affections and love of their brethren at Leyden was cordial and entire towards them, but they had little power to help them or themselves; and how the case stood between them and the merchants at their coming away hath already been declared.

What could now sustain them but the Spirit of God and His grace? May not and ought not the children of these fathers rightly say: "Our fathers were Englishmen which came over this great ocean, and were ready to perish in this wilderness; but they cried unto the Lord, and He heard their voice and looked on their adversity," etc. "Let them therefore praise the Lord, because He is good: and His mercies endure forever." "Yea, let them which have been redeemed of the Lord, shew how He hath delivered them from the hand of the oppressor. When they wandered in the desert wilderness out of the way, and found no city to dwell in, both hungry and thirsty, their soul was overwhelmed in them. Let them confess before the Lord His loving kindness and His wonderful works before the sons of men."

The Trial of John Peter Zenger. 1735

Prosecuting Attorney: The Case before the court is whether Mr. Zenger is guilty of libeling His Excellency the Governor of New York, and indeed the whole administration of the government. Mr. Hamilton has confessed the printing and publishing, and I think nothing is plainer than that the words in the information are scandalous, and tend to sedition, and to disquiet the minds of the people of this province. And if such papers are not libels, I think it may be said there can be no such thing as a libel.

Mr. Hamilton: May it please Your Honor, I cannot agree with Mr. Attorney. For though I freely acknowledge there are such things as libels, yet I must insist, at the same time, that what my client is charged with is not a libel. And I observed just now that Mr. Attorney, in defining a libel, made use of the words "scandalous, seditious, and tend to disquiet the people." But (whether with design or not I will not say) he omitted the word "false."

Prosecuting Attorney: I think I did not omit the word "false." But it has been said already that it may be a libel, notwithstanding it may be true.

Mr Hamilton: In this I must still differ with Mr. Attorney;... we are to be tried upon this information now before the court and jury, and to which we have pleaded not guilty, and by it we are charged printing and publishing a certain false, malicious, seditious, and scandalous libel. This word "false" must have some meaning or how came it there?...

Mr. Chief Justice [of the Court]: You cannot be admitted, Mr. Hamilton, to give the truth of a libel in evidence. A libel is not to be justified; for it is nevertheless a libel that it is true....

Mr Hamilton: I thank Your Honor. Then, gentlemen of the jury, it is to you we must now appeal, for witnesses to the truth of the facts we have offered, and are denied the liberty to prove. And let it not seem strange that I apply myself to you in this manner. I am warranted so to do both by law and reason.

The law supposes you to be summoned out of the neighborhood where the fact is alleged to be committed; and the reason... is because you are supposed to have the best knowledge of the fact that is to be tried. And were you to find a verdict against my client, you must take upon you to say the papers referred to in the information, and which we acknowledge we printed and published, are false, scandalous, and seditious.... According to my brief, the facts which we offer to prove were not committed in a corner; they are notoriously known to be true; and therefore in your justice lies our safety. And as we are denied the liberty of giving evidence to prove the truth of what we have published, I will beg leave to lay down, as a standing rule in such cases, that the suppressing of evidence ought always to be taken for the strongest evidence; and I hope it will have weight with you....

I hope to be pardoned, sir, for my zeal upon this occasion. It is an old and wise caution that when our neighbor's house is on fire, we ought to take care of our own. For though, blessed be God, I live in a government [Pennsylvania colony] where liberty is well understood, and freely enjoyed, yet experience has shown us all... that a bad precedent in one government is soon set up for an authority in another. And therefore I cannot but think it mine, and every honest man's duty, that (while we pay all due obedience to men in authority) we ought at the same time to be on our guard against power, wherever we apprehend that it may affect ourselves or our fellow subjects.

....Old and weak as I am, I should think it my duty, if required, to go to the utmost part of the land, where my service could be of any use, in assist--to quench the flame of prosecutions upon informations, set on foot by the government, to deprive a people of the right of remonstrating (and complaining too) of the arbitrary attempts of men in power. Men who injure and oppress the people under their administration provoke them to cry out and complain; and then make that very complaint the foundation for new oppressions and prosecutions. I wish I could say there were no instances of this kind.

But to conclude. The question before the court and you, gentlemen of the jury, is not of small nor private concern. It is not the cause of a poor printer, nor of New York alone, which you are now trying. No! It may, in its consequence, affect every freeman that lives under a British government on the main of America. It is the best cause. It is the cause of liberty. And I make no doubt but your upright conduct, this day, will not only entitle you to the love and esteem of your fellow citizens; but every man who prefers freedom to a life of slavery will bless and honor you, as men who have baffled the attempt of tyranny, and, by an impartial and uncorrupt verdict, have laid a noble foundation for securing to ourselves, our posterity, and our neighbors, that to which nature and the laws of our country have given us a right--the liberty both of exposing and opposing arbitrary power (in these parts of the world, at least) by speaking and writing the truth....

[The jury withdrew and in a small time returned. And being asked by the clerk whether they were agreed of their verdict, and whether John Peter Zenger was guilty of printing and publishing the libels in the information mentioned, they answered... NOT GUILTY; upon which there were three huzzas in the hall....]

The Causes of
Bacon's Rebellion

Carla Gardina Pestana
and Charles Coleman Finlay

INTRODUCTION

By 1675, the royal colony of Virginia concentrated its agricultural efforts on growing tobacco for export. Tobacco cultivation demanded a large labor force, and the planters relied mainly on English, Irish, and Scottish indentured servants, some of them poor young men and women, others convicts sentenced to a period of labor in the New World. When their terms of servitude expired, they wanted land for themselves, which put them in competition with plantation owners (their former masters) who wanted to expand their holdings to replace land that had been depleted by the overcultivation of tobacco. New land was becoming scarce, because the colony was reaching the limits of its boundaries. Beyond those boundaries lived various groups of Native Americans who opposed continued English expansion onto their lands. The royally appointed governor, Sir William Berkeley, sought to avoid further conflicts with the Indians by reaching boundary agreements with them. These agreements primarily hurt the ex-indentured servants and the newly arrived planters, since these people would benefit most if additional lands were made available for settlement. Some of these people went to live on (or beyond) the borders of the colony, where their presence sparked the hostilities that Berkeley sought to avoid.

In 1675 and early 1676, a series of confrontations occurred along the Potomac River in the Chesapeake region, pitting Doeg and Susquehannock Indians against these English planters. Nathaniel Bacon, a well-born Englishman who had recently migrated to Virginia, sought official sanction for a general attack against the natives. After Governor Berkeley refused to authorize

Bacon's request, Bacon led a group of volunteers to massacre one of the friendly tribes. When Berkeley declared Bacon a rebel and moved to arrest him, the young man launched an attack on the governor, and the entire colony collapsed into civil war. The rebels burned Jamestown, the capital, to the ground, and a period of plunder ensued in which partisans on both sides looted the homes and property of their enemies.

For most of 1676 Virginia was engulfed by civil war. The uprising against Berkeley, led by Bacon and named after him, was the largest armed revolt against English authority in the American colonies until the Revolution a century later. It was only put down after King Charles II dispatched an expeditionary force to quell the rebellion. After they had helped Berkeley restore order to the colony, the king's commissioners replaced Berkeley and sent him back to England to justify himself to the king. After an extended career (1642–52, 1660–77) as governor in the first royal colony in America, Berkeley died in disgrace in England shortly after his return there.

Although Berkeley's handling of the crisis (along with some of the policies that led up to it) resulted in his fall from power, the rebels were judged yet more harshly at the time. Many of them lost their lives after the rebellion was put down. During the revolutionary era, however, it became popular to present Bacon as the heroic forerunner of later Virginian revolutionaries like George Washington and Patrick Henry. More recently, scholars have been less inclined to side wholeheartedly with Bacon. They now tend to study the rebellion for what it reveals about serious divisions within late-seventeenth-century Chesapeake society. Bacon's Rebellion was the only colonial revolt to involve Native Americans, Europeans, and Africans. As such, it offers a glimpse of the social and political development of early Virginia.

CONTEMPORARY VIEWS OF THE REBELLION

Only a few of the participants left records about their roles in the rebellion, and those were mostly the wealthy men who served as leaders of either faction. While we know that several different groups of Native Americans were involved, that women participated actively in both the Bacon and Berkeley camps, and that the last rebels out in the field were mostly European indentured servants and African or African-American slaves, we have few, if any, records from these people to explain their actions. The motives of all parties can only be interpreted through the limited existing records. (Throughout these documents, archaic abbreviations have been silently edited for greater clarity.)

Tensions on the Frontier

In the aftermath of the rebellion, commissioners sent from England by the king interviewed people and collected information about the rebellion to discover why it happened. The following selection describes the conflicts with local Native Americans that sparked a desire for revenge in Bacon and other frontier dwellers. Taken from the commissioners' report entitled "A True Narrative of the Rise, Progresse, and Cessation of the Late Rebellion in Virginia . . ." in Narratives of the Insurrections, 1675–1690, *ed. Charles M. Andrews (New York, 1952), 105–7.*

Few or none had bin the Damages sustained by the English from the Indians, other than occasionally had happen'd sometimes upon private quarells and provocations, untill in July, 1675, certain Doegs and Susquahanok Indians on Maryland side, stealing some Hoggs from the English at Potomake on the Virginia shore (as the River divides the same), were pursued by the English in a Boate, beaten or kill'd and the hoggs retaken from them; whereupon the Indians repairing to their owne Towne, report it to their Superiors, and how that one [Thomas] Mathewes (whose hoggs they had taken) had before abused and cheated them, in not paying them for such Indian trucke [goods] as he had formerly bought of them, and that they took his hogs for Satisfaction [of the debt]. Upon this (to be Reveng'd on Mathews) a warr Captain with some Indians came over to Potomake and killed two of Mathewes his servants, and came also a second time and kill'd his sonne.

It happen'd hereupon that Major George Brent and Col. George Mason pursued some of the same Indians into Maryland, and marching directly up to the Indian Towne with a Party of 30 Virginians came to a certaine House and there killed an Indian King and 10 of his men upon the place; the rest of the Indians fled for their lives. . . .

The Indians persisting to Revenge themselves Inforted [fortified their position] in Maryland and now began to be bold and formidable to the English who Besieged them; their Boldness and daring behavior of late tymes and their promptnesse to Fire arms, being (indeed) wonderfull, over what they seem'd formerly indued with, which doubtlesse was of some advantage extraordinary to them considering their Small Body, [and the fact that] the Virginians and Marylanders that Besieged them being said to make neer a thousand men. The siege held 7 weekes, during which tyme the English lost 50 men, besides some Horses which the Indians tooke, and serv'd themselves to subsist on. But Provisions growing very scarce with them during this siege the Indians sent out 5 greate men to Treate of Peace, who were not Permitted to return to the Fort, but being kept Prisoners Some tyme were at last murdered by the English.

At length (whether through negligence or cowardize) the Indians made theire escape through the English, with all their wives, children and goods of value, wounding and killing some at their sally and going off. After which the English returning (as Report Saith), the Marylanders composed a Peace with the Salvages, and soe diverted the warr from themselves. . . .

But about the beginning of January, 1675–6, a Party of those abused Susquahanocks in Revenge of the Maryland businesse came suddainly down upon the weak Plantations at the head of Rappahanock and Potomaque and killed at one time 36 persons and then immediately (as their Custome is) ran off into the woods.

Berkeley Declares Bacon a Rebel

When Governor William Berkeley refused to authorize attacks against the Susquehannocks, Nathaniel Bacon, a wealthy planter, took matters into his own hands, leading a group of volunteers in a massacre of friendly Indians. In the selection below, Berkeley defends his own actions and declares Bacon a rebel. Originally printed in the Collections of the Massachusetts Historical Society, *4th Series, (Boston, 1871) 9:178–81.*

Since that time that I returned into the Country [as Governor of Virginia: about 1660], I call the great God, Judge of all things in heaven and earth to wittness, that I doe not know of any thing relateive to this Country, wherein I have acted unjustly, corruptly, or negligently, in distributeing equall Justice to all men, & takeing all possible care to preserue [preserve] their proprietys, & defend them from their barbarous enimies. . . .

And now I will state the Question betwixt me as a Governor and Mr Bacon, and say that if any enimies should invade England, any Councellor Justice of peace, or other inferiour officer, might raise what forces they could to protect his Majesty's subiects [subjects], But I say againe, if after the Kings knowledge of this inuasion, any the greatest peere [or nobleman] of England, should raise forces against the kings p'hibition this would be now, & ever was in all ages & Nations accompted [accounted as] treason. Nay I will goe further, that though this peere was truly zealous for the preservation of his King, & subiects, and had better & greater abillitys than all the rest of his fellow subiects, to doe his King and Country seruice, yett if the King (though by false information) should suspect the contrary, itt were treason in this Noble peere to p'ceed after the King's prohibition, and for the truth of this I appeale to all the laws of England, and the Laws and constitutions of all other Nations in the world. . . .

Now my friends I have lived 34 yeares amongst you, as vncorrupt and dilligent as ever [a] Governor was, Bacon is a man of two yeares amongst you, his p'son and qualities vnknowne to most of you, & to all men else, by any vertuous action that ever I heard of, And that very action which he boasts of [the massacre of the Occaneechee Indians], was sickly & fooleishly, & as I am informed treacherously carried to the dishonnor of the English Nation, yett in itt, he lost more men then I did in three yeares Warr [against an Indian uprising several decades earlier], and by the grace of God will putt myselfe to the same daingers & troubles againe when I have brought Bacon to acknowledge the Laws are above him, and I doubt not but by God's assistance to have better success then Bacon hath had, the reason of my hopes are, that I will take Councell of wiser men then my selfe, but Mr Bacon hath none about him, but the lowest of the people.

Yett I must further enlarge, that I cannot without your helpe, doe any thinge in this but dye in defence of my King, his laws, & subiects, which I will cheerefully doe, though alone I doe itt, and considering my poore fortunes, I can not leave my poore Wife and friends a better legacy then by dyeing for my King & you: for his sacred Majesty will easeily distinguish betweene Mr Bacons actions & myne, and Kinges have long Armes, either to reward or punish. . . .

Lastly my most assured ffriends I would have preserued those Indians that I knew were howerly att our mercy, to have beene our spyes and intelligence, to finde out our bloody enimies, but as soone as I had the least intelligence that they alsoe were trecherous enimies, I gave out Comissions to distroy them all as the Comissions themselues will speake itt.

To conclude, I have don what was possible both to friend and enimy, have granted Mr Bacon three pardons, which he hath scornefully reiected, suppoaseing himselfe stronger to subuert [the laws] than I and you [are] to maineteyne the Laws, by which onely and Gods assisting grace and mercy, all men must hope for peace and safety. I will add noe more though much more is still remaineing to Justifie me & condemne Mr Bacon, but to desier that this declaration may be read in every County Court in the Country.

The Queen of Pamunkey
Negotiates for Her People

---

*Once Bacon began attacking the frontier Indians, Virginia's leaders sought assistance from the Pamunkeys, the most powerful of the tributary, or "friendly," Indians. In the following passage, Thomas Mathew, an eyewitness, relates how and why the Queen of Pamunkey tried to keep her people from becoming involved. Taken from Thomas Mathew, "The Beginning, Progress, and Conclusion of Bacon's Rebellion . . .," re-*printed in, Tracts and Other Papers, Relating Principally to the Origin, Settlement, and Progress of the Colonies in North America . . . , ed. Peter Force, (Washington, D.C., 1836) 1:14–15.

Our comittee being sat, the Queen of Pamunky (descended from Oppechankenough a former Emperor of Virginia) was introduced, who entred the chamber with a comportment gracefull to admiration, bringing on her right hand an Englishman interpreter, and on the left her son a stripling twenty years of age, she having round her head a plat of black and white wampum peague three inches broad in imitation of a crown, and was cloathed in a mantle of dress't deer skins with the hair outwards and the edge cut round 6 inches deep which made strings resembling twisted frenge from the shoulders to the feet; thus with grave courtlike gestures and a majestick air in her face, she walk'd up our long room to the lower end of the table, where after a few intreaties she sat down; th' interpreter and her son standing by her on either side as they had walked up, our chairman asked her what men she woud [would] lend us for guides in the wilderness and to assist us against our enemy Indians, she spake to th' interpreter to inform her what the chairman said, (tho' we believed she understood him) he told us she bid him ask her son to whom the English tongue was familiar, and who was reputed the son of an English colonel, yet neither woud he speak to or seem to understand the chairman but th' interpreter told us, he referred all to his mother, who being againe urged she after a little musing with an earnest passionate countenance as if tears were ready to gush out and a fervent sort of expression made a harangue about a quarter of an hour often, interlacing (with a high shrill voice and vehement passion) these words "Tatapatamoi Chepiack, i.e. Tatapatamoi dead["] Coll. Hill being next me, shook his head, I ask'd him what was the matter, he told me all she said was too true to our shame, and that his father was generall in that battle, where diverse years before Tatapatamoi her husband had led a hundred of his Indians in help to th' English against our former enemy Indians, and was there slaine with most of his men; for which no compensation (at all) had been to that day rendered to her wherewith she now upbraided us.

Her discourse ending and our morose chairman not advancing one cold word towards asswaging the anger and grief her speech . . . nor taking any notice of all she had said, . . . he rudely push'd againe the same question "what Indians will you now contribute, &c.?["] of this disregard she signified her resentment by a disdainfull aspect, and turning her head half aside, sate mute till that same question being press'd, a third time, she not returning her face to the board, answered with a low slighting voice in her own language "six,["] but being further importun'd she sitting a little while sullen, without uttering a word between said "twelve,["] tho' she then had a hundred and fifty Indian men, in her town, and so rose up and gravely walked away, as [if] not pleased with her treatment.

Bacon Justifies Rebellion on Behalf of "the People"

Within months, the colony divided into factions that supported either Berkeley or Bacon, and both sides took up arms. On 30 July 1676, Bacon issued "The Declaration of the People," in which he defended his actions and attacked the policies of Berkeley's government. Reprinted from the Collections of the Massachusetts Historical Society, *4th Series, (Boston, 1871), 9:184–85.*

1st. For haveing . . . raised greate unjust taxes vpon the Comonality for the aduancement of private favorites & other sinister ends, but [without having] . . . in any measure aduanced this hopefull Colony either by fortifications Townes or Trade.

2d. For haveing abused & rendred contemptable the Magistrates of Justice, by aduanceing to places of Judicature, scandalous and Ignorant favorites.

3. For haveing wronged his Majestys prerogative & interest, by assumeing Monopolony of the Beaver trade, & for haveing in that unjust gaine betrayed & sold his Majestys Country & the lives of his loyall subiects to the barbarous heathen.

4. For haveing, protected, favoured, & Imboldned the Indians against his Majestys loyall subiects, never contriveing, requireing, or appointing any due or proper meanes of satisfaction for theire many Inuasions, robbories, & murthers comitted vpon vs.

5. For haveing when the Army of English was just vpon the track of those Indians, who now in all places burne, spoyle, murther & when we might with ease have distroyed them who then were in open hostillity, for then haveing expressly countermanded, & sent back our Army, by passing his word for the peaceable demeanour of the said Indians, who imediately p'secuted theire evill intentions, comitting horred murthers & robberies in all places, being p'tected by the said ingagement & word past of him the said Sir Wm Berkeley, haveing ruined & laid desolate a greate part of his Majestys Country, & have now drawne themselves into such obscure & remote places, & are by theire success soe imboldned & confirmed, by theire confederacy soe strengthned that the cryes of blood are in all places, & the terror, & constirnation of the people soe greate, are now become, not onely a difficult, but a very formidable enimy, who might att first with ease haue beene distroyed.

6th. And lately when vpon the loud outcryes of blood the Assembly had with all care raised & framed an Army for the preventing of further mischiefe & safeguard of this his Majestys Colony.

7th. For haveing with onely the privacy of some few favorites, without acquainting the people, onely by the alteration of a figure, forged a Comission, by we know not what hand, not onely without, but even against the consent of the people, for the raiseing & effecting civill warr & destruction, which being happily & without blood shed prevented, for haveing the second time attempted the same, thereby calling downe our forces from the defence of the fronteeres & most weekely expoased places.

8. For the prevention of civill mischeife & ruin amongst ourselues, whilst the barbarous enimy in all places did invade, murther & spoyle vs, his majestys most faithfull subiects.

Edward Hill Explains His Opposition to Nathaniel Bacon

Colonel Edward Hill, a Berkeley loyalist, vigorously suppressed the rebellion in Charles City County where he lived. When other planters in the area criticized his brutality, he countered with a description of the treatment he and his family received from the rebels, which he clearly believed justified his own actions. The following excerpt is taken from the Virginia Magazine of History and Biography, *3 (1895–1896): 250.*

I must with trouble and sorrow say that I am grieved to see the spirit of rebellion soe strong and fresh in the hearts of these people that would make it a grievance of the County for to obey those just comands which I received from his honor [the governor], and I should think theire true grievance should be that they were soe active and mischievous as they were from the beginning of the rebellion to the end thereof, and were the first that against the King's Governor's comands went out upon the Occaneechees, were the very men to help Bacon to force his comission, and marched a hundred miles out of theire own country [county] as low as Lower Norfolk to fight the king's loyall subjects, and over into Gloucester, and indeed all over the country, and in fine were the first in armes, and the laste that opposed and faced the King's Governor's power, yet these noe grievances, And I bless God, and truely rejoice in the great goodness and mercy of our most gracious king that they are pardoned; but me thinks with modesty they mought [might] have given me leave to have had my grievances that my house was plundered of all I had, my sheep all destroyed, my hoggs and cattle killed, all my grain taken and destroyed, wheat, barley, oates, & Indian graine, to the quantity of seven, or eight hundred bushels, and to compleat theire jollity draw my brandy, Butts of wyne and syder [cider, a mildly alcoholic beverage] by payles full, and [toasting] to every health instead of burning theire powder [shooting off their guns], burnt my writings, bills, bonds, acc'ts to the true vallue of forty thousand pounds of tobacco and to finish theire barbarism, take my wife bigg with child [pregnant] prisoner, beat her with my Cane, tare [tore] her childbed linen out of her hands, and with her ledd away my children where they must live on corne and water and lye on the ground.

Indentured Servants and Slaves Resist Surrender

Along with poor freemen, indentured servants and slaves who had deserted their masters formed a large part of Bacon's army. As the rebellion collapsed, they still held the fort at West Point. As the passage below indicates, Berkeley and his supporters were not above lying to trick such people into putting down their arms. Thomas Grantham was a ship captain who helped Berkeley suppress the uprising. From "A Narrative of the Indian and Civil Wars in Virginia . . .," in Tracts and Other Papers . . ., *ed. Peter Force, 1:44–45.*

What number of soulders was, at this time, in Garrisson at West Point, I am not certaine: It is saide about 250, sumed up in freemen, sarvants and slaves; these three ingredience being the compossition of Bacons Army, ever since that the Governour left Towne. These was informed (to prepare the way) two or three days before that Grantham came to them, that there was a treaty on foote betwene there Generall, and the Governour; and that Grantham did manely promote the same, as he was a parson [person] that favoured the cause, that they were contending for.

When that Grantham arived, amongst these fine fellowes, he was receved with more then an ordnary respect; which he haveing repade, with a suteable deportment, he acquaints them with his commission, which was to tell them, that there was a peace concluded betwene the Governour and their Generall; an since himself had (in some measure) used his indeviours, to bring the same to pass, hee begged of the Governour, that he might have the honor to com and acquaint them with the terms; which he saide was such, that they had all cause to rejoyce at, than any ways to thinke hardly of the same; there being a compleate satisfaction to be given (by the Articles of agreement) according to every ones particuler intress; which he sumed up under these heads. And first, those that were now in Arms (and free men) under the Generall, were still to be retained in Arms, if they so pleased, against the Indians. Secondly, and for those who had a desire for to return hom, to their owne abodes, care was taken for to have them satisfide, for the time they had bin out, according to the alowance made the last Assembley. And lastly, those that were sarvants in Arms, and behaved themselves well, in their imployment, should emediately receve discharges from their Indentures, signed by the Governour or Sequetary of State; and their Masters to receve, from the publick, a valluable satisfaction, for every sarvant, so set free (marke the words) proportionably to the time that they have to sarve.

Upon these terms, the soulders forsake West Point, and goe with Grantham to kiss the Governours hands (still at Tindells point) and to receve the benefitt of the Articles, mentioned by Grantham; where when they came (which was by water, themselves in one vessill, and their arms in another; and so contrived by Grantham, as he tould me himselfe, upon good reason) the sarvants and slaves was sent hom to their Masters, there to stay till the Governour had leasure to signe their discharges; or to say better, till they were free according to the custom of the countrey [which meant finishing their indentures, plus serving extra time for being runaways], the rest was made prissoners, or entertained by the Governour, as hee found them inclined.

Mrs. Cheisman's
Attempt to Save Her Husband

Mrs. Cheisman's husband was an officer in Bacon's army who was captured at the end of the rebellion. The selection below describes her effort to protect her husband from a death sentence by claiming responsibility for his rebellious actions. Assuming she honestly stated her views in this interview, she stands as one of the female supporters of the rebellion whom we can identify. If this account had not been recorded by an anonymous participant, we would not know today that Mrs. Cheisman existed (and we shall probably never know her first name). Her husband was never tried for his crime, dying in prison of "feare, griefe, or bad useage," as the author of this narrative put it. Excerpted from "A Narrative of the Indian and Civil Wars in Virginia . . .," in Tracts and Other Papers . . ., *ed. Peter Force, 1:34*

There is one remarkable passage reported of this Major Cheismans Lady [or wife], which because it sounds to the honor of her sex, and consequently of all loveing Wives, I will not deny it a roome in this Narrative.

When that the Major was brought into the Governours presence, and by him demanded, what made him to ingage in Bacons designes? Before that the Major could frame an answer to the Governours demand; his Wife steps in and tould his honour that it was her provocations that made her Husband joyne in the cause that Bacon contended for; ading, that if he had not bin influenced by her instigations, he had never don that which he had done. Therefore (upon her bended knees) she desired of his honour, that since what her husband had done, was by her meanes, and so, by consequence, she most guilty, that she might be hanged, and he pardoned. Though the Governour did know, that what she had saide, was neare to the truth, yet he said litle to her request.

Thomas Hansford's Execution

Thomas Hansford, who was a colonel in Bacon's army, was captured by Berkeley supporters as the rebellion collapsed. The excerpt below, describes his capture and death. Taken from the same anonymous "A Narrative of the Indian and Civil Wars in Virginia . . .," printed in Tracts and Other Papers . . ., *ed. Peter Force, vol. 1:33.*

[P]resently after that he [Thomas Hansford, a soldier] came to Accomack, he had the ill luck to be the first Verginian borne that dyed [meaning the first person of English descent born in Virginia to die] upon a paire of Gallows. When that he came to the place of

Execution (which was about a mile removed from his prison) he seemed very well resolved to undergo the utmost mallize [malaise] of his not over kinde Destinies, onely complaineing of the maner of his death. Being observed neather at the time of his tryall (which was by a Court Martiall) nor afterwards, to supplicate any other faviour, than that he might be shot like a soulder, and not to be hanged like a Dog. But it was tould him, that what he so passionately petitioned for could not be granted, in that he was not condemned as he was merely a soldier, but as a Rebell, taken in Arms, against the king, whose laws had ordained him that death. During the short time he had to live after his sentence he approved to his best advantage for the wellfare of his soul, by repentance and contrition for all his sins, in generall, excepting his Rebellion, which he would not acknowledge; desireing the people at the place of execution, to take notis that he dyed a loyal subject, and a lover of his countrey; and that he had never taken up arms, but for the destruction of the Indians, who had murthered so many Christians.

Questions

---

1. *Why did Berkeley believe it significant that only "the lowest of the people" supported Bacon?*
2. *Do you think that Bacon was really speaking on behalf of the "people" when he issued the "Declaration"?*
3. *What motivated the various individuals whose actions are described or whose words are quoted in these documents?*
4. *Do you think there was one rebellion or several rebellions, according to the accounts you have read?*
5. *How did the rebellion appear from the perspective of various Native American groups who fought against or refused to fight against Bacon?*

FURTHER READING

Thomas Wertenbaker's Torchbearer of the Revolution: The Story of Bacon's Rebellion in Virginia *(Princeton, 1940) and Wilcomb Washburn's* The Governor and The Rebel: A History of Bacon's Rebellion in Virginia *(Chapel Hill, 1957) are still the two most important full-length books on Bacon's Rebellion.* 1676: The End of American Independence *(New York, 1984), written by Stephen Saunders Webb, connects Bacon's Rebellion with other developments in English-Indian relations on the North American continent that occurred simultaneously. Warren M. Billings has re-explored the long-term economic and political conditions that led to the conflict in "The Causes of Bacon's Rebellion: Some Suggestions," an article in the October 1970 issue of the* Virginia Magazine of History and Biography. *Martha W. McCartney examines in detail the Queen of Pamunkey and her role in Virginia politics before, during, and after Bacon's Rebellion in "Cockacoeske, Queen of Pamunkey: Diplomat and Suzerain," an essay in* Powhatan's Mantle: Indians in the Colonial Southeast, *ed. Peter H. Wood, Gregory A. Waselko, and M. Thomas Hatley (Lincoln, Nebraska, 1989).*

The First Great Awakening

Frank Lambert

INTRODUCTION

The first Great Awakening was a religious revival that swept through the British North American colonies in the 1730s and 1740s. Huge crowds attended preaching services and large numbers of people claimed conversion experiences, leading a group of evangelicals to declare that America was witnessing an extraordinary outpouring of God's grace unlike anything seen since the Protestant Reformation. Mainly drawn from New England Congregationalists and Middle Colony Presbyterians, the revivalists were more than disinterested observers; they hoped to promote the spread of revival throughout the British North Atlantic world.

Awakeners believed that American religion, at least as they understood and expressed it, was in a state of decline. They thought that many colonists had endangered their souls by embracing Enlightenment notions that reduced salvation to a matter of right reason and good works rather than the grace of God. And they feared that others had been enticed by the growing consumer market to make a bad bargain, exchanging everlasting treasures for ephemeral baubles. To reverse these dangerous trends, revivalists preached with great fervor an old message: the necessity of each individual's undergoing a conversion experience, or, as they called it, a spiritual New Birth. Much of the preaching was hellfire, and London evangelical Isaac Watts spoke for many American revivalists when he advocated the use of "all Methods to rouse and awaken the cold, the stupid, the sleepy Race of Sinners." While the revivalists' message was old, their methods were innovative. They held mass meetings inside churches as well as anywhere large numbers gathered—spaces like village commons, marketplaces, and court-houses were popular meeting places.

34

They hyped their meetings through newspaper advertising, and they published testimonials that heralded their successes.

The Awakening was both transatlantic and local in scope. It started in tiny, remote villages and towns in East Jersey and western Massachusetts during the mid-1730s. At the outset, these revivals were similar to scores of spiritual awakenings that had occurred periodically from the 1670s through the 1720s. But George Whitefield's arrival and preaching up and down the Atlantic seaboard transformed the revival into something new: an intercolonial event, indeed the first national movement before a nation existed. Huge crowds gathered to hear the much-publicized preacher from London, as many as 20,000 in Philadelphia and Boston. For six months prior to his landing at Lewiston, Delaware, on October 30, 1739, colonial newspapers had provided readers with a steady stream of stories about the masses he attracted in England and the opposition to his preaching.

While the preaching of itinerants like George Whitefield was dramatic and received much attention, scores of local pastors helped promote the Great Awakening. One of the most effective was Jonathan Edwards, pastor at Northampton, Massachusetts. Unlike Whitefield's extemporaneous, theatrical performances, Edwards read his sermons in a quiet, even voice that nevertheless had an equally chilling effect on audiences. His highly reasoned discourse entitled Sinners in the Hands of an Angry God *depicted men and women suspended above the abyss, upheld only by God's mercy. It never failed to evoke emotional outbursts from listeners, causing some to cry aloud in anguish over the prospects of falling into the fiery pit.*

Not everyone thought the Great Awakening was a good thing, and indeed, all did not agree that what was occurring was even a revival. Some focused on what they considered to be the revival's erroneous ideas and disorderly practices and cited some of the most outrageous behavior of revival preachers and their followers. Their favorite target of ridicule was James Davenport, an itinerant revivalist, who on one occasion at New London, Connecticut, started a bonfire and called on his audience to toss in "heretical" books and "worldly" clothing. While acknowledging that some practices surrounding the Great Awakening were excessive, supporters concluded that recent events did in fact constitute a remarkable work of God. As evidence that the revival had divine origins, they pointed to the enormous crowds that materialized to hear the gospel, the suddenness with which the awakening erupted and spread, and the geographic reach of the movement. They compared the awakening to God's outpouring on the Day of Pentecost as described in the Bible in the Acts of the Apostles.

Though the Great Awakening created no new denominations, it left a lasting imprint on American culture. The revival inspired evangelicals to establish a number of colleges to train ministers for the gospel, including Princeton, Dartmouth, and Brown. By emphasizing the personal nature of the New Birth, the awakening empowered lay men and women to challenge the authority of unconverted pastors. Some separated themselves from their congregations and founded new churches. The revivals also created an intercolonial community of evangelicals and demonstrated to ordinary men and women that they could join together and make common cause regardless of geographical and denominational boundaries. Some historians have argued that this intercolonial cooperation inspired revolutionaries to forge larger connections. Finally, the **First** *Great Awakening inspired nineteenth-century revivalists who, like Jonathan Edwards and George Whitefield, led a* **Second** *Great Awakening that began in Kentucky and Tennessee in 1801 and by the 1830s had spread throughout much of the United States. Thus, the eighteenth-century awakening was the beginning of an American revival tradition that extends to the present as seen, for example, in the Evangelical Crusades of Billy Graham.*

Any discussion of colonial religion confronts students with unfamiliar terms, and the Great Awakening has its own peculiar vocabulary. Revival supporters were often referred to as "New Lights," originally a pejorative label suggesting the advocacy of innovative and perhaps fabricated doctrines. "Old Lights" were those who opposed the revival and claimed that they adhered to traditional teachings. New Lights ignored denominational distinctions and challenged the authority of "established" churches, those endowed by colonial legislatures with exclusive legal privi-

leges and public tax support. In about half the colonies the "Anglican Church" or "Church of England" enjoyed establishment status. When "itinerant" evangelists, preachers who traveled from place to place, entered their parishes, clergymen of established churches won legislative protection through laws demanding that itinerants could preach only after securing licenses.

Contemporary Views of the Great Awakening

The documents from which the following pieces are excerpted enable us to view the Great Awakening from several different perspectives. They therefore illustrate what some historians have claimed: there was not a single Great Awakening but many great awakenings. That is, individuals experienced the revivals within local communities and through personal circumstances. Some, like George Whitefield, Gilbert Tennent, and Jonathan Edwards, were architects of the awakenings. Others, like Nathan Cole, were among the thousands who got caught up in the excitement of reading accounts of revival in distant places and then with great anticipation finally became participants themselves. And still others, like Benjamin Franklin, were skeptical of the awakeners' theological claims and critical of some of their practices.

Whitefield Comes to Town!

For all of its large crowds, the Great Awakening was an intensely personal experience for thousands of men and women. One whose life was profoundly touched by the revival was a Connecticut farmer, Nathan Cole, who became a Baptist preacher. In this colorful account, Cole describes the day in 1740 that George Whitefield first came to his community, a much-anticipated and long-remembered event. Excerpt from Leonard W. Labaree, "George Whitefield Comes to Middletown," William and Mary Quarterly, 3d Series, 7 (October, 1950): 590–91.

Now it pleased God to send Mr Whitefield into this land; and my hearing of his preaching at Philadelphia, like one of the Old apostles, and many thousands flocking to hear him preach the Gospel; and great numbers were converted to Christ; I felt the Spirit of God drawing me by conviction; I longed to see and hear him, and wished he would come this way. I heard he was come to New York and the Jerseys and great multitudes flocking after him under great concern for their Souls which brought on my Concern more and more hoping soon to see him but next I heard he was at long Island; then at Boston and next at Northampton; then on a Sudden, in the morning about 8 or 9 of the Clock there came a messenger and said Mr Whitfield preached at Hartford and Weathersfield yesterday and is to preach at Middletown this morning at ten of the Clock, I was in my field at Work, I dropt my tool that I had in my hand and ran home to my wife telling her to make ready quickly to go and hear Mr Whitfield preach at Middletown then run to my pasture for my horse with all my might; fearing that I should be too late; having my horse I with my wife soon mounted the horse and went forward as fast as I thought the horse could bear, and when my horse got much out of breath I would get down and put my wife on the Saddle and bid her ride as fast as she could and not Stop or Slack for me except I bad her and so I would run untill I was much out of breath; and then mount my horse again, and so I did several times to favour my horse; we improved every moment to get along as if we were fleeing for our lives; all the while fearing we should be too late to hear the Sermon, for we had twelve miles to ride double in little more than an hour and we went round by the upper housen parish and when we came within about half a mile or a mile of the Road that comes down from Hartford weathersfield and Stepney to Middletown; on high land I saw before me a Cloud or fogg rising; I first thought it came from the great River, but as I came nearer the Road, I heard a noise something like a low rumbling thunder and presently found it was the noise of Horses feet coming down the Road and this Cloud was a Cloud of dust made by the Horses feet; it arose some Rods into the the [sic] air over the tops of Hills and trees and when I came within about 20 rods of the Road, I could see men and horses Sliping along in the Cloud like shadows and as I drew nearer it seemed like a steady Stream of horses and their riders, scarcely a horse more than his length behind another, all of a Lather and foam with sweat, their breath rolling out of their nostrils every Jump; every horse seemed to go with all his might to carry his rider to hear news from heaven for the saving of Souls, it made me tremble to see the Sight, how the world was in a Struggle; I found a Vacance between two horses to Slip in mine and my Wife said law our Cloaths will be all spoiled see how they look, for they were so Covered with dust, that they looked almost all of a Colour Coats, hats, Shirts, and horses: We went down in the Stream but heard no man speak a word all the way for 3 miles but every one pressing forward in great haste and when we got to Middletown old meeting house there was a great Multitude it was said to be 3 or 4000 of people Assembled together; we dismounted and shook of our dust; and the ministers were then Coming to the meeting house; I turned and looked towards the Great River and saw the ferry boats Running swift backward and forward bringing Over loads of people and the Oars Rowed nimble and quick; every thing men horses and boats seemed to be Struggling for life; the land and banks over the river looked black with people and horses all along the 12 miles I saw no man at work in his field, but all seemed to be gone—When I saw Mr. Whitfield come upon the Scaffold he lookt almost Angelical; a young, Slim, slender youth before some thousands of people with a bold undaunted Countenance, and my hearing how God was with him every where as he came along it Solemnized my mind; and put me into a trembling fear before he began to preach; for he looked as if he was Cloathed with Authority from the Great God; and a sweet sollome solemnity sat upon his brow And my hearing him preach, gave me a heart wound; By Gods blessing: my old Foundation was broken up, and I saw that my righteousness would not save me.

Suspended Above Hell's Fire

The revivalists' sermons were aimed at awakening men and women from their spiritual slumbers. Awakeners believed that many persons had become too "secure," that is, too smug in their own good works instead of depending solely on God's grace for their salvation. The idea, then, was for preachers to make the terrors of sin and damnation real to their listeners. No one was more effective in making hell frightfully graphic than Jonathan Edwards. He explained to his audience at Enfield, Connecticut, on July 8, 1741, that he hoped that the discourse would be useful in "awakening . . . unconverted persons in this congregation." Extracted from Jonathan Edwards, Sinners in the Hands of an Angry God *(Boston, 1741), 14–16.*

The Bow of God's Wrath is bent, and the Arrow made ready on the String, and Justice bends the Arrow at your Heart, and strains the Bow, and it is nothing but the meer Pleasure of God, and that of an angry God, without any Promise or Obligation at all, that keeps the Arrow one moment from being made drunk with your Blood.

Thus are all you that never passed under a great Change of heart, by the mighty Power of the SPIRIT of GOD upon your Souls; all that were never born again, and made new Creatures, and raised from being dead in Sin, to a State of new, and before altogether unexperienced Light and Life, (however you may have reformed your Life in many Things, and may have had religious Affections, and may keep up a Form of Religion in your Families and Closets, and in the House of God, and may be strict in it,) you are thus in the Hands of an angry God; 'tis nothing but his meer Pleasure that keeps you from being this Moment swallowed up in everlasting Destruction.

However unconvinced you may now be of the Truth of what you hear, by & by you will be fully convinced of it. Those that are gone from being in the like Circumstances with you, see that it was so with them; for Destruction came suddenly upon most of them, when they expected nothing of it, and while they were saying, *Peace and Safety*: Now they see, that those Things that they depended on for Peace and Safety, were nothing but thin Air and empty Shadows.

The God that holds you over the Pit of Hell, much as one holds a Spider, or some loathsome Insect, over the Fire, abhors you, and is dreadfully provoked; his Wrath towards you burns like Fire; he looks upon you as worthy of nothing else, but to be cast into the Fire; he is of purer Eyes than to bear to have you in his Sight; you are ten thousand Times so abominable in his Eyes as the most hateful venomous Serpent is in ours. You have offended him infinitely more than ever a stubborn Rebel did his Prince: and yet 'tis nothing but his Hand that holds you from falling into the Fire every Moment: 'Tis to be ascribed to nothing else, that you did not go to Hell the last Night; that you was suffer'd to awake

41

again in this World, after you closed your Eyes to sleep: and there is no other Reason to be given why you have not dropped into Hell since you arose in the Morning, but that God's Hand has held you up: There is no other Reason to be given why you han't gone to Hell since you have sat here in the House of God, provoking his pure Eyes by your sinful wicked Manner of attending his solemn Worship: Yea, there is nothing else that is to be given as a Reason, why you don't this very Moment drop down into Hell.

O Sinner! Consider the fearful Danger you are in: 'Tis a great Furnace of Wrath, a wide and bottomless Pit, full of the Fire of Wrath, that you are held over in the Hand of that God, whose Wrath is provoked and incensed as much against you as against many of the Damned in Hell: You hang by a slender Thread, with the Flames of divine Wrath flashing about it, and ready every Moment to singe it, and burn it asunder; and you have no Interest in any Mediator, and nothing to lay hold of to save yourself, nothing to keep off the Flames of Wrath, nothing of your own, nothing that you ever have done, nothing that you can do, to induce God to spare you one Moment.

A "Dead Ministry"

Unlike earlier colonial revivalists who charged parishioners with abandoning the faith of their forbears, the mid-eighteenth-century awakeners shifted the blame for religious decline to the ministers. To them, too many pastors had not undergone a conversion experience themselves and were, therefore, incapable of leading others into the New Birth. No one made this point more forcefully than did Gilbert Tennent in the following sermon. Excerpted from Gilbert Tennent, The Danger of an Unconverted Ministry *(Boston, 1742), 11–12 and 14–15.*

Then what a Scrole & Scene of Mourning, and Lamentation, and Wo, is opened! because of the Swarms of Locusts, the Crowds of Pharisees, that have as *covetously* as *cruelly*, crept into the Ministry, in this adulterous Generation! who as nearly resemble the Character given of the old Pharisees, in the Doctrinal Part of this Discourse, as one Crow's Egg does another. It is true some of the modern Pharisees have learned to prate a little more *orthodoxly* about the New Birth, than their Predecessor *Nicodemus*, who are, in the mean Time, as great Strangers to the feeling Experience of it, as he. They are blind who see not this to be the Case of the Body of the Clergy, of this Generation. And O! that our Heads were Waters, and our Eyes a Fountain of Tears, that we could *Day* and *Night* lament, with the utmost Bitterness, the doleful Case of the poor Church of God, upon this account.

From what has been said, we may learn, That such who are contented under a *dead Ministry*, have not in them the Temper of that Saviour they profess. It's an awful Sign, that they are as blind as Moles, and as dead as Stones, without any spiritual Taste and Relish. And alas! isn't this the Case of Multitudes? If they can get one, that has the Name of a Minister, with a Band, and a black Coat or Gown to carry on a *Sabbath-days* among them, although never so coldly, and *insuccessfully;* if he is free from gross Crimes in Practice, and takes good Care to keep at a due Distance from their Consciences, and is never troubled about his Insuccessfulness; O! think the poor Fools, that is a fine Man indeed; our Minister is a prudent charitable Man, he is not always harping upon Terror, and sounding Damnation in our Ears, like some rash-headed Preachers, who by their uncharitable Methods, are ready to put poor People out of their Wits, or to run them into Despair; O! how terrible a Thing is that Dispair! Ay, our Minister, honest Man, gives us good Caution against it. Poor silly Souls! consider *seriously* these Passages, of the Prophet, *Jeremiah* 5.30, 31. . . .

If the Ministry of natural Men be as it has been represented; Then it is both lawful and expedient to go from them to hear Godly Persons; yea, it's so far from being sinful to do this, that one who lives under a pious Minister of lesser Gifts, after having honestly endeavour'd to get Benefit by his Ministry, and yet gets little or none, but doth find real Benefit and more Benefit elsewhere; I say, he may *lawfully* go, and that *frequently,* where he gets most Good to his precious Soul, after regular Application to the Pastor where he lives, for his Consent, and proposing the Reasons thereof; when this is done in the Spirit of Love and Meekness, without Contempt of any, as also without rash *Anger* or vain *Curiosity.* . . .

If the great Ends of Hearing may be attained as well, and better, by Hearing of another Minister than our own; then I see not, why we should be under a fatal Necessity of hearing him, I mean our Parish-Minister, perpetually, or generally. Now, what are, or ought to be, the Ends of Hearing, but the Getting of Grace, and Growing in it? . . . Well then, and may not these Ends be obtained out of our Parish-line? *Faith* is said to come by *Hearing*, Rom. 10. But the Apostle doesn't add, *Your Parish-Minister.* Isn't the same Word preach'd out of our Parish? and is there any Restriction in the Promises of blessing the Word to those only, who keep within their Parish-line ordinarily? If there be, I have not yet met with it; yea, I can affirm, that so far as Knowledge can be had in such Cases, I have known Persons to get saving Good to their Souls, by Hearing over their Parish-line; and this makes me earnest in Defence of it. . . .

Now, if it be lawful to withdraw from the Ministry of a pious Man, in the Case aforesaid; how much more, from the Ministry of a natural Man? Surely, it is both lawful and expedient, for the Reasons offered in the Doctrinal Part of this Discourse: To which let me add a few Words more.

To trust the Care of our Souls to those who have little or no Care for their own, to those who are both unskilful and unfaithful, is contrary to the common Practice of considerate Mankind, relating to the Affairs of their Bodies and Estates; and would signify, that we set light by our Souls, and did not care what became of them. For if the Blind lead the Blind, will they not both fall into the Ditch?

The Grand Itinerant

Devout revivalists revered George Whitefield's published journals as evidence that he was indeed an instrument of God in promoting a great awakening across the land. Published in 20 editions from 1739 to 1741 in the colonies, his followers made them best sellers. Opponents viewed the same works as shameless self-promotion, the work of one who was a Pedlar in Divinity, as he roved the countryside "selling" his brand of religion. In the following extracts, Whitefield describes his reception in northern cities. Taken from [Banner of Truth Trust], George Whitefield's Journals *(London, 1960), 343, 348–49, 359–60, 460–61, and 472.*

Thursday, November 8. [Philadelphia, 1739] Read prayers and preached to a more numerous congregation than I have yet seen here. Dined with an honest, open-hearted, true Israelitish Quaker; and had a sweet opportunity with him and his family, of talking about Jesus Christ *and Him crucified*. Preached at six in the evening, from the Court House stairs to about six thousand people. I find the number that came on Tuesday to my house greatly increased and multiplied. The inhabitants were very solicitous for me to preach in another place besides the church; for it is quite different here from what it is in England. There, the generality of people think a sermon cannot be preached well without; here, they do not like it so well if delivered within the church walls. Lord, grant that I may become all things to all men, that I may gain some; and preach the Gospel in every place and in every manner, as well as to every creature. . . .

Thursday, November 15. [New York City]. Several came to see me at my lodgings, who also gave me kind invitations to their houses. Waited upon Mr. Vessey [Commissary of Church of England in New York]; but wished, for his own sake, he had behaved in a more Christian manner. He seemed to be full of anger and resentment, and before I asked him for the use of his pulpit, denied it. He desired to see my Letters of Orders, and, when I told him they were left at Philadelphia, he asked me for a licence. I answered, I never heard that the Bishop of London gave any licence to any one who went to preach the Gospel in Georgia; but that I was presented to the living of Savannah by the trustees, and upon that presentation had letters Dismissory from my lord of London, which I thought was sufficient authority. But this was by no means satisfactory to him; he charged me with breaking my oath, with breaking the Canon, which enjoins ministers and churchwardens not to admit persons into their pulpit without a licence. How can I break that, when I am neither a churchwarden, nor have any church hereabouts to admit any one into? Upon this, knowing that he was a frequenter of public houses, I reminded him of that Canon which forbids the clergy to go to any such places. This, though spoken in the spirit of meekness, stirred him up more. He charged me with making a disturbance in Philadelphia, and sowing and causing divisions in other places. "But you," he said, "have a necessity laid upon you to preach." I told him I had, for the clergy and laity of our Church seemed to be settled on their lees; but that my end in preaching was not to sow divisions, but to propagate the pure Gospel of Jesus Christ. He said, "they did not want my assistance." I replied, if they preached the Gospel, I wished them good luck in the Name of the Lord; but as he had denied me the church without my asking the use of it, I would preach in the fields, for all places were alike to me." . . .

Wednesday, Nov. 28 [Philadelphia]. . . . In the morning, notice had been given that I should preach my farewell sermon in the afternoon. But the church, (though as large as most of our London churches), being not large enough to contain a fourth part of the people, we adjourned to the fields, and I preached for an hour-and-a-half from a balcony, to upwards of ten thousand hearers, who were very attentive. . . .

One of the printers [Benjamin Franklin] has told me he has taken above two hundred subscriptions for printing my *Sermons* and *Journals.* Another printer [Andrew Bradford] told me he might have sold a thousand *Sermons,* if he had them; I therefore gave two extempore discourses to be published. Lord, give them Thy blessing. . . .

Monday, September 22 [Boston, 1740] Preached this morning at the Rev. Mr. Webb's meeting-house, to six thousand hearers in the house, besides great numbers standing about the doors. Most wept for a considerable time. . . .

In the afternoon I went to preach at the Rev. Mr. Checkley's meeting-house; but God was pleased to humble us by a very awful providence. The meeting-house being filled, though there was no real danger, on a sudden all the people were in an uproar, and so unaccountably surprised, that some threw themselves out of the windows, others threw themselves out of the gallery, and others trampled upon one another; so that five were actually killed, and others dangerously wounded. I happened to come in the midst of the uproar, and saw two or three lying on the ground in a pitiable condition. God was pleased to give me presence of mind; so that I gave notice I would immediately preach upon the common. The weather was wet, but many thousands followed in the field, to whom I preached from these words, "Go out into the highways and hedges, and compel them to come in." . . .

Sunday, October 12. . . . Went with the Governor, in his coach, to the common, where I preached my farewell sermon to near twenty thousand people,—a sight I have not seen since I left Blackheath,—and a sight, perhaps never seen before in America. It being nearly dusk before I had done, the sight was more solemn. Numbers, great numbers, melted into tears, when I talked of leaving them. I was very particular in my application, both to rulers, ministers, and people, and exhorted my hearers steadily to imitate the piety of their forefathers; so that I might hear, that with one heart and mind, they were striving together for the faith of the Gospel.

Benjamin Franklin's Skeptical Appraisal

Benjamin Franklin found Whitefield's sermons far too emotional for his tastes, preferring a more rationalist approach to religion. Nevertheless, the Philadelphia printer became one of Whitefield's greatest promoters by printing his journals and sermons and publicizing the revival in the Pennsylvania Gazette *and the several other colonial newspapers in which he had a financial interest. Moreover, Franklin and the London evangelist became lifelong friends, with Whitefield often staying in Franklin's home while preaching in Philadelphia. In the following passage, Franklin offers a critical but sympathetic assessment of the evangelist. From J. A. Leo Lemay and P. M. Zall, eds.,* The Autobiography of Benjamin Franklin: A Genetic Text *(Knoxville, 1981), 103–7.*

In 1739 arriv'd among us from England the Rev. Mr Whitefield who had made himself remarkable there by preaching as an itinerant Preacher. He was at first permitted to preach in some of our Churches; but the Clergy taking a Dislike to him, soon refus'd him their Pulpits and he was oblig'd to preach in the Fields. The Multitudes of all Sects and Denominations that attended his Sermons were enormous, and it was matter of Speculation to me who was one of the Number, to observe the extraordinary Influence of his Oratory on his Hearers, and how much they admir'd & respected him, notwithstanding his Abuse of them, by assuring them they were naturally *half Beasts and half Devils*. It was wonderful to see the Change soon made in the Manners of our Inhabitants; from being thoughtless or indifferent about Religion, it seem'd as if all the World were growing Religious; so that one could not walk thro' the Town in an Evening without Hearing Psalms sung in different Families of every Street. And it being found inconvenient to assemble in the open Air, subject to its Inclemencies, the Building of a House to meet-in was no sooner propos'd and Persons appointed to receive Contributions, but sufficient Sums were soon receiv'd to procure the Ground and erect the Building which was 100 feet long & 70 broad, about the Size of Westminster-hall; and the Work was carried on with such Spirit as to be finished in a much shorter time than could have been expected. Both House and Ground were vested in Trustees, expressly for the Use of any Preacher of any religious Persuasion who might desire to say something to the People of Philadelphia, the Design in building not being to accommodate any particular Sect, but the Inhabitants in general, so that even if the Mufti of Constantinople were to send a Missionary to preach Mahometanism to us, he would find a Pulpit at his Service.

Mr Whitfield, in leaving us, went preaching all the Way thro' the Colonies to Georgia. The Settlement of that Province had lately been begun; but instead of being made with hardy Husbandmen accustomed to Labour, the only People fit for such an Enterprise, it was with Families of broken Shopkeepers and other insolvent Debtors, many of indolent & idle habits, taken out of the [jails], who being set down in the Woods, unqualified for clearing Land, & unable to endure the Hardships of a new Settlement, perished in Numbers, leaving many helpless Children unprovided for. The Sight of their miserable Situation inspired the benevolent Heart of Mr Whitefield with the Idea of building an Orphan House there, in which they might be supported and educated. Returning northward he preach'd up this Charity, & made large Collections;—for his Eloquence had a wonderful Power over the Hearts & Purses of his Hearers, of which I myself was an Instance. I did not disapprove of the Design, but as Georgia was then destitute of Materials & Workmen, and it was propos'd to send them from Philadelphia at a great Expence, I thought it would have been better to have built the House here & brought the Children to it. This I advis'd, but he was resolute in his first Project, and rejected my Counsel, and I thereupon refus'd to contribute. I happened soon after to attend one of his Sermons, in the Course of which I perceived he intended to finish with a Collection, & I silently resolved he should get nothing from me. I had in my

Pocket a Handful of Copper, Money, three or four silver Dollars, and five Pistoles in Gold. As he proceeded I began to soften, and concluded to give the Coppers. Another Stroke of his Oratory made me asham'd of that, and determin'd me to give the Silver; & he finish'd so admirably, that I empty'd my Pocket wholly into the Collector's Dish, Gold and all. . . .

Some of Mr Whitfield's Enemies affected to suppose that he would apply these Collections to his own private Emolument; but I, who was intimately acquainted with him, (being employ'd in printing his Sermons and Journals, &c.) never had the least Suspicion of his Integrity, but am to this day decidedly of Opinion that he was in all his Conduct, a perfectly *honest Man*. And methinks my Testimony in his Favour ought to have the more Weight, as we had no religious Connection. He us'd indeed to pray for my Conversion, but never had the Satisfaction of believing that his Prayers were heard. Ours was a mere civil Friendship, sincere on both Sides, and lasted to his Death.

The following Instance will show something of the Terms on which we stood. Upon one of his Arrivals from England at Boston, he wrote to me that he should come soon to Philadelphia, but knew not where he could lodge when there, as he understood his old kind Host Mr Benezet was remov'd to Germantown. My Answer was; You know my House, if you can make shift with its scanty Accommodations you will be most heartily welcome. He reply'd, that if I made that kind Offer for Christ's sake, I should not miss of a Reward.—And I return'd, *Don't let me be mistaken; it was not for Christ's sake, but for your sake.* . . .

He had a loud and clear Voice, and articulated his Words & Sentences so perfectly that he might be heard and understood at a great Distance, especially as his Auditories, however numerous, observ'd the most exact Silence. He preach'd one Evening from the Top of the Court House Steps, which are in the Middle of Market Street, and on the West Side of Second Street which crosses it at right angles. Both Streets were fill'd with his Hearers to a considerable Distance. Being among the hindmost in Market Street, I had the Curiosity to learn how far he could be heard, by retiring down the Street towards the River, and I found his Voice distinct till I came near Front-Street, when some Noise in that Street, obscur'd it. Imagining then a Semi-Circle, of which my Distance should be the Radius, and that it were fill'd with Auditors, to each of whom I allow'd two square feet, I computed that he might well be heard by more than Thirty-Thousand. This reconcil'd me to the Newspaper Accounts of his having preach'd to 25000 People in the Fields, and to the [ancient] Histories of Generals haranguing whole Armies, of which I had sometimes doubted.

By hearing him often I came to distinguish easily between Sermons newly compos'd, & those which he had often preach'd in the Course of his Travels. His Delivery of the latter was so improv'd by frequent Repetitions, that every Accent, every Emphasis, every Modulation of Voice, was so perfectly well turn'd and well plac'd, that without being interested in the Subject, one could not help being pleas'd with the Discourse, a Pleasure of much the same kind with that receiv'd from an excellent Piece of Musick. This is an Advantage itinerant Preachers have over those who are stationary: as the latter cannot well improve their Delivery of a Sermon by so many Rehearsals.

His Writing and Printing from time to time gave great Advantage to his Enemies. Unguarded Expressions and even erroneous Opinions del^d in Preaching might have been afterwards explain'd, or qualify'd by supposing others that might have accompany'd them; or they might have been deny'd; But *litera scripta manet.* Critics attack'd his Writings violently, and with so much Appearance of Reason as to diminish the Number of his Votaries, and prevent their Encrease: So that I am of Opinion, if he had never written any thing he would have left behind a much more numerous and important Sect. And his Reputation might in that case have been still growing, even after his Death; as there being nothing of his Writing on which to found a Censure; and give him a lower Character, his Proselites [followers] would be left at Liberty to feign for him as great a Variety of Excellencies, as their enthusiastic Admiration might wish him to have possessed.

Competing Claims: A "Work of God" or "Errors and Disorders"

Public opinion surrounding the Great Awakening spanned a broad spectrum. Newspapers and pamphlets in the 1740s were filled with editorials and commentaries both favorable and unfavorable. In the summer of 1743, a print war broke out in Boston between revivalists and anti-revivalists over how to characterize the awakenings. The following excerpts from rival declarations printed give a flavor of the diversity and intensity of competing interpretations. The anti-revivalist interpretation appeared in The Testimony of the Pastors of the Churches in the province of the Massachusetts-Bay in New-England, at their Annual Convention in Boston, May 25, 1743, Against several Errors in Doctrines, and Disorders in Practices . . . *(Boston, 1743), 6. The pro-revivalist response appeared in* The Testimony and Advice of an Assembly of Pastors of Churches in New-England, at a Meeting in Boston July 7, 1743. Occasion'd By the late happy Revival of Religion in many Parts of the Land *(Boston, 1743), 6–7, 10.*

We, the *Pastors* of the *Churches* of Christ in the Province of the Massachusetts-Bay in New-England, at our *annual* Convention, *May* 25th. 1743, taking into Consideration several *Errors in Doctrine*, and *Disorders in Practice*, that have of late obtained *in various Parts of the Land*, look upon our selves bound, in *Duty* to our great Lord and Master, Jesus Christ, and in *Concern* for the *Purity* and *Welfare* of these Churches, in the most public Manner, to bear our *Testimony* against them.

. . . As to *Errors in Doctrine;* we observe, that some in our Land look upon what are called *secret Impulses* upon their Minds, without due Regard to the *written Word*, the *Rule* of their Conduct; . . . we judge [this teaching is] contrary to the pure Doctrines of the Gospel, and testified against and confuted, by Arguments fetched from *Scripture* and *Reason*, by our venerable *Fathers*, in the Acts of the *Synod* of August 1637. . . .

As to *Disorders in Practice*, we judge, the *Itinerancy*, as it is called, by which either *ordained Ministers*, or *young Candidates*, go from Place to Place, and without the Knowledge, or contrary to the Leave of the *stated* Pastors in such Places, assemble their People to hear *themselves* preach, arising, we fear, from too great an Opinion of *themselves*, and an uncharitable Opinion of *those Pastors*, and a Want of Faith in the great *Head* of the Churches, is a Breach of *Order*, and contrary to the *Scriptures*. . . .

Six weeks later, pro-revivalists responded:

We, whose Names are hereunto annexed, Pastors of Churches in *New-England*, . . . think it *our* indispensable Duty . . . to declare, to the Glory of sovereign Grace, our full Perswasion, either from what we have seen our selves, or received upon credible Testimony, That there has been a *happy* and *remarkable Revival of Religion in many Parts of this Land, thro' an uncommon divine Influence;* after a long Time of great Decay and Deadness. . . .

Tho' the Work of Grace wro't on the Hearts of Men by the Word and Spirit of GOD, and which has been more or less carried on in the Church from the Beginning, is always the same for Substance, and agrees, at one Time and another, in one Place or Person and another, as to the main Strokes and Lineaments of it, yet the *present Work* appears to be remarkable and extraordinary,

On Account of the *Numbers wrought upon*—We never before saw so many brought under Soul-Concern, and with Distress making the Inquiry, *What must we do to be saved?* And these Persons of all Characters and Ages.—With Regard to the *Suddenness* and *quick Progress* of it—Many Persons and Places were surprized with the gracious Visit together, or near about the same Time; . . .

Thus we have freely declar'd our Tho'ts as to the Work of GOD so remarkably reviv'd in many Parts of this Land—And now, We desire to *bow the Knee in Thanksgiving to the God and Father of our Lord Jesus Christ,* that our *Eyes have seen,* and our *Ears heard* such Things. And while these are our Sentiments, we must necessarily be grieved at any Accounts sent abroad, representing this Work as all *Enthusiasm, Delusion,* and *Disorder.*

Response of the Laymen

Finally, a group of laymen published their own pamphlet expressing their displeasure with the rancorous exchanges between the rival groups of ministers. That publication was The Testimony and Advice of a Number of Laymen Respecting Religion, and the Teachers of It. Addressed to the Pastors of New-England *(Boston, 1743), 1–2.*

Whereas the Pastors of this Land at their two last Meetings, have bore at one Time their Testimony against Errors and Disorders, prevailing among us, and at the other Time have bore their open and conjunct Testimony to the signal Display of God's Grace, and the late plentiful Effusions of the divine Spirit among us; *And whereas,* the Testimony of the Assembly of Pastors of the

Massachusetts Bay in *New-England,* and the Testimony of the Assembly of Pastors of Churches in *New-England,* are publish'd from different Principles, Sentiments and Designs, give contradictory Accounts of the State of Religion in these Parts, show the great Prevalence of a party Spirit, and have a tendency to perplex the Minds of the weak and unstable, and thereby to throw us into Confusions and Divisions; *And whereas,* they have a Tendency to set the Laity of this Province in a very disadvantageous Light in distant Parts, whereby Foreigners will be apt to entertain a contemptible Opinion of them; *And whereas,* every Layman is under indispensable Obligations to check Error, and to promote Truth, to the utmost of his Power . . . lest any should be carried away by their Dissimulation: It hath seem'd proper to us a Number of Laymen of this Province (from a Desire of publishing the Truth as disinterested Persons, which Ministers are not, and in order to set our Characters right in Foreign Parts . . .) to give our open and conjunct Testimony and Advice, respecting the State of Religion, and the Teachers of it in this Province.

Questions

1. *Contemporaries characterized George Whitefield's* Journals *as either evidence that the revival was a work of God or a piece of shameless self-promotion, depending upon the commentator's perspective on religious events. Evaluate those critiques based on your reading of the excerpts. Why did Whitefield publish his journals? More generally, what was the role of print in a revival that featured dynamic preaching?*

2. *How did the Great Awakening and the Enlightenment differ in their respective appeals to colonial Americans? In what ways were they similar?*

3. *What was the role of "hell-fire" preaching in the revivals? Why were men and women attracted to revivalist preachers and why were they willing to listen to sermons filled with terror?*

FURTHER READING

Older works that focus on the Great Awakening in particular regions include: Edwin Gaustad, The Great Awakening in New England *(New York, 1957); Wesley Gewehr,* The Great Awakening in Virginia, 1740–1790 *(Durham, N.C., 1930); C. C. Goen,* Revivalism and Separatism in New England: Strict Congregationalists and Separate Baptists in the Great Awakening *(New Haven, 1962); and Charles Maxson,* The Great Awakening in the Middle Colonies *(Chicago, 1920).*

Recent treatments of the revivals as an intercolonial and/or transatlantic movement: Michael Crawford, Seasons of Grace: Colonial New England's Revival Tradition in Its British Context *(New York, 1991); Timothy D. Hall,* Contested Boundaries: Itinerancy and the Reshaping of the Colonial Religious World *(Durham, N.C., 1994); Leigh Schmidt,* Holy Fairs: Scottish Communions and American Revivals in the Early Modern Period *(Princeton, 1989); W. R. Ward,* The Protestant Evangelical Awakening *(Cambridge, Eng., 1992); Marilyn Westerkamp,* Triumph of the Laity: Scots-Irish Piety and the Great Awakening, 1625–1760 *(New York, 1988).*

For works on George Whitefield, see Frank Lambert, "Pedlar in Divinity": George Whitefield and the Transatlantic Revivals, 1737–1770 *(Princeton, 1994); Harry Stout,* The Divine Dramatist: George Whitefield and the Rise of Modern Evangelicalism *(Grand Rapids, Mich., 1991).*

Works on the Great Awakening and the American Revolution: Alan Heimert, Religion and the American Mind: From the Great Awakening to the Revolution *(Cambridge, Mass., 1966); David Lovejoy,* Religious Enthusiasm in the New World: Heresy to Revolution *(Cambridge, Mass., 1985).*

The Struggle over the Constitution: Federalists vs. Anti-Federalists

Saul Cornell

INTRODUCTION

The publication of the Constitution prompted Americans from all walks of life to participate in a lively public debate over the meaning of republican government and the nature of constitutionalism. The meaning of the Constitution has been debated since it was first proposed more than two hundred years ago. While most Americans today venerate the Constitution, there was substantial opposition to the Constitution when it was first proposed.

Three issues dominated the debate over ratification: the absence of a bill of rights, the meaning of federalism, and the role of democracy in the new government. The Philadelphia Convention that proposed the Constitution did not include a basic declaration of rights. The Bill of Rights was only added during the First Congress and might never have been added had not Anti-Federalists demanded substantial amendments. Apart from the controversy over the absence of a bill of rights, Federalists and Anti-Federalists argued over the scope of power ceded to the new government. This debate raised questions about the distribution of authority between the states and the new federal government. Another controversial issue was the Anti-Federalist claim that the constitution created an aristocratic government. Federalists disputed this charge and defended the republican character of the new government.

No essay produced during this controversy has exerted a more profound impact on subsequent generations than The Federalist. *Judges and lawyers routinely consult* The Federalist *for insights into the original meaning of the Constitution. While Federalists may have won the battle over ratification, Anti-Feder-*

alist concerns have shaped the language of dissent within the American constitutional tradition. Jeffersonian and Jacksonian thought each owed a significant debt to Anti-Federalist ideas. In contemporary America, their ideas have been rediscovered by the political right and left, who have been drawn to different aspects of Anti-Federalist thought.

DEBATING AND RATIFYING THE CONSTITUTION

Interpreting a document as complex as the Constitution has proven to be an exceedingly difficult task for historians, political scientists, and judges. The debate over ratification involved hundreds of delegates to state conventions and thousands of voters, as well as countless essays and letters, some of which were published in the press and others of which circulated in private. The documents below illustrate some of the sources that historians have used either to prove or refute the claim that the Constitution represented a rejection of the Revolution's principles.

Hamilton Introduces the Federalist Argument

The Federalist Papers were published pseudonymously under the pen name of Publius. By choosing to sign the essays with a name drawn from classical antiquity, the true authors of the essays, Alexander Hamilton, John Jay, and James Madison, hoped to impress readers with their commitment to the ideals of republicanism. The following is the first installment of The Federalist. *Taken from Alexander Hamilton, "The Federalist No. 1" in* The Federalist: A Commentary on the Constitution of the United States, *ed. Paul Leicester Ford (New York, 1898), 1-7.*

October 27, 1787

To the People of the State of New York:

After an unequivocal experience of the inefficiency of the subsisting federal government, you are called upon to deliberate

THE

FEDERALIST:

ADDRESSED TO THE

PEOPLE OF THE STATE OF
NEW-YORK.

NUMBER I.

Introduction.

AFTER an unequivocal experience of the inefficacy of the subsisting federal government, you
are called upon to deliberate on a new constitution for
the United States of America. The subject speaks its
own importance; comprehending in its consequences,
nothing less than the existence of the UNION, the
safety and welfare of the parts of which it is composed, the fate of an empire, in many respects, the
most interesting in the world. It has been frequently
remarked, that it seems to have been reserved to the
people of this country, by their conduct and example,
to decide the important question, whether societies of
men are really capable or not, of establishing good
government from reflection and choice, or whether
they are forever destined to depend, for their political
constitutions, on accident and force. If there be any
truth in the remark, the crisis, at which we are arrived,
may with propriety be regarded as the era in which
A   that

A page of The Federalist *encouraging
ratification of the new United States
Constitution. (Courtesy of the Library of
Congress.)*

on a new Constitution for the United States of America. The subject speaks its own importance; comprehending in its consequences nothing less than the existence of the UNION, the safety and welfare of the parts of which it is composed, the fate of an empire in many respects the most interesting in the world. It has been frequently remarked that it seems to have been reserved to the people of this country, by their conduct and example, to decide the important question, whether societies of men are really capable or not of establishing good government from reflection and choice, or whether they are forever destined to depend for their political constitutions on accident and force. If there be any truth in the remark, the crisis at which we are arrived may with propriety be regarded as the era in which that decision is to be made; and a wrong election of the part we shall act may, in this view, deserve to be considered as the general misfortune of mankind.

This idea will add the inducements of philanthropy to those of patriotism, to heighten the solicitude which all considerate and good men must feel for the event. Happy will it be if our choice should be directed by a judicious estimate of our true interests, unperplexed and unbiased by considerations not connected with the public good. But this is a thing more ardently to be wished than seriously to be expected. The plan offered to our deliberations affects too many particular interests, innovates upon too many local institutions, not to involve in its discussion a variety of objects foreign to its merits, and of views, passions, and prejudices little favorable to the discovery of truth.

Among the most formidable of the obstacles which the new Constitution will have to encounter may readily be distinguished the obvious interest of a certain class of men in every State to resist all changes which may hazard a diminution of the power, emolument, and consequence of the offices they hold under the State establishments; and the perverted ambition of another class of men, who will either hope to aggrandize themselves by the confusions of their country, or will flatter themselves with fairer prospects of elevation from the subdivision of the empire into several partial confederacies than from its union under one government.

It is not, however, my design to dwell upon observations of this nature. I am well aware that it would be disingenuous to resolve indiscriminately the opposition of any set of men (merely because their situations might subject them to suspicion) into interested or ambitious views. Candor will oblige us to admit that even such men may be actuated by upright intentions; and it cannot be doubted that much of the opposition which has made its appearance, or may hereafter make its appearance, will spring from sources, blameless, at least, if not respectable—the honest errors of minds led astray by preconceived jealousies and fears. So numerous indeed and so powerful are the causes which serve to give a false bias to the judgment, that we, upon many occasions, see wise and good men on the wrong as well as on the right side of questions of the first magnitude to society. This circumstance, if duly attended to, would furnish a lesson of moderation to those who are ever so much persuaded of their being in the right in any controversy. And a further reason for caution, in this respect, might be drawn from the reflection that we are not always sure that those who advocate the truth are influenced by purer principles than their antagonists. Ambition, avarice, personal animosity, party opposition, and many other motives not more laudable than these, are apt to operate as well upon those who support as those who oppose the right side of a question. Were there not even these inducements to moderation, nothing could be more ill-judged than that intolerant spirit which has, at all times, characterized political parties. For in politics, as in religion, it is equally absurd to aim at making proselytes by fire and sword. Heresies in either can rarely be cured by persecution.

And yet, however just these sentiments will be allowed to be, we have already sufficient indications that it will happen in this as in all former cases of great national discussion. A torrent of angry and malignant passions will be let loose. To judge from the conduct of the opposite parties, we shall be led to conclude that they will mutually hope to evince the justness of their opinions, and to increase the number of their converts by the loudness of their declamations and by the bitterness of their invectives. An enlightened zeal for the energy and efficiency of government will be stigmatized as the offspring of a temper fond of despotic power and hostile to the principles of liberty. An overscrupulous jealousy of danger to the rights of the people, which is more commonly the fault of the head than of the heart, will be represented as mere pretense and artifice, the stale bait for popularity at the expense of the public good. It will be forgotten, on the one hand, that jealousy is the usual concomitant of love, and that the noble enthusiasm of liberty is apt to be infected with a spirit of narrow and illiberal distrust. On the other hand, it will be equally forgotten that the vigor of government is essential to the security of liberty; that, in the contemplation of a sound and well-informed judgment, their interest can never be separated; and that a dangerous ambition more often lurks behind the specious mask of zeal for the rights of the people than under the forbidding appearance of zeal for the firmness and efficiency of government. History will teach us that the former has been found a much more certain road to the introduction of despotism than the latter, and that of those men who have overturned the liberties of republics, the greatest number have begun their career by paying an obsequious court to the people; commencing demagogues, and ending tyrants.

In the course of the preceding observations, I have had an eye, my fellow-citizens, to putting you upon your guard against all attempts, from whatever quarter, to influence your decision in a matter of the utmost moment to your welfare, by any impressions other than those which may result from the evidence of truth. You will, no doubt, at the same time have collected from the general scope of them, that they proceed from a source not unfriendly to the new Constitution. Yes, my countrymen, I own to you that, after having given it an attentive consideration, I am clearly of opinion it is your interest to adopt it. I am convinced that this is the safest course for your liberty, your dignity, and your happiness. I affect not reserves which I do not feel. I will not amuse you with an appearance of deliberation when I have decided. I frankly acknowledge to you my convictions, and I will freely lay before you the reasons on which they are founded. The consciousness of good intentions disdains ambiguity. I shall not, however, multiply professions on his head. My motives must remain in the depository of my own breast. My arguments will be open to all, and may be judged of by all. They shall at least be offered in a spirit which will not disgrace the cause of truth.

I propose, in a series of papers, to discuss the following interesting particulars:—*The utility of the UNION to your political prosperity—The insufficiency of the present Confederation to preserve that Union—The necessity of a government at least equally energetic with the one proposed, to the attainment of this object—The conformity of the proposed Constitution to the true principles of republican government—Its analogy to your own State constitution*—and lastly, *The additional security which its adoption will afford to the preservation of that species of government, to liberty, and to property.*

In the progress of this discussion I shall endeavor to give a satisfactory answer to all the objections which shall have made their appearance, that may seem to have any claim to your attention. . . .

PUBLIUS.

The Virginia Ratification Debates

The contest for ratification of the Constitution was closely fought. The selection below is from the debates in the constitutional convention of Virginia, which ratified the Constitution in June 1788 by a vote of 89 to 79. The Anti-Federalist position is aired first. Excerpted from The Debates, Resolutions, and Other Proceedings, in Convention, on the adoption of the Federal Constitution . . . *(Washington, 1828), 2:46–47, 56–58.*

Mr. HENRY.—Mr. Chairman, the public mind, as well as my own, is extremely uneasy at the proposed change of government. . . . I consider myself as the servant of the people of this commonwealth, as a centinel over their rights, liberty, and happiness. I represent their feelings, when I say, that they are exceedingly uneasy, being brought from that state of full security, which they enjoyed, to the present delusive appearance of things. A year ago, the mind of our citizens were at perfect repose. Before the meeting of the late federal convention at Philadelphia, a general peace, and an universal tranquillity prevailed in this country; but, since that period, they are exceedingly uneasy and disquieted. When I wished for an appointment to this convention, my mind was extremely agitated for the situation of public affairs. I conceive the republic to be in extreme danger. If our situation be thus uneasy, whence has arisen this fearful jeopardy? It arises from this fatal system—it arises from a proposal to change our government—a proposal that goes to the utter annihilation of the most solemn engagements of the states; a proposal of establishing nine states into a confederacy, to the eventual exclusion of four states. . . . Was our civil polity, or public justice, endangered or sapped: Was the real existence of the country threatened—or was this preceded by a mournful progression of events? This proposal of altering our federal government is of a most alarming nature: make the best of this new government—say it is composed by any thing but inspiration—you ought to be extremely cautious, watchful, jealous of your liberty; for instead of securing your rights, you may lose them forever. If a wrong step be now made, the republic may be lost forever. If this new government will not come up to the expectation of the people, and they should be disappointed—their liberty will be lost, and tyranny must and will arise. I repeat it again, and I beg gentlemen to consider, that a wrong step made now will plunge us into misery, and our republic will be lost. . . . I have the highest veneration for those gentlemen; but, sir, give me leave to demand, what right had they to say, *We, the People?* My political curiosity, exclusive of my anxious solicitude for the public welfare, leads me to ask, who authorized them to speak the language of, *We, the People,* instead of *We, the States?* States are the characteristics, and the soul of a confederation. If the states be not the agents of this compact, it must be one great consolidated national government, of the people of all the states. I have the highest respect for those gentlemen who formed the convention, and were some of them not here, I would express some testimonial of esteem for them. America had on a former occasion put the utmost confidence in them; a confidence which was well placed: and I am sure, sir, I would give up any thing to them; I would cheerfully confide in them as my representatives. But, sir, on this great occasion, I would demand the cause of their conduct. . . . The people gave them no power to use their name. That they exceeded their power is perfectly clear. . . .

[Next the Federalist view was articulated.]

Mr. PENDLETON.—Mr. Chairman, my worthy friend (Mr. HENRY) has expressed great uneasiness in his mind, and informed us, that a great many of our citizens are also extremely uneasy, at the proposal of changing our government: but that a year ago, before this fatal system was thought of, the public mind was at perfect repose. It is necessary to inquire, whether the public mind was at ease on the subject, and if it be since disturbed, what was the cause? What was the situation of this country, before the meeting of the federal convention? Our general government was totally inadequate to the purpose of its institution; our commerce decayed; our finances deranged; public and private credit destroyed: these and many other national evils, rendered necessary the meeting of that convention. If the public mind was then at ease, it did not result from a conviction of being in a happy and easy situation: it must have been an inactive unaccountable stupor. The federal convention devised the paper on your table, as a remedy to remove our political diseases. What has created the public uneasiness since? Not public reports, which are not to be depended upon; but mistaken apprehensions of danger, drawn from observations on governments which do not apply to us. When we come to inquire into the origin of most governments of the world, we shall find, that they are generally dictated by a conqueror at the point of the sword, or are the offspring of confusion, when a great popular leader taking advantage of circumstances, if not producing them, restores order at the expence of liberty, and becomes the tyrant over the people. It may well be supposed, that in forming a government of this sort, it will not be favourable to liberty: the conqueror will take care of his own emoluments, and have little concern for the interest of the people. In either case, the interest and ambition of a despot, and not the good of the people, have given the tone to the government. A government thus formed, must necessarily create a continual war between the governors and governed. Writers consider the two parties (the people and tyrants) as in a state of perpetual warfare, and sounded the alarm to the people. But what is our case? We are perfectly free from sedition and war: we are not yet in confusion: we are left to consider our real happiness and security: we want to secure these objects: we know they cannot be attained without government. Is there a single man in this committee of a contrary opinion?. . . There is no quarrel between government and liberty; the former is the shield and protector of the latter. The war is between government and licentiousness, faction, turbulence, and other violations of the rules of society, to preserve liberty. Where is the cause of alarm? We, the people, possessing all power, form a government, such as we think will secure happiness: and suppose in adopting this plan we should be mistaken in the end; where is the cause of alarm on that quarter? In the same plan we point out an easy and quiet method of reforming what may be found amiss. . . .

But an objection is made to the form: the expression, We, the people, is thought improper. Permit me to ask the gentleman, who made this objection, who but the people can delegate powers? Who but the people have a right to form government? The expression is a common one, and a favorite one with me: the representatives of the people, by their authority, is a mode wholly inessential. If the objection be, that the union ought to be not of the people, but of the state governments, then I think the choice of the former, very happy and proper.—What have the state governments to do with it? . . . It has been said that it has carried us through a dangerous war to a happy issue. Not that confederation, but common danger and the spirit of America, were the bonds of our union: union and unanimity, and not that insignificant paper, carried us through that dangerous war. "United, we stand—divided, we fall!" echoed and re-echoed through America, from congress to the drunken carpenter; was effectual, and procured the end of our wishes, though now forgot by gentlemen, if such there be, who incline to let go this strong hold, to catch at feathers; for such all substituted projects may prove.

This spirit had nearly reached the end of its power when relieved by peace. It was the spirit of America, and not the confederation, that carried us through the war: thus I prove it. The moment of peace showed the imbecility of the federal government: . . . The inefficacy of the general government warranted an idea that we had no government at all. Improvements were proposed and agreed to by twelve states, but were interrupted, because the little state of Rhode Island refused to accede to them; this was a further proof of the imbecility of that government; need I multiply instances to shew that it is wholly ineffectual for the purposes of its institution? Its whole progress since the peace proves it.

The Federalist Defense of the Constitution

James Madison provided one of the most intellectually sophisticated defenses of the Constitution. Madison's argument has since become a classic statement of American constitutional principles. The following is excerpted from James Madison, "Federalist No. 10, " in The Federalist: A Commentary on the Constitution of the United States, *ed. Paul Leicester Ford (New York, 1898), 54–60, 62–63.*

November 22, 1787

To the People of the State of New York

Among the numerous advantages promised by a well-constructed Union, none deserves to be more accurately developed than its tendency to break and control the violence of faction. . . . Complaints are everywhere heard from our most considerate and virtuous citizens, equally the friends of public and private faith and of public and personal liberty, that our governments are too unstable, that the public good is disregarded in the conflicts of rival parties, and that measures are too often decided, not according to the rules of justice and the rights of the minor party, but by the superior force of an interested and overbearing majority. . . .

By a faction I understand a number of citizens, whether amounting to a majority or minority of the whole, who are united and actuated by some common impulse of passion, or of interest, adverse to the rights of other citizens, or to the permanent and aggregate interests of the community. . . .

There are again two methods of removing the causes of faction: the one, by destroying the liberty which is essential to its existence; the other, by giving to every citizen the same opinions, the same passions, and the same interests. . . .

The latent causes of faction are thus sown in the nature of man; and we see them everywhere brought into different degrees of activity, according to the different circumstances of civil society. A zeal for different opinions concerning religion, concerning government, and many other points, as well of speculation as of practice; an attachment to different leaders ambitiously contending for pre-eminence and power; or to persons of other descriptions whose fortunes have been interesting to the human passions, have, in turn, divided mankind into parties, inflamed them with mutual animosity, and rendered them much more disposed to vex and oppress each other than to co-operate for their common good. . . . But the most common and durable source of factions has been the various and unequal distribution of property. Those who hold and those who are without property have ever formed distinct interests in society. Those who are creditors, and those who are debtors, fall under a like discrimination. A landed interest, a manufacturing interest, a mercantile interest, a moneyed interest, with many lesser interests, grow up of necessity in civilized nations, and divide them into different classes actuated by different sentiments and views. The regulation of these various and interfering interests forms the principal task of modern legislation and involves the spirit of party and faction in the necessary and ordinary operations of the government. . . .

It is in vain to say that enlightened statesmen will be able to adjust these clashing interests and render them all subservient to the public good. Enlightened statesmen will not always be at the helm. . . .

The inference to which we are brought is that the *causes* of faction cannot be removed and that relief is only to be sought in the means of controlling its *effects.* . . .

By what means is this object attainable? Evidently by one of two only: Either the existence of the same passion or interest in a majority at the same time must be prevented, or the majority, having such coexistent passion or interest, must be rendered, by their number and local situation, unable to concert and carry into effect schemes of oppression. . . .

From this view of the subject it may be concluded that a pure democracy, by which I mean a society consisting of a small number of citizens, who assemble and administer the government in person, can admit of no cure for the mischiefs of faction. . . . Hence it is that such democracies have ever been spectacles of turbulence and contention; have ever been found incompatible with personal security or the rights of property; and have in general been as short in their lives as they have been violent in their deaths. . . .

A republic, by which I mean a government in which the scheme of representation takes place, opens a different prospect and promises the cure for which we are seeking. Let us examine the points in which it varies from pure democracy, and we shall comprehend both the nature of the cure and the efficacy which it must derive from the Union.

The two great points of difference between a democracy and a republic are: first, the delegation of the government in the latter, to a small number of citizens elected by the rest; secondly, the greater number of citizens and greater sphere of country over which the latter may be extended.

The effect of the first difference is, on the one hand, to refine and enlarge the public views by passing them through the medium of a chosen body of citizens, whose wisdom may best discern the true interest of their country and whose patriotism and love of justice will be least likely to sacrifice it to temporary or partial considerations. . . .

The other point of difference is the greater number of citizens and extent of territory which may be brought within the compass of republican than of democratic government; and it is this circumstance principally which renders factious combinations less to be dreaded in the former than in the latter. The smaller the society, the fewer probably will be the distinct parties and interests composing it; the fewer the distinct parties and interests, the more frequently will a majority be found of the same party; and the smaller the number of individuals composing a majority, and the smaller the compass within which they are placed, the more easily will they concert and execute their plans of oppression. Extend the sphere and you take in a greater variety of parties and interests; you make it less probable that a majority of the whole will have a common motive to invade the rights of other citizens; or if such a common motive exists, it will be more difficult for all who feel it to discover their own strength and to act in unison with each other. . . .

The influence of factious leaders may kindle a flame within their particular States but will be unable to spread a general conflagration through the other States. A religious sect may degenerate into a political faction in a part of the Confederacy; but the variety of sects dispersed over the entire face of it must secure the national councils against any danger from that source. A rage for paper money, for an abolition of debts, for an equal division of property, or for any other improper or wicked project, will be less apt to pervade the whole body of the Union than a particular member of it, in the same proportion as such a malady is more likely to taint a particular county or district than an entire State.

In the extent and proper structure of the Union, therefore, we behold a republican remedy for the diseases most incident to republican government. . . .

PUBLIUS.

The Anti-Federalist Critique of the Constitution

The Centinel essays were among the most widely reprinted Anti-Federalist attacks on the Constitution. Authored by Pennsylvania's Samuel Bryan, the essays rejected the calm disinterested tone favored by many Anti-Federalists in favor of a more polemical style. The following document is excerpted from The Documentary History of the Ratification of the Constitution, *vol. 13,* Commentaries on the Constitution: Public and Private, *ed. John P. Kaminski and Gaspare J. Saladino, (Madison, 1981), 1:332, 334–35.*

I shall now proceed to the examination of the (proposed plan of government, and I trust, shall make it appear to the meanest capacity, that it has none of the essential requisites of a free government; . . . that it is a most daring attempt to establish a despotic aristocracy among freemen, that the world has ever witnessed.) . . .

. . . [I]f the United States are to be melted down into one empire, it becomes you to consider, whether such a government, however constructed, would be eligible in so extended a territory; and whether it would be practicable, consistent with freedom? It is the opinion of the greatest writers, that a very extensive country cannot be governed on democratical principles, on any other plan, than a confederation of a number of small republics, possessing all the powers of internal government, but united in the management of their foreign and general concerns.

It would not be difficult to prove, that any thing short of despotism, could not bind so great a country under one govern-

69

ment; and that whatever plan you might, at the first setting out, establish, it would issue in a despotism.

If one general government could be instituted and maintained on principles of freedom, it would not be so competent to attend to the various local concerns and wants, of every particular district; as well as the peculiar governments, who are nearer the scene, and possessed of superior means of information, besides, if the business of the *whole* union is to be managed by one government, there would not be time. Do we not already see, that the inhabitants in a number of larger states, who are remote from the seat of government, are loudly complaining of the inconveniencies and disadvantages they are subjected to on this account, and that, to enjoy the comforts of local government, they are separating into smaller divisions. . . .

Thus, we see, the house of representatives, are on the part of the people to balance the senate, who I suppose will be composed of the *better sort,* the *well born,* &c. The number of the representatives . . . appears to be too few, either to communicate the requisite information, of the wants, local circumstances and sentiments of so extensive an empire, or to prevent corruption and undue influence, in the exercise of such great powers.

Ratification Of The Federal Constitution 1787 - 1788

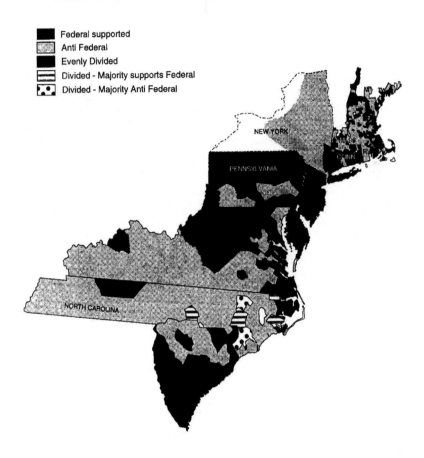

Reprinted from *The Other Founders: Antifederalism and the American Constitutional Tradition* by Saul Cornell (Chapel Hill: University of North Carolina Press, forthcoming).

Questions

1. *What are the essential points of conflict between the Anti-Federalists and the Federalists?*
2. *Does it make sense to view the Anti-Federalists as the spokesmen for democracy?*
3. *When historians interpret texts, they usually ask two questions: Who is the author? Who is the intended audience? With these questions in mind, what rhetorical strategies does Publius use in* Federalist 1 *to persuade his readers?*
4. *How does the approach of Publius compare to that of Centinel?*

FURTHER READING

Gordon S. Wood's The Creation of the American Republic, 1776– 1787 *(Chapel Hill, 1969) is a study of the transformation of American political ideas in the period between the Revolution and the Constitution that puts the conflict between Federalists and Anti-Federalists in the larger context of evolving ideas about republicanism. Forrest McDonald's work explores the intellectual influences shaping the participants in the struggle over the Constitution; see* Novus Ordo Seclorum: the Intellectual Origins of the Constitution *(Lawrence, Kansas, 1985). Richard B. Morris describes the immediate political and social context of the debate over the Constitution in* The Forging of the Union, 1781–1789 *(New York, 1987). Finally, the essays in Richard Beeman's volume cover a variety of topics including: Madison's political thought, slavery, Shays's Rebellion, and the legacy of Anti-Federalism; see Richard Beeman et al.,* Beyond Confederation: Origins of the Constitution and American National Identity *(Chapel Hill, 1987).*

Washington's Farewell Address 1796

1796

Friends and Citizens:

The period for a new election of a citizen to administer the executive government of the United States being not far distant, and the time actually arrived when your thoughts must be employed in designating the person who is to be clothed with that important trust, it appears to me proper, especially as it may conduce to a more distinct expression of the public voice, that I should now apprise you of the resolution I have formed, to decline being considered among the number of those out of whom a choice is to be made.

I beg you, at the same time, to do me the justice to be assured that this resolution has not been taken without a strict regard to all the considerations appertaining to the relation which binds a dutiful citizen to his country; and that in withdrawing the tender of service, which silence in my situation might imply, I am influenced by no diminution of zeal for your future interest, no deficiency of grateful respect for your past kindness, but am supported by a full conviction that the step is compatible with both.

The acceptance of, and continuance hitherto in, the office to which your suffrages have twice called me have been a uniform sacrifice of inclination to the opinion of duty and to a deference for what appeared to be your desire. I constantly hoped that it would have been much earlier in my power, consistently with motives which I was not at liberty to disregard, to return to that retirement from which I had been reluctantly drawn. The strength of my inclination to do this, previous to the last election, had even led to the preparation of an address to declare it to you; but mature reflection on the then perplexed and critical posture of our affairs with foreign nations, and the unanimous advice of persons entitled to my confidence, impelled me to abandon the idea.

I rejoice that the state of your concerns, external as well as internal, no longer renders the pursuit of inclination incompatible with the sentiment of duty or propriety, and am persuaded, whatever partiality may be retained for my services, that, in the present circumstances of our country, you will not disapprove my determination to retire.

The impressions with which I first undertook the arduous trust were explained on the proper occasion. In the discharge of this trust, I will only say that I have, with good intentions, contributed towards the organization and administration of the government the best exertions of which a very fallible judgment was capable. Not unconscious in the outset of the inferiority of my qualifications, experience in my own eyes, perhaps still more in the eyes of others, has strengthened the motives to diffidence of myself; and every day the increasing weight of years admonishes me more and more that the shade of retirement is as necessary to me as it will be welcome. Satisfied that if any circumstances have given peculiar value to my services, they were temporary, I have the consolation to believe that, while choice and prudence invite me to quit the political scene, patriotism does not forbid it.

In looking forward to the moment which is intended to terminate the career of my public life, my feelings do not permit me to suspend the deep acknowledgment of that debt of gratitude which I owe to my beloved country for the many honors it has conferred upon me; still more for the steadfast confidence with which it has supported me; and for the opportunities I have thence enjoyed of manifesting my inviolable attachment, by services faithful and persevering, though in usefulness unequal to my zeal. If benefits have resulted to our country from these services, let it always be remembered to your praise, and as an instructive example in our annals, that under circumstances in which the passions, agitated in every direction, were liable to mislead, amidst appearances sometimes dubious, vicissitudes of fortune often discouraging, in situations in which not unfrequently want of success has countenanced the spirit of criticism, the constancy of your support was the essential prop of the efforts, and a guarantee of the plans by which they were effected. Profoundly penetrated with this idea, I shall carry it with me to my grave, as a strong incitement to unceasing vows that heaven may continue to you the choicest tokens of its beneficence; that your union and brotherly affection may be perpetual; that the free Constitution, which is the work of your hands, may be sacredly maintained; that its administration in every department may be stamped with wisdom and virtue; that, in fine, the happiness of the people of these States, under the auspices of liberty, may be made complete by so careful a preservation and so prudent a use of this blessing as will acquire to them the glory of recommending it to the applause, the affection, and adoption of every nation which is yet a stranger to it.

Here, perhaps, I ought to stop. But a solicitude for your welfare, which cannot end but with my life, and the apprehension of danger, natural to that solicitude, urge me, on an occasion like the present, to offer to your solemn contemplation, and to recommend to your frequent review, some sentiments which are the result of much reflection, of no inconsiderable observation, and which appear to me all-important to the permanency of your felicity as a people. These will be offered to you with the more freedom, as you can only see in them the disinterested warnings of a parting friend, who can possibly have no personal motive to bias his counsel. Nor can I forget, as an encouragement to it, your indulgent reception of my sentiments on a former and not dissimilar occasion.

Interwoven as is the love of liberty with every ligament of your hearts, no recommendation of mine is necessary to fortify or confirm the attachment.

The unity of government which constitutes you one people is also now dear to you. It is justly so, for it is a main pillar in the edifice of your real independence, the support of your tranquility at home, your peace abroad; of your safety; of your prosperity; of that very liberty which you so highly prize. But as it is easy to foresee that, from different causes and from different quarters, much pains will be taken, many artifices employed to weaken in your minds the conviction of this truth; as this is the point in your political fortress against which the batteries of internal and external enemies will be most constantly and actively (though often covertly and insidiously) directed, it is of infinite moment that you should properly estimate the immense value of your national union to your collective and individual happiness; that you should cherish a cordial, habitual, and immovable attachment to it; accustoming yourselves to think and speak of it as of the palladium of your political safety and prosperity; watching for its preservation with jealous anxiety; discountenancing whatever may suggest even a suspicion that it can in any event be abandoned; and indignantly frowning upon the first dawning of every attempt to alienate any portion of our country from the rest, or to enfeeble the sacred ties which now link together the various parts.

For this you have every inducement of sympathy and interest. Citizens, by birth or choice, of a common country, that country has a right to concentrate your affections. The name of American, which belongs to you in your national capacity, must always exalt the just pride of patriotism more than any appellation derived from local discriminations. With slight shades of difference, you have the same religion, manners, habits, and political principles. You have in a common cause fought and triumphed together; the independence and liberty you possess are the work of joint counsels, and joint efforts of common dangers, sufferings, and successes.

But these considerations, however powerfully they address themselves to your sensibility, are greatly outweighed by those which apply more immediately to your interest. Here every portion of our country finds the most commanding motives for carefully guarding and preserving the union of the whole.

The North, in an unrestrained intercourse with the South, protected by the equal laws of a common government, finds in the productions of the latter great additional resources of maritime and commercial enterprise and precious materials of manufacturing industry. The South, in the same intercourse, benefiting by the agency of the North, sees its agriculture grow and its commerce expand. Turning partly into its own channels the seamen of the North, it finds its particular navigation invigorated; and, while it contributes, in different ways, to nourish and increase the general mass of the national navigation, it looks forward to the protection of a maritime strength, to which itself is unequally adapted. The East, in a like intercourse with the West, already finds, and in the progressive improvement of interior communications by land and water, will more and more find a valuable vent for the commodities which it brings from abroad, or manufactures at home. The West derives from the East supplies requisite to its growth and comfort, and, what is perhaps of still greater consequence, it must of necessity owe the secure enjoyment of indispensable outlets for its own productions to the weight, influence, and the future maritime strength of the Atlantic side of the Union, directed by an indissoluble community of interest as one nation. Any other tenure by which the West can hold this essential advantage, whether derived from its own separate strength, or from an apostate and unnatural connection with any foreign power, must be intrinsically precarious.

While, then, every part of our country thus feels an immediate and particular interest in union, all the parts combined cannot fail to find in the united mass of means and efforts greater strength, greater resource, proportionably greater security from external danger, a less frequent interruption of their peace by foreign nations; and, what is of inestimable value, they must derive from union an exemption from those broils and wars between themselves, which so frequently afflict neighboring countries not tied together by the same governments, which their own rival ships alone would be sufficient to produce, but which opposite foreign alliances, attachments, and intrigues would stimulate and embitter. Hence, likewise, they will avoid the necessity of those overgrown military establishments which, under any form of government, are inauspicious to liberty, and which are to be regarded as particularly hostile to republican liberty. In this sense it is that your union ought to be considered as a main prop of your liberty, and that the love of the one ought to endear to you the preservation of the other.

These considerations speak a persuasive language to every reflecting and virtuous mind, and exhibit the continuance of the Union as a primary object of patriotic desire. Is there a doubt whether a common government can embrace so large a sphere? Let experience solve it. To listen to mere speculation in such a case were criminal. We are authorized to hope that a proper organization of the whole with the auxiliary agency of governments for the respective subdivisions, will afford a happy issue to the experiment. It is well worth a fair and full experiment. With such powerful and obvious motives to union, affecting all parts of our country, while experience shall not have demonstrated its impracticability, there will always be reason to distrust the patriotism of those who in any quarter may endeavor to weaken its bands.

In contemplating the causes which may disturb our Union, it occurs as matter of serious concern that any ground should have been furnished for characterizing parties by geographical discriminations, Northern and Southern, Atlantic and Western; whence designing men may endeavor to excite a belief that there is a real difference of local interests and views. One of the expedients of party to acquire influence within particular districts is to misrepresent the opinions and aims of other districts. You cannot shield yourselves too much against the jealousies and heartburnings which spring from these misrepresentations; they tend to render alien to each other those who ought to be bound together by fraternal affection. The inhabitants of our Western country have lately had a useful lesson on this head; they have seen, in the negotiation by the Executive, and in the unanimous ratification by the Senate, of the treaty with Spain, and in the universal satisfaction at that event, throughout the United States, a decisive proof how unfounded were the suspicions propagated among them of a policy in the General Government and in the Atlantic States unfriendly to their interests in regard to the Mississippi; they have been witnesses to the formation of two treaties, that with Great Britain, and that with Spain, which secure to them everything they could desire, in respect to our foreign relations, towards confirming their prosperity. Will it not be their wisdom to rely for the preservation of these advantages on the Union by which they were procured ? Will they not henceforth be deaf to those advisers, if such there are, who would sever them from their brethren and connect them with aliens?

To the efficacy and permanency of your Union, a government for the whole is indispensable. No alliance, however strict, between the parts can be an adequate substitute; they must inevitably experience the infractions and interruptions which all alliances in all times have experienced. Sensible of this momentous truth, you have improved upon your first essay, by the adoption of a constitution of government better calculated than your former for an intimate union, and for the efficacious management of your common concerns. This government, the offspring of our own choice, uninfluenced and unawed, adopted upon full investigation and mature deliberation, completely free in its principles, in the distribution of its powers, uniting security with energy, and containing within itself a provision for its own amendment, has a just claim to your confidence and your support. Respect for its authority, compliance with its laws, acquiescence in its measures, are duties enjoined by the fundamental maxims of true liberty. The basis of our political systems is the right of the people to make and to alter their constitutions of government. But the **Constitution** which at any time exists, till changed by an explicit and authentic act of the whole people, is sacredly obligatory upon all. The very idea of the power and the right of the people to establish government presupposes the duty of every individual to obey the established government.

All obstructions to the execution of the laws, all combinations and associations, under whatever plausible character, with the real design to direct, control, counteract, or awe the regular deliberation and action of the constituted authorities, are destructive of this fundamental principle, and of fatal tendency. They serve to organize faction, to give it an artificial and extraordinary force; to put, in the place of the delegated will of the nation the will of a party, often a small but artful and enterprising minority of the community; and, according to the alternate triumphs of different parties, to make the public administration the mirror of the ill-concerted and incongruous projects of faction, rather than the organ of consistent and wholesome plans digested by common counsels and modified by mutual interests.

However combinations or associations of the above description may now and then answer popular ends, they are likely, in the course of time and things, to become potent engines, by which cunning, ambitious, and unprincipled men will be enabled to subvert the power of the people and to usurp for themselves the reins of government, destroying afterwards the very engines which have lifted them to unjust dominion.

Towards the preservation of your government, and the permanency of your present happy state, it is requisite, not only that you steadily discountenance irregular oppositions to its acknowledged authority, but also that you resist with care the spirit of innovation upon its principles, however specious the pretexts. One method of assault may be to effect, in the forms of the **Constitution**, alterations which will impair the energy of the system, and thus to undermine what cannot be directly overthrown. In all the changes to which you may be invited, remember that time and habit are at least as necessary to fix the true character of governments as of other human institutions; that experience is the surest standard by which to test the real tendency of the existing constitution of a country; that facility in changes, upon the credit of mere hypothesis and opinion, exposes to perpetual change, from the endless variety of hypothesis and opinion; and remember, especially, that for the efficient management of your common interests, in a country so extensive as ours, a government of as much vigor as is consistent with the perfect security of liberty is indispensable. Liberty itself will find in such a government, with powers properly distributed and adjusted, its surest guardian. It is, indeed, little else than a name, where the government is too feeble to withstand the enterprises of faction, to confine each member of the society within the limits prescribed by the laws, and to maintain all in the secure and tranquil enjoyment of the rights of person and property.

I have already intimated to you the danger of parties in the State, with particular reference to the founding of them on geographical discriminations. Let me now take a more comprehensive view, and warn you in the most solemn manner against the baneful effects of the spirit of party generally.

This spirit, unfortunately, is inseparable from our nature, having its root in the strongest passions of the human mind. It exists under different shapes in all governments, more or less stifled, controlled, or repressed; but, in those of the popular form, it is seen in its greatest rankness, and is truly their worst enemy.

The alternate domination of one faction over another, sharpened by the spirit of revenge, natural to party dissension, which in different ages and countries has perpetrated the most horrid enormities, is itself a frightful despotism. But this leads at length to a more formal and permanent despotism. The disorders and miseries which result gradually incline the minds of men to seek security and repose in the absolute power of an individual; and sooner or later the chief of some prevailing faction, more able or more fortunate than his competitors, turns this disposition to the purposes of his own elevation, on the ruins of public liberty.

Without looking forward to an extremity of this kind (which nevertheless ought not to be entirely out of sight), the common and continual mischiefs of the spirit of party are sufficient to make it the interest and duty of a wise people to discourage and restrain it.

It serves always to distract the public councils and enfeeble the public administration. It agitates the community with ill-founded jealousies and false alarms, kindles the animosity of one part against another, foments occasionally riot and insurrection. It opens the door to foreign influence and corruption, which finds a facilitated access to the government itself through the channels of party passions. Thus the policy and the will of one country are subjected to the policy and will of another.

There is an opinion that parties in free countries are useful checks upon the administration of the government and serve to keep alive the spirit of liberty. This within certain limits is probably true; and in governments of a monarchical cast, patriotism may look with indulgence, if not with favor, upon the spirit of party. But in those of the popular character, in governments purely elective, it is a spirit not to be encouraged. From their natural tendency, it is certain there will always be enough of that spirit for every salutary purpose. And there being constant danger of excess, the effort ought to be by force of public opinion, to mitigate and assuage it. A fire not to be quenched, it demands a uniform vigilance to prevent its bursting into a flame, lest, instead of warming, it should consume.

It is important, likewise, that the habits of thinking in a free country should inspire caution in those entrusted with its administration, to confine themselves within their respective constitutional spheres, avoiding in the exercise of the powers of one department to encroach upon another. The spirit of encroachment tends to consolidate the powers of all the departments in one, and thus to create, whatever the form of government, a real despotism. A just estimate of that love of power, and proneness to abuse it, which predominates in the human heart, is sufficient to satisfy us of the truth of this position. The necessity of reciprocal checks in the exercise of political power, by dividing and distributing it into different depositaries, and constituting each the guardian of the public weal against invasions by the others, has been evinced by experiments ancient and modern; some of them in our country and under our own eyes. To preserve them must be as necessary as to institute them. If, in the opinion of the people, the distribution or modification of the constitutional powers be in any particular wrong, let it be corrected by an amendment in the way which the **Constitution** designates. But let there be no change by usurpation; for though this, in one instance, may be the instrument of good, it is the customary weapon by which free governments are destroyed. The precedent must always greatly overbalance in permanent evil any partial or transient benefit, which the use can at any time yield.

Of all the dispositions and habits which lead to political prosperity, religion and morality are indispensable supports. In vain would that man claim the tribute of patriotism, who should labor to subvert these great pillars of human happiness, these firmest props of the duties of men and citizens. The mere politician, equally with the pious man, ought to respect and to cherish them. A volume could not trace all their connections with private and public felicity. Let it simply be asked: Where is the security for property, for reputation, for life, if the sense of religious obligation desert the oaths which are the instruments of investigation in courts of justice ? And let us with caution indulge the supposition that morality can be maintained without religion. Whatever may be conceded to the influence of refined education on minds of peculiar structure, reason and experience both forbid us to expect that national morality can prevail in exclusion of religious principle.

It is substantially true that virtue or morality is a necessary spring of popular government. The rule, indeed, extends with more or less force to every species of free government. Who that is a sincere friend to it can look with indifference upon attempts to shake the foundation of the fabric?

Promote then, as an object of primary importance, institutions for the general diffusion of knowledge. In proportion as the structure of a government gives force to public opinion, it is essential that public opinion should be enlightened.

As a very important source of strength and security, cherish public credit. One method of preserving it is to use it as sparingly as possible, avoiding occasions of expense by cultivating peace, but remembering also that timely disbursements to prepare for danger frequently prevent much greater disbursements to repel it, avoiding likewise the accumulation of debt, not only by shunning occasions of expense, but by vigorous exertion in time of peace to discharge the debts which unavoidable wars may have occasioned, not ungenerously throwing upon posterity the burden which we ourselves ought to bear. The execution of these maxims belongs to your representatives, but it is necessary that public opinion should co-operate. To facilitate to them the performance of their duty, it is essential that you should practically bear in mind that towards the payment of debts there must be revenue; that to have revenue there must be taxes; that no taxes can be devised which are not more or less inconvenient and unpleasant; that the intrinsic embarrassment, inseparable from the selection of the proper objects (which is always a choice of difficulties), ought to be a decisive motive for a candid construction of the conduct of the government in making it, and for a spirit of acquiescence in the measures for obtaining revenue, which the public exigencies may at any time dictate.

Observe good faith and justice towards all nations; cultivate peace and harmony with all. Religion and morality enjoin this conduct; and can it be, that good policy does not equally enjoin it 7 It will be worthy of a free, enlightened, and at no distant period, a great nation, to give to mankind the magnanimous and too novel example of a people always guided by an exalted justice and benevolence. Who can doubt that, in the course of time and things, the fruits of such a plan would richly repay any temporary advantages which might be lost by a steady adherence to it ? Can it be that Providence has not connected the permanent felicity of a nation with its virtue ? The experiment, at least, is recommended by every sentiment which ennobles human nature. Alas! is it rendered impossible by its vices?

In the execution of such a plan, nothing is more essential than that permanent, inveterate antipathies against particular nations, and passionate attachments for others, should be excluded; and that, in place of them, just and amicable feelings towards all should be cultivated. The nation which indulges towards another a habitual hatred or a habitual fondness is in some degree a slave. It is a slave to its animosity or to its affection, either of which is sufficient to lead it astray from its duty and its interest. Antipathy in one nation against another disposes each more readily to offer insult and injury, to lay hold of slight causes of umbrage, and to be haughty and intractable, when accidental or trifling occasions of dispute occur. Hence, frequent collisions, obstinate, envenomed, and bloody contests. The nation, prompted by ill-will and resentment, sometimes impels to war the government, contrary to the best calculations of policy. The government sometimes participates in the national propensity, and adopts through passion what reason would reject; at other times it makes the animosity of the nation subservient to projects of hostility instigated by pride, ambition, and other sinister and pernicious motives. The peace often, sometimes perhaps the liberty, of nations, has been the victim.

So likewise, a passionate attachment of one nation for another produces a variety of evils. Sympathy for the favorite nation, facilitating the illusion of an imaginary common interest in cases where no real common interest exists, and infusing into one the enmities of the other, betrays the former into a participation in the quarrels and wars of the latter without adequate inducement or justification. It leads also to concessions to the favorite nation of privileges denied to others which is apt doubly to injure the nation making the concessions; by unnecessarily parting with what ought to have been retained, and by exciting jealousy, ill-will, and a disposition to retaliate, in the parties from whom equal privileges are withheld. And it gives to ambitious, corrupted, or deluded citizens (who devote themselves to the favorite nation), facility to betray or sacrifice the interests of their own country, without odium, sometimes even with popularity; gilding, with the appearances of a virtuous sense of obligation, a commendable deference for public opinion, or a laudable zeal for public good, the base or foolish compliances of ambition, corruption, or infatuation.

As avenues to foreign influence in innumerable ways, such attachments are particularly alarming to the truly enlightened and independent patriot. How many opportunities do they afford to tamper with domestic factions, to practice the arts of seduction, to mislead public opinion, to influence or awe the public councils 7 Such an attachment of a small or weak towards a great and powerful nation dooms the former to be the satellite of the latter.

Against the insidious wiles of foreign influence (I conjure you to believe me, fellow-citizens) the jealousy of a free people ought to be constantly awake, since history and experience prove that foreign influence is one of the most baneful foes of republican government. But that jealousy to be useful must be impartial; else it becomes the instrument of the very influence to be avoided, instead of a defense against it. Excessive partiality for one foreign nation and excessive dislike of another cause those whom they actuate to see danger only on one side, and serve to veil and even second the arts of influence on the other. Real patriots who may resist the intrigues of the favorite are liable to become suspected and odious, while its tools and dupes usurp the applause and confidence of the people, to surrender their interests.

The great rule of conduct for us in regard to foreign nations is in extending our commercial relations, to have with them as little political connection as possible. So far as we have already formed engagements, let them be fulfilled with perfect good faith. Here let us stop. Europe has a set of primary interests which to us have none; or a very remote relation. Hence she must be engaged in frequent controversies, the causes of which are essentially foreign to our concerns. Hence, therefore, it must be unwise in us to implicate ourselves by artificial ties in the ordinary vicissitudes of her politics, or the ordinary combinations and collisions of her friendships or enmities.

Our detached and distant situation invites and enables us to pursue a different course. If we remain one people under an efficient government. the period is not far off when we may defy material injury from external annoyance; when we may take such an attitude as will cause the neutrality we may at any time resolve upon to be scrupulously respected; when belligerent nations, under the impossibility of making acquisitions upon us, will not lightly hazard the giving us provocation; when we may choose peace or war, as our interest, guided by justice, shall counsel.

Why forego the advantages of so peculiar a situation? Why quit our own to stand upon foreign ground? Why, by interweaving our destiny with that of any part of Europe, entangle our peace and prosperity in the toils of European ambition, rivalship, interest, humor or caprice?

It is our true policy to steer clear of permanent alliances with any portion of the foreign world; so far, I mean, as we are now at liberty to do it; for let me not be understood as capable of patronizing infidelity to existing engagements. I hold the maxim no less applicable to public than to private affairs, that honesty is always the best policy. I repeat it, therefore, let those engagements be observed in their genuine sense. But, in my opinion, it is unnecessary and would be unwise to extend them.

Taking care always to keep ourselves by suitable establishments on a respectable defensive posture, we may safely trust to temporary alliances for extraordinary emergencies.

Harmony, liberal intercourse with all nations, are recommended by policy, humanity, and interest. But even our commercial policy should hold an equal and impartial hand; neither seeking nor granting exclusive favors or preferences; consulting the natural course of things; diffusing and diversifying by gentle means the streams of commerce, but forcing nothing; establishing (with powers so disposed, in order to give trade a stable course, to define the rights of our merchants, and to enable the government to support them) conventional rules of intercourse, the best that present circumstances and mutual opinion will permit, but temporary, and liable to be from time to time abandoned or varied, as experience and circumstances shall dictate; constantly keeping in view that it is folly in one nation to look for disinterested favors from another; that it must pay with a portion of its independence for whatever it may accept under that character; that, by such acceptance, it may place itself in the condition of having given equivalents for nominal favors, and yet of being reproached with ingratitude for not giving more. There can be no greater error than to expect or calculate upon real favors from nation to nation. It is an illusion, which experience must cure, which a just pride ought to discard.

In offering to you, my countrymen, these counsels of an old and affectionate friend, I dare not hope they will make the strong and lasting impression I could wish; that they will control the usual current of the passions, or prevent our nation from running the course which has hitherto marked the destiny of nations. But, if I may even flatter myself that they may be productive of some partial benefit, some occasional good; that they may now and then recur to moderate the fury of party spirit, to warn against the mischiefs of foreign intrigue, to guard against the impostures of pretended patriotism; this hope will be a full recompense for the solicitude for your welfare, by which they have been dictated.

How far in the discharge of my official duties I have been guided by the principles which have been delineated, the public records and other evidences of my conduct must witness to you and to the world. To myself, the assurance of my own conscience is, that I have at least believed myself to be guided by them.

In relation to the still subsisting war in Europe, my proclamation of the twenty-second of April, 1793, is the index of my plan. Sanctioned by your approving voice, and by that of your representatives in both houses of Congress, the spirit of that measure has continually governed me, uninfluenced by any attempts to deter or divert me from it.

After deliberate examination, with the aid of the best lights I could obtain, I was well satisfied that our country, under all the circumstances of the case, had a right to take, and was bound in duty and interest to take, a neutral position. Having taken it, I determined, as far as should depend upon me, to maintain it, with moderation, perseverance, and firmness.

The considerations which respect the right to hold this con duct, it is not necessary on this occasion to detail. I will only observe that, according to my understanding of the matter, that right, so far from being denied by any of the belligerent powers, has been virtually admitted by all.

The duty of holding a neutral conduct may be inferred, without anything more, from the obligation which justice and humanity impose on every nation, in cases in which it is free to act, to maintain inviolate the relations of peace and amity towards other nations.

The inducements of interest for observing that conduct will best be referred to your own reflections and experience. With me a predominant motive has been to endeavor to gain time to our country to settle and mature its yet recent institutions, and to progress without interruption to that degree of strength and consistency which is necessary to give it, humanly speaking, the command of its own fortunes.

Though, in reviewing the incidents of my administration, I am unconscious of intentional error, I am nevertheless too sensible of my defects not to think it probable that I may have committed many errors. Whatever they may be, I fervently beseech the Almighty to avert or mitigate the evils to which they may tend. I shall also carry with me the hope that my country will never cease to view them with indulgence; and that, after forty five years of my life dedicated to its service with an upright zeal, the faults of incompetent abilities will be consigned to oblivion, as myself must soon be to the mansions of rest.

Relying on its kindness in this as in other things, and actuated by that fervent love towards it, which is so natural to a man who views in it the native soil of himself and his progenitors for several generations, I anticipate with pleasing expectation that retreat in which I promise myself to realize, without alloy, the sweet enjoyment of partaking, in the midst of my fellow-citizens, the benign influence of good laws under a free government, the ever-favorite object of my heart, and the happy reward, as I trust, of our mutual cares, labors, and dangers.

Geo. Washington.

Jeffersonian Republicans vs. Federalists: The Struggle over the Sedition Act

Saul Cornell

INTRODUCTION

The 1790s were a period of intense partisan conflict. The notion of party politics was anathema to the Framers of the Constitution, who viewed party as a form of factionalism that was incompatible with republican virtue. Nothing better captured the antipathy to party than Washington's decision to include both Jefferson and Hamilton in his cabinet. Ultimately, Hamilton proved more adept at influencing Washington and his agenda to strengthen the new federal government and forced a realignment in politics. With the adoption of the Bill of Rights, former Anti-Federalists shifted their attentions to the dangers posed by Hamilton's program. Anti-Federalists joined forces with an important group of former Federalists who opposed Hamilton to form the Democratic-Republicans. Although many of the most important state leaders of the Democratic-Republican movement were former Anti-Federalists, the most important theorists of the opposition were the former Federalist James Madison and Thomas Jefferson. Many of the issues raised during the debate over ratification of the Constitution resurfaced a scant few years after its adoption. The conflict between the Jeffersonians and the Federalists during the 1790s cut across a broad range of issues including economics, foreign policy, law, and domestic policy.

One of the most important divisions between the Jeffersonians, who were known at the time as Democratic-Republicans, and the Federalists arose over the question of constitutional interpretation. Two key questions resurfaced time and again. What powers had the Constitution granted to the new government? How ought judges, lawmakers, and the executive interpret the text of the Constitution? For Democratic-Republicans the

Constitution was a document intended to provide a limited grant of authority. To preserve this ideal, it was vital to interpret the text of the Constitution in a strict—almost literal—manner. Federalists, by contrast, believed that within its sphere of authority the federal government had broad powers to achieve its objectives.

No issue proved more controversial during the 1790s than conflict over the Alien and Sedition Acts. This debate was not only one of the most important episodes in the struggle to protect freedom of the press, it also was a key moment in the emergence of the notion of states' rights. The material presented below deals with the constitutionality of the Sedition Act and with the political struggle between Jeffersonians and Federalists.

THE DEBATE OVER THE SEDITION ACT

Federalist fears about the threat of sedition were intensified by the rising tension between the United States and France. The Jeffersonians were closely identified with the French cause, and Federalists took every opportunity to denounce their opponents as champions of French atheism and anarchism. Suspicion of French influence among the Jeffersonians led the Federalists to pass a strict federal sedition law. The debate between Federalists and Jeffersonians on the legality of the Sedition Act reveals a number of important philosophical differences between these two groups. The conflict over this issue provides an excellent illustration of the profound divisions that arose within a decade of the ratification of the U.S. Constitution.

Sir William Blackstone Defines Seditious Libel

The English jurist, Sir William Blackstone, compiled the most influential study of the English common law. American judges and lawyers in the revolutionary era consulted Blackstone as a standard reference work. In the period after the Revolution a number of radical thinkers attacked aspects of Blackstone's jurisprudence because of its anti-republican character. In particular, a number of legal reformers believed that his view of seditious libel was inappropriate for a republican government in which the people, not the monarch, were sovereign. Abridged from Sir William Blackstone, Commentaries on the Laws of England *(London, 1765–69), Book 4 (1769), Chapter 11, 150–53. Punctuation has been altered to clarify meaning.*

Of a nature very similar to challenges are *libels, libelli famosi,* which, taken in their largest and most extensive sense, signify any writings, pictures, or the like, of an immoral or illegal tendency; but, in the sense under which we are now to consider them, are malicious defamations of any person, and especially a magistrate, made public by either printing, writing, signs, or pictures, in order to provoke him to wrath or expose him to public hatred, contempt, and ridicule. The direct tendency of these libels is the breach of the public peace, by stirring up the objects of them to revenge, and perhaps to bloodshed. The communication of a libel to any one person is a publication in the eye of the law; and therefore the sending of an abusive letter to a man is as much a libel as if it were openly printed, for it equally tends to a breach of the peace. For the same reason it is immaterial, with respect to the essence of a libel, whether the matter of it be true or false, since the provocation, and not the falsity, is the thing to be punished criminally; though, doubtless, the falsehood of it may aggravate its guilt, and enhance its punishment. . . .

In this, and the other instances which we have lately considered, where blasphemous, immoral, treasonable, schismatical, seditious, or scandalous libels are punished by the English law, some with a greater, others with a less degree of severity, the *liberty of the press,* properly understood, is by no means infringed or violated. The liberty of the press is indeed essential to the nature of a free state; but this consists in laying no *previous* restraints upon publications, and not in freedom from censure for criminal matter when published. Every freeman has an undoubted right to lay what sentiments he pleases before the public; to forbid this, is to destroy the freedom of the press; but if he publishes what is improper, mischievous, or illegal, he must take the consequence of his own temerity. To subject the press to the restrictive power of a licenser, as was formerly done, both before and since the revolution [meaning the English revolution of 1642–1660], is to subject all freedom of sentiment to the prejudices of one man, and make him the arbitrary and infallible judge of all controverted points in learning, religion, and government. But to punish (as the law does at present) any dangerous or offensive writings, which, when published, shall on a fair and impartial trial be adjudged of a pernicious tendency, is necessary for the preservation of peace and good order, of government and religion, the only solid foundations of civil liberty. Thus the will of individuals is still left free; the abuse only of that free will is the object of legal punishment. Neither is any restraint hereby laid upon freedom of thought or enquiry: liberty of private sentiment is still left; the disseminating or making public, of bad sentiments, destructive of the ends of society, is the crime which society corrects. A man (says a fine writer on this subject) may be allowed to keep poisons in his closet, but not publicly vend them as cordials. . . . So true will it be found, that to censure the licentiousness, is to maintain the liberty of the press.

Jeffersonian Republican Congressman Albert Gallatin Attacks the Sedition Act

---

Gallatin was a leading spokesman for the Jeffersonian Republican forces in Congress. His speech captures a number of the essential philosophical and constitutional beliefs of the Jeffersonians. His argument seeks to dismantle the Federalist case in favor of the Sedition Act. Excerpted from Annals of Congress, *5th Cong., 2d sess. (July 5 and 10, 1798), 2:2107, 2109, 2159–60, 2162.*

Does the situation of the country, at this time, require that any law of this kind should pass? Do there exist such new and alarming symptoms of sedition, as render it necessary to adopt, in addition to the existing laws, any extraordinary measure for the purpose of suppressing unlawful combinations, and of restricting the freedom of speech and of the press? For such were the objects of the bill, whatever modifications it might hereafter receive. . . .

Was the gentleman afraid, or rather was Administration afraid, that in this instance error could not be successfully opposed by truth? The American Government had heretofore subsisted, it had acquired strength, it had grown on the affection of the people, it had been fully supported without the assistance of laws similar to the bill now on the table. It had been able to repel opposition by the single weapon of argument. And at present, when out of ten presses in the country nine were employed on the side of Administration, such is their want of confidence in the purity of their own views and motives, that they even fear the unequal contest, and require the help of force in order to suppress the limited circulation of the opinions of those who did not approve all their measures. One of the paragraphs says, that it will soon become a question whether there will be more liberty at Philadelphia or Constantinople. . . .

. . . It was in order to remove these fears [that the Constitution could be interpreted to permit the government to suppress free speech], that the amendment, which declares that Congress shall pass no law abridging the freedom of speech or the liberty of the press, was proposed and adopted—an amendment which was intended as an express exception to any supposed general power of *passing laws*, &c., vested in Congress by the other clause. The sense, in which he and his friends understood this amendment, was that Congress could not pass any law to punish any real or supposed abuse of the press. The construction given to it by the supporters of the bill was, that it did not prevent them to punish what they called the licentiousness of the press, but merely forbade their laying any previous restraints upon it. It appeared to him preposterous to say, that to punish a certain act was not an abridgement of the liberty of doing that act. It appeared to him that it was an insulting evasion of the Constitution for gentlemen to say, "We claim no power to abridge the liberty of the press; *that,* you shall enjoy unrestrained. You may write and publish what you please, but if you publish anything against us, we will punish you for it. So long as we do not prevent, but only punish your writings, it is no abridgment of your liberty of writing and printing." Congress were by that amendment prohibited from passing any law abridging, &c.; they were, therefore, prohibited from adding any restraint, either by previous restrictions, or by subsequent punishment, or by any alteration of the proper jurisdiction, or of the mode of trial, which did not exist before; in short, they were under an obligation of leaving that subject where they found it—of passing no law, either directly or indirectly, affecting that liberty. . . .

. . . Whilst, therefore, they [the Federalists] support the bill in its present shape, do they not avow that the true object of the law is to enable one party to oppress the other; that they mean to have the power to punish printers who may publish against them, whilst their opponents will remain alone, and without redress, exposed to the abuse of Ministerial prints? Is it not their object to frighten and suppress all presses which they consider as contrary to their views; to prevent a free circulation of opinion; to suffer the people at large to hear only partial accounts, and but one side of the question; to delude and deceive them by partial information, and, through those means, to perpetuate themselves in power?

The Federalists Defend the Sedition Act

Harrison Gray Otis was a leading Federalist politician from Massachusetts. His defense of the constitutionality of the Sedition Act demonstrates the continuing importance of Blackstone to American legal thought. This account of Otis's speech before Congress is taken from Annals of Congress, *5th Cong., 2d sess. (July 10, 1798), 2:2145–48.*

Mr. OTIS said the professions of attachment to the Constitution, made by the gentleman from Virginia [Republican John Nicholas, a critic of the sedition bill], are certainly honorable to him; and he could not believe that an attachment so deeply engrafted as he states his to be would be shaken by this bill. The gentleman had caught an alarm on the first suggestion of a sedition bill, which had not yet subsided; and though the present bill is perfectly harmless, and contains no provision which is not practised upon under the laws of the several States in which gentlemen had been educated, and from which they had drawn most of their ideas of jurisprudence, yet the gentleman continues to be dissatisfied with it.

. . . In the first place, had the Constitution given Congress cognizance over the offences described in this bill prior to the adoption of the amendments to the Constitution? and, if Congress had that cognizance before that time, have those amendments taken it away? With respect to the first question, it must be allowed that every independent Government has a right to preserve and defend itself against injuries and outrages which endanger its existence; for, unless it has this power, it is unworthy the name of a free Government, and must either fall or be subordinate to some other protection. Now some of the offences delineated in the bill are of this description. Unlawful combinations to oppose the measures of Government, to intimidate its officers, and to excite insurrections, are acts which tend directly to the destruction of the

Constitution, and there could be no doubt that the guardians of that Constitution are bound to provide against them. And if gentlemen would agree that these were acts of a criminal nature, it follows that all means calculated to produce these effects, whether by speaking, writing, or printing, were also criminal. . . .

It was . . . most evident to his mind, that the Constitution of the United States, prior to the amendments that have been added to it, secured to the National Government the cognizance of all the crimes enumerated in the bill, and it only remained to be considered whether those amendments divested it of this power. . . . "Congress shall make no law abridging the freedom of speech and of the press." The terms "freedom of speech and of the press," he supposed, were a phraseology perfectly familiar in the jurisprudence of every State, and of a certain and technical meaning. It was a mode of expression which we had borrowed from the only country in which it had been tolerated. . . . In support of this doctrine, he quoted *Blackstone's Commentaries,* under the head of libels, . . . in several of the State constitutions, the liberty of speech and of the press were guarded by the most express and unequivocal language, the Legislatures and Judicial departments of those States had adopted the definitions of the English law, and provided for the punishment of defamatory and seditious libels.

The Sedition Act

The Constitution details treason as the levying of war against the United States or the giving of aid and comfort to the enemy in time of war. Even though America had not declared war on France, the original version of the Sedition Act defined adherence to the French cause as treason, carrying a penalty of death. The final version of the act, less severe, passed by a slim three-vote majority in the House. The text of the Sedition Act is taken from Public Statutes at Large of the United States of America. . . *(Boston, 1848), 1:596–97.*

SECTION 1. *Be it enacted by the Senate and House of Representatives of the United States of America, in Congress assembled,* That if any persons shall unlawfully combine or conspire together, with intent to oppose any measure or measures of the government of the

United States, which are or shall be directed by proper authority, or to impede the operation of any law of the United States, or to intimidate or prevent any person holding a place or office in or under the government of the United States, from undertaking, performing or executing his trust or duty; and if any person or persons, with intent as aforesaid, shall counsel, advise or attempt to procure any insurrection, riot, unlawful assembly, or combination, whether such conspiracy, threatening, counsel, advice, or attempt shall have the proposed effect or not, he or they shall be deemed guilty of a high misdemeanor, and on conviction, before any court of the United States having jurisdiction thereof, shall be punished by a fine not exceeding five thousand dollars, and by imprisonment during a term not less than six months nor exceeding five years; and further, at the discretion of the court may be holden to find sureties for his good behaviour in such sum, and for such time, as the said court may direct.

SEC. 2. *And be it further enacted*, That if any person shall write, print, utter or publish, or shall cause or procure to be written, printed, uttered or published, or shall knowingly and willingly assist or aid in writing, printing, uttering or publishing any false, scandalous and malicious writing or writings against the government of the United States, or either house of the Congress of the United States, or the President of the United States, with intent to defame the said government, or either house of the said Congress, or the said President, or to bring them, or either of them, into contempt or disrepute; or to excite against them, or either or any of them, the hatred of the good people of the United States, or to stir up sedition within the United States, or to excite any unlawful combinations therein, for opposing or resisting any law of the United States, or any act of the President of the United States, done in pursuance of any such law, or of the powers in him vested by the constitution of the United States, or to resist, oppose, or defeat any such law or act, or to aid, encourage or abet any hostile designs of any foreign nation against the United States, their people or government, then such person, being thereof convicted before any court of the United States having jurisdiction thereof, shall be punished by a fine not exceeding two thousand dollars, and by imprisonment not exceeding two years.

SEC. 3. *And be it further enacted and declared*, That if any person shall be prosecuted under this act, for the writing or publishing any libel aforesaid, it shall be lawful for the defendant, upon the trial of the cause, to give in evidence in his defence, the truth of the matter contained in the publication charged as a libel. And the jury who shall try the cause, shall have a right to determine the law and the fact, under the direction of the court, as in other cases.

SEC. 4. *And be it further enacted,* That this act shall continue and be in force until the third day of March, one thousand eight hundred and one, and no longer: *Provided,* that the expiration of the act shall not prevent or defeat a prosecution and punishment of any offence against the law, during the time it shall be in force.

APPROVED, July 14, 1798.

Thomas Cooper Is Tried for Sedition

Cooper, an ardent supporter of the Jeffersonian movement, published a volume entitled Political Essays *(1799) and was the editor of a newspaper in Pennsylvania. The judge in the case, Samuel Chase of Maryland, had been a leading Anti-Federalist during the struggle over the Constitution. Frightened by the radicalism of the French Revolution, Chase became a staunch Federalist during the 1790s. Abridged from "Trial of Thomas Cooper, for a Seditious Libel. In the Circuit Court of the United States for the Pennsylvania District. Philadelphia, 1800" in* State Trials of the United States . . ., *ed. Francis Wharton (Philadelphia, 1849), 659, 663–65, 670–71, 677, 679.*

THE libellous matter complained of was as follows:—

"Nor do I see any impropriety in making this request of Mr. Adams. At that time he had just entered into office; he was hardly in the infancy of political mistake; even those who doubted his capacity thought well of his intentions. Nor were we yet saddled with the expense of a permanent navy, or threatened, under his auspices, with the existence of a standing army. Our credit was not yet reduced so low as to borrow money at eight per cent. in time of peace, while the unnecessary violence of official expressions might justly have provoked a war. Mr. Adams had not yet projected his embassies to Prussia, Russia and the Sublime Porte, nor had he yet interfered, as President of the United States, to influence the decisions of a court of justice—a stretch of authority which the monarch of Great Britain would have shrunk from—an interference without precedent, against law and against mercy. This melancholy case of Jonathan Robbins, a native citizen of America, forcibly impressed by the British, and delivered up, with the advice of Mr. Adams, to the mock trial of a British court-martial, had not yet astonished the republican citizens of this free country; a case too little known, but of which the people ought to be fully apprised, before the election, and they shall be.". . .

Mr. COOPER then addressed the jury as follows:. . .

But I hope, in the course of this trial, I shall be enabled to prove to your satisfaction, that I have published nothing which truth will not justify. That the assertions for which I am indicted are free from malicious imputation, and that my motives have been honest and fair. . . .

You, and all who hear me, well know that this country is divided, and almost equally divided, into two grand parties; usually termed, whether properly or improperly, *Federalists* and *Anti-Federalists*: and that the governing powers of the country are ranked in public opinion under the former denomination—of these divisions, the one wishes to increase, the other to diminish, the powers of the executive; the one thinks that the people (the democracy of the country) has too much, the other too little, influence on the measures of government: the one is friendly, the other hostile, to a standing army and a permanent navy: the one thinks them necessary to repel invasions and aggressions from without, and commotions within; the other, that a well-organized militia is a sufficient safeguard for all that an army could protect, and that a navy is more dangerous and expensive than any benefit derived from it can compensate; the one thinks the liberties of our country endangered by the licentiousness, the other, by the restrictions of the press. Such are some among the leading features of these notorious divisions of political party. It is evident, Gentlemen of the Jury, that each will view with a jealous eye the positions of the other, and that there cannot but be a bias among the partisans of the one side, against the principles and doctrines inculcated by the other. . . .

But in the present state of affairs, the press is open to those who will praise, while the threats of the law hang over those who blame the conduct of the men in power. Indiscriminate approbation of the measures of the executive is not only unattacked, but fostered, and received with the utmost avidity; while those who venture to express a sentiment of opposition must do it in fear and trembling, and run the hazard of being dragged like myself before the frowning tribunal, erected by the Sedition Law. Be it so; but surely this anxiety to protect public character must arise from fear of attack.—That conduct which will not bear investigation will naturally shun it; and whether my opinions are right or wrong, as they are stated in the charge, I cannot help thinking they would have been better confuted by evidence and argument than by indictment. Fines and imprisonment will produce conviction neither in the mind of the sufferer nor of the public.

Nor do I see how the people can exercise on rational grounds their elective franchise, if perfect freedom of discussion of public characters be not allowed. Electors are bound in conscience to reflect and decide who best deserves their suffrages; but how can they do it, if these prosecutions in *terrorem* close all the avenues of information, and throw a veil over the grossest misconduct of our periodical rulers? . . .

Judge CHASE then charged the jury as follows:—Gentlemen of the jury—When men are found rash enough to commit an offence such as the traverser is charged with, it becomes the duty of the government to take care that they should not pass with impunity. It is my duty to state to you the law on which this indictment is preferred, and the substance of the accusation and defence.

Thomas Cooper, the traverser, stands charged with having published a false, scandalous and malicious libel against the President of the United States, in his official character as President. There is no civilized country that I know of, that does not punish such offences; and it is necessary to the peace and welfare of this country, that these offences should meet with their proper punishment, since ours is a government founded on the opinions and confidence of the people. . . .

All governments which I have ever read or heard of punish libels against themselves. If a man attempts to destroy the confidence of the people in their officers, their supreme magistrate, and their legislature, he effectually saps the foundation of the government. A republican government can only be destroyed in two ways; the introduction of luxury, or the licentiousness of the press. This latter is the more slow, but most sure and certain, means of bringing about the destruction of the government. The legislature of this country, knowing this maxim, has thought proper to pass a law to check this licentiousness of the press: by a clause in that law it is enacted—(Judge C. here read the second section of the Sedition Law.) . . .

After the jury had returned with a verdict of Guilty . . . Mr. Cooper attended, and the court sentenced him to pay a fine of four hundred dollars; to be imprisoned for six months, and, at the end of that period, to find surety for his good behaviour, himself in a thousand, and two sureties in five hundred dollars each.

A Jeffersonian Jurist
Rejects Blackstonian Principles

St. George Tucker set out to adapt Blackstone's Commentaries *to the realities of American law and society. His discussion of the differences between English common law and American constitutionalism exerted an enormous influence on Jeffersonian jurisprudence. Selected from St. George Tucker,* Blackstone's Commentaries: With Notes of Reference to the Constitution and Laws, of the Federal Government of the United States; and the Commonwealth of Virginia *(Philadelphia, 1803), appendix to vol. 1, part 2, 15–16, 20, 29–30.*

The consequences of this act [the Sedition Act], as might have been foreseen, were a general astonishment, and dissatisfaction, among all those who considered the government of the United States, as a limited system of government; in it's nature altogether federal, and essentially different from all others which might lay claim to unlimited powers; or even to national, instead of federal authority. The constitutionality of the act was accordingly very generally denied, or questioned by them. They alleged, that it is to the freedom of the press, and of speech, that the American nation is indebted for it's liberty, it's happiness, it's enlightened state, nay more, for it's existence. That in these states the people are the only sovereign: that the government established by themselves, is for their benefit; that those who administer the government, whether it be that of the state, or of the federal union, are the agents and servants of the people, not their rulers or tyrants. That these agents must be, and are, from the nature and principles of our governments, responsible to the people, for their conduct. That to enforce this responsibility, it is indispensibly necessary that the people should inquire into the conduct of their agents;

that in this inquiry, they must, or ought to scrutinize their motives, sift their intentions, and penetrate their designs; and that it was therefore, an unimpeachable right in them to censure as well as to applaud; to condemn or to acquit; and to reject, or to employ them again, as the most severe scrutiny might advise. That as no man can be forced into the service of the people against his own will and consent; so if any man employed by them in any office, should find the tenure of it too severe, because responsibility is inseparably annexed to it, he might retire: if he can not bear scrutiny, he might resign: if his motives, or designs, will not bear sifting; or if censure be too galling to his feelings, he might avoid it in the shades of domestic privacy. . . .

. . . [I]n the United States the case is altogether different [than it is in Great Britain]. The people, not the government, possess the absolute sovereignty. The legislature, no less than the executive, is under limitations of power. Encroachments are regarded as possible from the one, as well as from the other. Hence in the United States, the great and essential rights of the people, are secured against legislative, as well as against executive ambition. They are secured, not by laws paramount to prerogative; but by constitutions paramount to laws. This security of the freedom of the press requires, that it should be exempt, not only from previous restraint by the executive, as in Great-Britain; but from legislative restraint also; and this exemption, to be effectual, must be an exemption, not only from the previous inspection of licencers, but from the subsequent penalty of laws. . . . A further difference between the two governments was also insisted on. In Great-Britain, it is a maxim, that the king, an hereditary, not a responsible magistrate, can do no wrong; and that the legislature, which in two thirds of it's composition, is also hereditary, not responsible, can do what it pleases. In the United States, the executive magistrates are not held to be infallible, nor the legislatures to be omnipotent; and both being elective, are both responsible.

. . . Whoever makes use of the press as the vehicle of his sentiments on any subject, ought to do it in such language as to shew he has a deference for the sentiments of others; that while he asserts the right of expressing and vindicating his own judgment, he acknowledges the obligation to submit to the judgment of those whose authority he cannot legally, or constitutionally dispute. In his statement of facts he is bound to adhere strictly to the truth; for any deviation from the truth is both an imposition upon the public, and an injury to the individual whom it may respect. In his restrictures on the conduct of men, in public stations, he is bound to do justice to their characters, and not to criminate them without substantial reason. The right of character is a sacred and invaluable right, and is not forfeited by accepting a public employment. Whoever knowingly departs from any of these maxims is guilty of a crime against the community, as well as against the person injured; and though both the letter and the spirit of our federal constitution wisely prohibit the congress of the United States from making any law, by which the freedom of speech, or of the press, may be exposed to restraint or persecution under the authority of the federal government, yet for injuries done the reputation of any person, as *an individual*, the state-courts are always open, and may afford ample, and competent redress as the records of the courts of this commonwealth abundantly testify.

Jefferson Defends His Vision of Liberty and Republicanism

In his first Inaugural Address (1801), Jefferson sought to heal the nation's political wounds and articulate the essential principles of America's political creed. Excerpted from A Compilation of the Messages and Papers of the Presidents, *comp. James D. Richardson (Washington, 1910), 1:310–12.*

During the contest of opinion through which we have passed the animation of discussions and of exertions has sometimes worn an aspect which might impose on strangers unused to think freely and to speak and to write what they think; but this being now decided by the voice of the nation, announced according to the rules of the Constitution, all will, of course, arrange themselves under the will of the law, and unite in common efforts for the common good. All, too, will bear in mind this sacred principle, that though the will of the majority is in all cases to prevail, that will to be rightful must be reasonable; that the minority possess their equal rights, which equal law must protect, and to violate would be oppression. Let us, then, fellow-citizens, unite with one heart and one mind. Let us restore to social intercourse that harmony and affection without which liberty and even life itself are but dreary things. And let us reflect that, having banished from our land that religious intolerance under which mankind so long bled and suffered, we have yet gained little if we countenance a political intolerance as despotic, as wicked, and capable of as bitter and bloody persecutions. During the throes and convulsions of the ancient world, during the agonizing spasms of infuriated man, seeking through blood and slaughter his long-lost liberty, it was not wonderful that the agitation of the billows should reach even this distant and peaceful shore; that this should be more felt and feared by some and less by others, and should divide opinions as to measures of safety. But every difference of opinion is not a difference of principle. We have called by different names brethren of the same principle. We are all Republicans, we are all Federalists. If there be any among us who would wish to dissolve this Union or to change its republican form, let them stand undisturbed as monuments of the safety with which error of opinion may be tolerated where reason is left free to combat it. I know, indeed, that some honest men fear that a republican government can not be strong, that this Government is not strong enough; but would the honest patriot, in the full tide of successful experiment, abandon a government which has so far kept us free and firm on the theoretic and visionary fear that this Government, the world's best hope, may by possibility want energy to preserve itself? I trust not. I believe this, on the contrary, the strongest Government on earth. I believe it the only one where every man, at the call of the law, would fly to the standard of the law, and would meet invasions of the public order as his own personal concern. Sometimes it is said that man can not be trusted with government of himself. Can he, then, be trusted with the government of others? Or have we found angels in the forms of kings to govern him? Let history answer this question.

Let us, then, with courage and confidence pursue our own Federal and Republican principles, our attachment to union and representative government. . . .

. . . Equal and exact justice to all men, of whatever state or persuasion, religious or political; peace, commerce, and honest friendship with all nations, entangling alliances with none; the support of the State governments in all their rights, as the most competent administrations for our domestic concerns and the surest bulwarks against antirepublican tendencies; the preservation of the General Government in its whole constitutional vigor, as the sheet anchor of our peace at home and safety abroad; a jealous care of the right of election by the people—a mild and safe corrective of abuses which are lopped by the sword of revolution where peaceable remedies are unprovided; absolute acquiescence in the decisions of the majority, the vital principle of republics, from which is no appeal but to force, the vital principle and immediate parent of despotism; a well-disciplined militia, our best reliance in peace and for the first moments of war, till regulars may relieve them; the supremacy of the civil over the military authority; economy in the public expense, that labor may be lightly burthened; the honest payment of our debts and sacred preservation of the public faith; encouragement of agriculture, and of commerce as its handmaid; the diffusion of information and arraignment of all abuses at the bar of the public reason; freedom of religion; freedom of the press, and freedom of person under the protection of the habeas corpus, and trial by juries impartially selected. These principles form the bright constellation which has gone before us and guided our steps through an age of revolution and reformation. The wisdom of our sages and blood of our heroes have been devoted to their attainment. They should be the creed of our political faith, the text of civic instruction, the touchstone by which to try the services of those we trust; and should we wander from them in moments of error or of alarm, let us hasten to retrace our steps and to regain the road which alone leads to peace, liberty, and safety.

Questions

---

1. *What exactly was the doctrine of seditious libel and how did it function in American and English legal theory? In Jeffersonian legal theory? In Federalist legal theory?*
2. *Were the Federalists justified in passing the sedition law in legal terms? In political terms?*
3. *Is the controversy over the Sedition Act best thought of as a controversy over civil liberties or over federalism?*

FURTHER READING

Richard Buel explores the ideological tensions between Jeffersonians and Federalists in Securing the Revolution: Ideology in American Politics, 1789–1815 *(Ithaca, 1972). Leonard Levy's* Emergence of a Free Press *(New York, 1985) demonstrates the importance of Blackstonian ideals before the outbreak of the sedition crisis. Norman Rosenberg's* Protecting the Best Men: An Interpretive History of the Law of Libel *(Chapel Hill, 1986) examines the way seditious libel functioned within the context of the debate over republican constitutional ideas. Stanley Elkins's and Eric McKitrick's detailed narrative history,* The Age of Federalism *(New York, 1993), provides a panoramic overview of the political issues of the 1790s.*

The Development of American Political Parties, 1815-1840: The Emergence of the Whigs and the Democrats

Jean Harvey Baker

INTRODUCTION

The most significant contribution of Americans to the development of democracy in their own government and in that of other nation-states has been the political party and the associated idea that competition between parties benefits democracy. But the understanding that any rivalry between two or occasionally more organizations encourages citizens' participation and enhances their involvement developed slowly. There is no mention of political parties in the U.S. Constitution. No article considers them; no clause controls their behavior, although today political parties are essential instruments of our government. Nor did the founders from Washington to Adams support such organizations, believing them disruptive factions that infringed on the free choice expected of independent freemen. But even as the leaders of the early Republic claimed that parties threatened the stability of the new nation, their dependence on some kind of organization to run the government, choose leaders, and win elections was apparent. Especially in the U.S. Congress, legislators, including future president James Madison, acted as partisans supporting certain issues and fighting to pass legislation that was opposed by a persistent bloc they understood to be their opponents. But as emerging partisans these early Americans still argued against parties, when they thought of them at all. Their hope was to create a civil society in which factions and discord withered away. In the English poet Alexander Pope's words, "Where order in variety we see/And where, though all things differ, all agree."

For a time—during the so-called Era of Good Feelings from 1817-1825— such harmony ruled. But even during this period the emergence of local divisions over offices and legislation could be glimpsed through the prevailing antiparty rhetoric. The virtues of a permanent organization to contest elections, take positions on issues, bring forth candidates, and even serve as a social association were more and more obvious. Especially during the eight years of Andrew Jackson's presidency (1828-36) a shift in attitude and behavior could be seen, as first the Democrats and then the Whigs created permanent organizations. These early parties were different from the Federalists and Republicans of the previous generation. And while they demonstrated some, though not all, of the crucial characteristics that we have come to associate with modern parties, they were also different from twentieth-century parties. By 1840 the Democrats and the Whigs had developed into national organizations with loyal, disciplined followers, admired leaders, closely fought election contests, and a body of values that separated them—at least in the eye of their supporters—from each other. Whigs and Democrats also came to understand the concept of a loyal opposition in a democratic society, which meant that they might have to alternate power with their opponents. This module will explore how and why Americans changed their minds about parties, and what characterized parties in this Second American Party System.

CONTEMPORARY VIEWS OF PARTIES AND VOTING PATTERNS

When studying the emergence of parties, it is important to consider not just what historians say but also how contemporaries viewed these new organizations that so quickly became fixed institutions. The primary sources that follow include excerpts from political speeches and party platforms and reveal the attitudes of contemporary politicians. Additionally, a table analyzing voter turnouts is included because it is also crucial to consider the behavior of the all-male and overwhelmingly white electorate. Hence, voting returns should be seen as the testimony of Americans who did not leave written speeches or dissertations about their attitude toward parties. Figures on turnout and party selection display the interest that average American males had in the democratic system fostered by the competition between the Whigs and the Democrats.

Excerpts from Washington's Farewell Address (1796)

To the first generation of Americans, George Washington was indeed a hero. He had been an important commander in the French and Indian War. He had served in the Virginia House of Burgesses and later in the Continental Congress. In 1775 he was unanimously selected to command the Continental Army. Thirteen years later he was, again unanimously, elected president of the United States, a nation that he had done much to help create. After serving two terms and deciding not to seek a third, Washington delivered a farewell address in which he considered some of the main issues facing the nation. Among them was the threat of political parties, which despite his warning, had already developed over differences in Congress. Excerpted from James Richardson, ed., A Compilation of the Messages and Papers of the President (Washington, 1897), 1:210-11.

Let me . . . warn you against the baneful effects of party generally. . . . The alternate domination of one faction over another, sharpened by the spirit of revenge natural to party dissension, which in different ages and countries has perpetrated the most horrid enormities, is itself a frightful despotism. . . . the common and continual mischiefs of the spirit of party are sufficient to make it the interest and duty of a wise people to discourage and restrain it. . . .

It {the spirit of party} serves always to distract the public councils and enfeeble the public administration. It agitates the community with ill-founded jealousies and false alarms; kindles the animosity of one part against another; foments occasionally riot and insurrection. It opens the door to foreign influence and corruption, which find a facilitated access to the government itself through the channels of party passion. Thus the policy and the will of one country are subjected to the policy and will of another.

There is an opinion that parties in free countries are useful checks upon the administration of the government, and serve to keep alive the spirit of liberty. . . . in governments of a monarchical cast patriotism may look with indulgence . . . upon the spirit of party. But in those of the popular character, in governments purely elective, it is a spirit not to be encouraged. From their natural tendency it is certain there will always be enough of that spirit for every salutary purpose; and there being constant danger of excess, the effort ought not to be by force of opinion to mitigate and assuage it. A fire not to be quenched, it demands a uniform vigilance to prevent its bursting into a flame, lest, instead of warming, it should consume.

James Monroe and the Period of No Parties

Washington articulated a nearly universal opinion that persisted for a quarter century. Few voices in the early Republic supported the idea of political organizations or the benefits of party competition. At most there were fragmentary suggestions that factions and interest groups were natural expressions of difference. Generally Americans agreed with the Anglo-Irish political writer Edmund Burke that submitting individual preferences to the ideas of a party was a form of servitude. The ideal state followed principles of consensus and harmony, especially in a new political society where it was feared that public contention would shatter the young republic. James Monroe, the fourth president, spoke to this consensus in his first inaugural address delivered in 1817. Excerpted from James Richardson, ed., A Compilation of the Messages and Papers of the Presidents *(Washington, 1896), 2:10.*

Equally gratifying is it to witness the increased harmony of opinion which pervades our Union. Discord does not belong to our system. Union is recommended as well by the free and benign principles of our Government, extending its blessings to every individual, as by the other eminent advantages attending it. The American people have encountered together great dangers and sustained severe trials with success. They constitute one great family with a common interest. Experience has enlightened us on some questions of essential importance to the country.... To promote this harmony in accord with the principles of our republican Government and in a manner to give them the most complete effect, and to advance in all other respects the best interests of our Union, will be the object of my constant and zealous exertions.

A French Visitor Evaluates American Political Parties in 1835

The United States, argued these early leaders, did not need any parties. But increasingly practice did not conform to these ideals. The French aristocrat Alexis de Tocqueville, who had come to assess the American penal system in 1831, recognized the national taste for joining together in associations, some of which were inevitably based on political issues. In Democracy in America, *his famous analysis written in 1835, he discussed what he called "great parties," which were attached to important principles, and "small parties," which in his judgment were little more than interest groups. As a French aristocrat, de Tocqueville was accustomed to political movements during the French Revolution that intended the overthrow of the government, and from such a perspective almost all the Americans' domestic quarrels seemed "incomprehensible and puerile." Excerpted from Alexis de Tocqueville,* Democracy in America, *ed. J. P. Mayer and Max Lerner (New York, 1966), 122, 162–63.*

... The Americans are used to all sorts of elections. Experience has taught them what degree of agitation can be permitted and where whey should stop. The vast extent of the territory over which the inhabitants spread makes collisions between the various parties less probable and less dangerous there than elsewhere. Up to the present the political circumstances of the nation at election time have presented no real danger.

Nevertheless, one may consider the time of the Presidential election as a moment of national crisis. . . .

Moreover, in the United States as elsewhere, parties feel the need to rally around one man in order more easily to make themselves understood by the crowd. Generally, therefore, they use the Presidential candidate's name as a symbol; in him they personify their theories. Hence the parties have a great interest in winning the election, not so much in order to make their doctrines triumph by the President-elect's help, as to show, by his election, that their doctrines have gained a majority. . . .

. . . [T]oday there is no sign of great political parties in the United States. There are many parties threatening the future of the Union, but none which seem to attack the actual form of government and the general course of society. The parties that threaten the union rely not on principles but on material interests. In so vast a land these interests make the provinces into rival nations rather than parties . . .

Lacking great parties, the United States is creeping with small ones and public opinion is broken up ad infinitum about questions of detail. It is impossible to imagine the trouble they take to create parties; it is not an easy matter now. In the United States there is no religious hatred because religion is universally respected and no sect is predominant; there is no class hatred because the people is everything . . . ; and there is no public distress to exploit because the physical state of the country offers such an immense scope to industry that man has only to be left to himself to work marvels. . . . Hence all the skill of politicians consists in forming parties; in the United States a politician first tries to see what his own interest is and who have analogous interests which can be grouped around his own; he is next concerned to discover whether by chance there may not be somewhere in the world a doctrine or a principle that could conveniently be placed at the head of the new association to give it the right to put itself forward and circulate freely. . . .

Van Buren Supports Parties of Principles, Not Men

In the following excerpt, one of the chief architects of the Democratic party in the 1820s and 1830s discusses the development of political parties in a letter to newspaper editor Thomas Ritchie of the Richmond Enquirer. *Although the basic philosophy of political party organization was established by this time, its form, such as whether to nominate by convention or caucus, was not yet determined. In this letter Van Buren makes clear his opposition to any one-party system and argues against the "amalgamationist," one-party principles of James Monroe. He is also opposed to any system of politics that sets great men such as General Jackson above parties. Excerpted from* Martin Van Buren to Thomas Ritchie, 13 January 1817, Martin Van Buren Papers, Library of Congress, Washington, D. C.

[F]or myself I am not tenacious whether we have a congressional caucus or a general convention, so that we have either; the latter would remove the embarrassment of those who have or profess to have scruples, as to the former [it] would be fresher and perhaps more in unison with the spirit of the times. . . . The following, I think, justly be ranked among its probable advantages: It is the best and probably the only practicable mode of concentrating the entire vote of the opposition and of effecting what is of still great importance, the substantial re-organization of the Old Republican party. 2nd, its first result cannot be doubtful. Mr. Adams occupying the seat and being determined not to surrender it except in extremis will not submit his pretension to the convention . . .

. . . Instead of the question being between a northern and southern man, it would be whether or not the ties, which have heretofore bound together a great political party should be severed.

The difference between the two questions would be found to be immense in the elective field. Although a mere party consideration, it is not on that account to be less likely to be effectual. Considerations of this character not infrequently operate as efficiently as those which bear upon the most important questions of constitutional doctrine. Indeed Gen. Jackson has been so little in public life, that it will be not a little difficult to contrast his opinions on great questions with those of Mr. Adams. His letter to Mr. Monroe operates against him in New York by placing him in one respect on the same footing with the present incumbent. Hence the importance if not necessity of collateral matter to secure him a support there. . . .

We must always have party distinctions and the old ones are the best of which the nature of the case admits. Political combinations between the inhabitants in the different states are unavoidable. . . . The country has since flourished under a party thus constituted and may again. . . . Party attachment in former times furnished a complete antidote for sectional prejudices by producing counteracting feelings. . . .

Lastly, the effect of such a nomination on General Jackson can not fail to be considerable. His election, as the result of his military services without reference to party and so far as he alone is concerned and scarcely to principle would be one thing. His election as the result of a combined and concerted effort of a political party, holding in the main, to certain tenets and opposed to certain prevailing principles might be another and a far different thing. . . .

The press is the great lever by which all great movements in the political world must be sustained.

Van Buren Makes Political Parties an Essential Part of Democracy

Near the end of his life, Martin Van Buren began writing his autobiography. By that time he had served from 1837 to 1841 as president of the United States. Ironically, he had suffered a painful lesson about the power and whims of the political parties that he had done much to create when he was not renominated by the Democrats to be their presidential candidate in 1844. Still, his appreciation of political parties had grown during the period, and he believed that no free country could exist without political parties. Excerpted from John C. Fitzpatrick, ed., The Autobiography of Martin Van Buren *(New York, 1973), 125.*

I have been led to take a more extended notice of this subject by my repugnance to a species of cant against Parties in which too many are apt to indulge when their own side is out of power and to forget when they come in. I have not, I think, been considered even by opponents as particularly rancorous in my party prejudices, and might not perhaps have anything to apprehend from a comparison, in this respect, with my cotemporaries. But knowing, as all men of sense know, that political parties are inseparable from free governments, and that in many and material respects they are highly useful to the country, I never could bring myself for party purposes to deprecate their existence. Doubtless excesses frequently attend them and produce many evils, but not so many as are prevented by the maintenance of their organization and vigilance. The disposition to abuse power, so deeply planted in the human heart, can by no other means be more effectually checked; and it has always therefore struck me as more honorable and manly and more in harmony with the character of our People and of our Institutions to deal with the subject of Political Parties in a sincerer and wiser spirit—to recognize their necessity, to give them the credit they deserve, and to devote ourselves to improve and to elevate the principles and objects of our own and to support it ingenuously and faithfully.

Democratic Party Platforms in 1840

Among the important characteristics of the Whigs and the Democrats of the 1830s and 1840s was their commitment to certain positions that separated them from their opponents. Parties represented principles and purpose and were not just electoral machines based on the idea of electing a certain group of leaders to office. The Anti-Masons, a third party, are often credited with organizing the first national presidential nominating convention. The Democratic party, however, in a meeting held in Baltimore in 1840, adopted what would become an important and recurring practice—that is, a platform that was accepted by delegates to a national party convention. In 1840 Democrats accepted nine resolutions, three of which are included below. From Kirk Porter and Donald Johnson, eds., National Party Platforms, 1840-1964 *(Urbana, Ill., 1966), 2.*

1. Resolved, That the federal government is one of limited powers, derived solely from the constitution, and the grants of power shown therein, ought to be strictly construed by all the departments and agents of the government, and that it is inexpedient and dangerous to exercise doubtful constitutional powers. . . .

6. Resolved, That congress has no power to charter a national bank; that we believe such an institution one of deadly hostility to the best interests of the country, dangerous to our republican institutions and the liberties of the people, and calculated to place the business of the country within the control of a concentrated money power, and above the laws and the will of the people. . . .

9. Resolved, That the liberal principles embodied by Jefferson in the Declaration of Independence, and sanctioned in the constitution, which makes ours the land of liberty, and the asylum of the oppressed of every nation, have ever been cardinal principles in the democratic faith; and every attempt to abridge the present privilege of becoming citizens, and the owners of soil among us, ought to be resisted with the same spirit which swept the alien and sedition laws from our statute-book.

Mobilizing the Vote

By the 1840s the Whigs and the Democrats were well organized and mounted professional campaigns to get the vote out. Below is one example from 1840 that suggests that the Illinois Whigs were as well organized as any military force. The following is an excerpt from a letter from Abraham Lincoln to Madison Miller. Excerpted from Roy P. Basler, ed., The Collected Works of Abraham Lincoln *(New Brunswick, N.J., 1953), 1:180-81.*

The Whig county committee should

1st. Appoint one person in each county as county captain, and take his pledge to perform promptly all the duties assigned him.

Duties of the County Captain

1st. To procure from the poll-books a separate list for each Precinct of all the names of all those persons who voted the Whig ticket in August.

2nd. To appoint one person in each Precinct as Precinct Captain, and, by a personal interview with him, procure his pledge, to perform promptly all the duties assigned him.

3rd. To deliver to each Precinct Captain the list of names as above, belonging to his Precinct; and also a written list of his duties.

Duties of the Precinct Captain

1st. To divide the list of names delivered him by the County Captain into Sections of ten who reside most convenient to each other.

2nd. To appoint one person of each Section as Section Captain, and by a personal interview with him, procure his pledge to perform promptly all the duties assigned him.

3rd. To deliver to each Section Captain the list of names belonging to his Section and also a written list of his duties.

Duties of the Section Captain

1st. To see each man of his Section face to face, and procure his pledge that he will for no consideration (impossibilities excepted) stay from the polls on the first monday in November; and that he will record his vote as early on the day as possible.

2nd. To add to his Section the name of every person in his vicinity who did not vote with us in August, but who will vote with us in the fall, and take the same pledge of him, as from the others. 3rd. To *task* himself to procure at least the additional names to his Section.

Increasing Turnouts among the Electorate

Below is a table of the turnout among eligible voters in presidential elections that reveals the increasing participation of Americans in elections. Clearly the party system encouraged the enfranchised to take part in a democratic process. From Joel H.Silbey, The American Political Nation, 1838–1893 *(Stanford, 1991), 14, 29, 145.*

NATIONAL VOTING TURNOUT: PRESIDENTIAL ELECTIONS 1800-1840

YEAR	TURNOUT OF ELIGIBLE VOTERS (Percentage Rounded Off)
1800	31
1804	25
1808	37
1812	n.a.
1816	21
1820	10
1824	27
1828	57
1832	57
1836	56
1840	80

Questions

1. *To what extent are Washington's specific objections to political parties legitimate? Can you think of an example from his administration that displays his specific warnings?*

2. *Monroe's description of harmony for the American republic sounds idyllic. Is his metaphor of the United States as one great family realistic and/or worthy of emulation? Are there reasons why consensus is not something to pursue?*

3. *As a French aristocrat de Tocqueville's sense of parties was quite different than that of most Americans. How so? In what ways does his view of human nature conflict with that of Monroe? To what extent is a view of human nature an important backdrop to a position on the merits and demerits of political parties? What reasons does de Tocqueville give for the Americans not having "great" political parties? Do you agree?*

4. *Why shouldn't Americans simply vote for political candidates on the basis of their "personal popularity"?*

5. *What public issues seem to you to have had the most influence on the creation of the Second American Party System?*

Further Reading

Along with the shift in mainstream attitudes about political parties came an understanding that they were worthy of study. Contemporary accounts include Jabez Hammond, The History of Political Parties in the State of New York from the Ratification of the Federal Constitution to December, 1840, 2 vols. *(Buffalo, 1850); Martin Van Buren,* Inquiry into the Origin and Course of Political Parties in the United States *(New York, 1867); and Philip Friese,* An Essay on Party Showing Its Uses, Its Abuses, and Its Natural Dissolution . . . *(New York, 1856). The classic study of the American government contained in the* Federalist Papers *is worth examining for what it does not say about political parties. More recent examinations appear in Richard Hofstadter,* The Idea of a Party System: The Rise of Legitimate Opposition in the United States, 1789-1840 *(Berkeley, 1969); Richard McCormick,* The Second American Party System *(Chapel Hill, 1966); and Roy Nichols,* The Invention of the American Political Parties *(New York, 1967). Increasingly, the focus of attention has shifted to the voting behavior of the electorate, and among the pathbreaking investigations in this area is Ronald Formisano,* The Birth of Mass Political Parties: Michigan, 1827-1861 *(Princeton, 1971).*

Jacksonian Democracy

Daniel Feller

INTRODUCTION

The word "democracy" first came into widespread use during the presidency of Andrew Jackson (1829-1837). It was adopted both as a self-identifying label by Jackson's Democratic party and by European visitors (most notably the Frenchman Alexis de Tocqueville) who saw it as Americans' distinguishing national characteristic. From the outset, then, democracy's meaning was ambiguous, used sometimes to identify a political movement or program within American society and at others to describe the society as a whole. Still, however vaguely defined, the notion that America grew more democratic in Jackson's day became a commonplace, as expressed in the phrase "Jacksonian Democracy."

For historians seeking to understand both Jackson's party and his era, this label raises far more questions than it answers. For one thing, it begs the question of how democratic America really was in Jackson's day—or still is today, since Jacksonian Democracy is often taken as the model for our own. What does democracy mean? Is it a mere formal arrangement for electing leaders, or a political system that genuinely serves the needs and interests of "the people"? If the second, then how can we be sure what the people really want? Do elections always offer them clear alternatives? And what about those people who don't vote, or whose vote is bribed, coerced, or carelessly cast?

Even the phrase "the people" demands inspection. By the 1820s, most states had expanded the suffrage (the right to vote) from holders of property to all adult white males. Jackson, a great popular hero since his stunning victory over the British at New Orleans in the War of 1812, certainly benefited from this trend.

But neither he nor the Democratic party, which organized under his presidency in the 1830s, had initiated it. As their name implied, Jackson and the Democrats always claimed to represent the true interests of the people. They branded the opposing political party—the Whigs, led by Henry Clay—as "the aristocracy." Some historians have accepted this Democratic claim pretty much at face value, but others dismiss it as mere campaign propaganda. Certainly the Whigs themselves denied it. In elections from the late 1830s through the 1840s the two parties appeared to be nearly evenly matched in popular appeal.

Further, although the expanded suffrage did point toward a more broadly representative politics, from today's perspective Jacksonian Democracy seems as noteworthy for whom it left out as for whom it included. When politicians spoke of "the voice of the people," they did not include white women, the Native American tribes, or the slaves. Even the thousands of free blacks who legally had the right to vote suffered pervasive discrimination and were effectively deprived of this right in most parts of the country. Together these groups, though not among the voting "people," numbered well more than half the population. To complicate the issue, though both parties shunned demands for the abolition of slavery or for women's rights, the Whigs were generally more receptive to appeals for racial and sexual justice, and more sympathetic to the plight of the Indians, than were Andrew Jackson's Democrats. Overall, there is evidence to show that American politics and society were becoming not less but more exclusionary along racial and sexual lines in the era of "Jacksonian Democracy."

Still further perplexities arise when we consider the policy content of Jacksonian Democracy. The main issues of Jackson's presidency concerned the role that government should play in promoting and balancing the country's rapid economic development.

The chief tools available for economic intervention included a protective tariff on imported manufactures, subsidies for transportation projects such as roads and canals, and a federally chartered — but privately owned and managed—central bank. Henry Clay and the Whigs espoused all these policies, under the general heading of the "American System"—a comprehensive plan for ordered progress.

Jackson and the Democrats, however, opposed the System, and especially its centerpiece, the Bank of the United States. They demanded a simple, frugal government, divorced from connections with private enterprise. To achieve this laissez faire end, Jackson wielded his executive powers vigorously, especially the veto. In a prolonged struggle known as the "Bank War," he destroyed the Bank of the United States by vetoing its recharter and then removing the federal government's deposits from its vaults. He blocked transportation subsidies and successfully urged a reduction of the tariff. By the time he retired in 1837, the policy differences between the two parties were crystal-clear. Yet their significance has been endlessly disputed.

THE CONTEMPORARY EVIDENCE

Given the variety of opinions by historians, we are compelled to evaluate those opinions by retracing their steps and reviewing the primary sources. We need to examine carefully what politicians, especially Andrew Jackson, actually said. Immersing oneself in the sources is vital to comprehending Jacksonian Demoracy, or indeed any historical subject. And yet—as the selections here illustrate—even this strategy yields no simple answers.

A European View

In the 1820s and 1830s, many Europeans flocked to the United States to observe and report on the Americans' democratic experiment. One of them was Alexis de Tocqueville, a French aristocrat who toured the country in 1831-32 and subsequently published Democracy in America *in two volumes. Comprehensive and at times highly abstract, it is generally considered the most penetrating analysis of American society and character ever penned. In Tocqueville's eyes democracy was not the program of a particular movement or party within American society. It was a principle that pervaded and shaped the whole—and that would, for good or ill, eventually sweep the world. Excerpted from Alexis de Tocqueville,* Democracy in America, *trans. Phillips Bradley (New York, 1945), 1:3, 51-53, 57-58.*

Among the novel objects that attracted my attention during my stay in the United States, nothing struck me more forcibly than the general equality of condition among the people. I readily discovered the prodigious influence that this primary fact exercises on the whole course of society; it gives a peculiar direction to public opinion and a peculiar tenor to the laws; it imparts new maxims to the governing authorities and peculiar habits to the governed.

I soon perceived that the influence of this fact extends far beyond the political character and the laws of the country, and that it has no less effect on civil society than on the government; it creates opinions, gives birth to new sentiments, founds novel customs, and modifies whatever it does not produce. The more I advanced in the study of American society, the more I perceived that this equality of condition is the fundamental fact from which all others seem to be derived and the central point at which all my observations constantly terminated. . . .

It is not only the fortunes of men that are equal in America; even their acquirements partake in some degree of the same uniformity. I do not believe that there is a country in the world where, in proportion to the population, there are so few ignorant and at the same time so few learned individuals. Primary instruction is within the reach of everybody; superior instruction is scarcely to be obtained by any. . . .

In America the aristocratic element has always been feeble from its birth; and if at the present day it is not actually destroyed, it is at any rate so completely disabled that we can scarcely assign to it any degree of influence on the course of affairs.

The democratic principle, on the contrary, has gained so much strength by time, by events, and by legislation, as to have become not only predominant, but all-powerful. . . .

America, then, exhibits in her social state an extraordinary phenomenon. Men are there seen on a greater equality in point of fortune and intellect, or, in other words, more equal in their strength, than in any other country of the world, or in any age of which history has preserved the remembrance. . . .

At the present day the principle of the sovereignty of the people has acquired in the United States all the practical development that the imagination can conceive. . . .

In some countries a power exists which, though it is in a degree foreign to the social body, directs it, and forces it to pursue a certain track. In others the ruling force is divided, being partly within and partly without the ranks of the people. But nothing of the kind is to be seen in the United States; there society governs itself for itself. All power centers in its bosom, and scarcely an individual is to be met with who would venture to conceive or, still less, to express the idea of seeking it elsewhere. The nation participates in the making of its laws by the choice of its legislators, and in the execution of them by the choice of the agents of the executive government; it may almost be said to govern itself, so feeble and so restricted is the share left to the administration, so little do the authorities forget their popular origin and the power from which they emanate. The people reign in the American political world as the Deity does in the universe. They are the cause and the aim of all things; everything comes from them, and everything is absorbed in them.

Andrew Jackson: First Annual Message

In 1828 Andrew Jackson was elected president, defeating the incumbent John Quincy Adams of Massachusetts. The election displayed a clear sectional pattern; the Tennessean Jackson swept all the South and West while Adams carried New England. Beyond this sectional alignment, the reasons for Jackson's victory are unclear. While Jackson's campaign theme promoted Jacksonian Democrats as "the people" versus the Whig "aristocracy," the campaign itself focused far more attention on personalities and on Jackson's heroic image than it did on issues.

Jackson's first annual message to Congress in December 1829 (what today we call a State of the Union address) announced some enduring themes of his presidency and divulged some of the content of what became known as "Jacksonian Democracy." Jackson proposed a constitutional amendment to make presidents directly electable by the people, a measure he continued to urge without success. He announced that Indian tribes residing within the states must—treaty stipulations notwithstanding— either consent to remove westward beyond existing state boundaries or disband their tribal governments and submit to state authority. He intimated his dissatisfaction with the Bank of the United States and, without pronouncing a particular stance on the tariff and internal improvements, propounded a general philosophy of limited and frugal government. Lastly, in the passage below, he justified on democratic grounds his policy of removing many career government officials and replacing them with his own partisans—a practice that would later become notorious as the "spoils system." Excerpted from A Compilation of the Messages and Papers of the Presidents: 1789-1897, *ed.* James D. Richardson *(Washington, 1896), 2: 448-49, 452.*

There are, perhaps, few men who can for any great length of time enjoy office and power without being more or less under the influence of feelings unfavorable to the faithful discharge of their public duties. Their integrity may be proof against improper considerations immediately addressed to themselves, but they are apt to acquire a habit of looking with indifference upon the public interests and of tolerating conduct from which an unpracticed man would revolt. Office is considered as a species of property, and government rather as a means of promoting individual interests than as an instrument created solely for the service of the people. Corruption in some and in others a perversion of correct feelings and principles divert government from its legitimate ends and make it an engine for the support of the few at the expense of the many. The duties of all public officers are, or at least admit of being made, so plain and simple that men of intelligence may readily qualify themselves for their performance; and I can not but believe that more is lost by the long continuance of men in office than is generally to be gained by their experience. . . .

In a country where offices are created solely for the benefit of the people no one man has any more intrinsic right to official station than another. Offices were not established to give support to particular men at the public expense. No individual wrong is, therefore, done by removal, since neither appointment to nor continuance in office is matter of right. The incumbent became an officer with a view to public benefits, and when these require his removal they are not to be sacrificed to private interests. . . . He who is removed has the same means of obtaining a living that are enjoyed by the millions who never held office. . . .

. . . That this was intended to be a government of limited and specific, and not general, powers must be admitted by all, and it is our duty to preserve for it the character intended by its framers. If experience points out the necessity for an enlargement of these powers, let us apply for it to those for whose benefit it is to be exercised, and not undermine the whole system by a resort to

A portrait of Andrew Jackson during his second term. (Courtesy of Corbis Images.)

overstrained constructions. . . . The great mass of legislation relating to our internal affairs was intended to be left where the Federal Convention found it—in the State governments. Nothing is clearer, in my view, than that we are chiefly indebted for the success of the Constitution under which we are now acting to the watchful and auxiliary operation of the State authorities. . . . I can not, therefore, too strongly or too earnestly, for my own sense of its importance, warn you against all encroachments upon the legitimate sphere of State sovereignty.

Andrew Jackson: The Bank Veto

By 1832, when he stood successfully for re-election against Henry Clay, Jackson's stance on economic issues had become much more clearly defined. Beginning with the Maysville Road in 1830, he vetoed congressional subsidies to internal improvement projects, attacking them as constitutionally dubious, politically divisive, and recklessly expensive. In 1831 he came out for a lower tariff and "a reduction of our revenue to the wants of the Government."

In 1832, just months before the presidential election, Congress passed a bill to renew the charter of the Bank of the United States, which was due to expire in 1836. Jackson vetoed it, with a message that became the defining document of his presidency. Echoing Thomas Jefferson, he attacked the charter as an unconstitutional extension of congressional authority. He denied the Bank's efficacy in handling the government's finances and maintaining a stable currency and complained of its irresponsible management. The core of the message, however, was an attack on the Bank as an engine of privilege—an attack whose meaning and implications have been disputed ever since.

The veto was but the beginning of Jackson's Bank War. In the ensuing presidential contest both sides used Jackson's message as a campaign document. Jackson read his victory over Clay (a champion of the Bank) as encouragement to proceed further. After the election he removed the federal government's deposits from the Bank of the United States to selected state-chartered banks. By the end of his presidency his hostility toward the Bank of the United States had broadened into a general animus against all chartered banks, state or federal, and a conviction that banknote currency should be replaced in everyday transactions by gold and silver "hard money." Excerpted from A Compilation of the Messages and Papers of the Presidents: 1789-1897, *ed. James D. Richardson (Washington, 1896), 2:576-79, 590-91.*

The present corporate body, denominated the president, directors, and company of the Bank of the United States . . . enjoys an exclusive privilege of banking under the authority of the General Government, a monopoly of its favor and support, and, as a necessary consequence, almost a monopoly of the foreign and domestic exchange. The powers, privileges, and favors bestowed upon it in the original charter, by increasing the value of the stock far above its par value, operated as a gratuity of many millions to the stockholders.

. . . The act before me proposes another gratuity to the holders of the same stock, and in many cases to the same men, of at least seven millions more. . . . It is not our own citizens only who are to receive the bounty of our Government. More than eight millions of the stock of this bank are held by foreigners. By this act the American Republic proposes virtually to make them a present of some millions of dollars. For these gratuities to foreigners and to some of our own opulent citizens the act secures no equivalent whatever. . . .

. . . If we must have such a corporation, why should not the Government sell out the whole stock and thus secure to the people the full market value of the privileges granted? . . .

But this act does not permit competition in the purchase of this monopoly. . . . It appears that more than a fourth part of the stock is held by foreigners and the residue is held by a few hundred of our own citizens, chiefly of the richest class. For their benefit does this act exclude the whole American people from competition in the purchase of this monopoly and dispose of it for many millions less than it is worth. . . .

The fourth section . . . secures to the State banks a legal privilege in the Bank of the United States which is withheld from all private citizens. If a State bank in Philadelphia owe the Bank of the United States and have notes issued by the St. Louis branch, it can pay the debt with those notes, but if a merchant, mechanic, or other private citizen be in like circumstances he can not by law pay his debt with those notes, but must sell them at a discount or send them to St. Louis to be cashed. This boon conceded to the State banks, though not unjust in itself, is most odious because it does not measure out equal justice to the high and the low, the rich and the poor. To the extent of its practical effect it is a bond of union among the banking establishments of the nation, erecting them into an interest separate from that of the people. . . .

It is to be regretted that the rich and powerful too often bend the acts of government to their selfish purposes. Distinctions in society will always exist under every just government. Equality of talents, of education, or of wealth can not be produced by human institutions. In the full enjoyment of the gifts of Heaven and the fruits of superior industry, economy, and virtue, every man is equally entitled to protection by law; but when the laws undertake to add to these natural and just advantages artificial distinctions, to grant titles, gratuities, and exclusive privileges, to make the rich richer and the potent more powerful, the humble members of society—the farmers, mechanics, and laborers—who have neither the time nor the means of securing like favors to themselves, have a right to complain of the injustice of their Government. There are no necessary evils in government. Its evils exist only in its abuses. If it would confine itself to equal protection, and, as Heaven does its rains, shower its favors alike on the high and the low, the rich and the poor, it would be an unqualified blessing. In the act before me there seems to be a wide and unnecessary departure from these just principles.

Nor is our Government to be maintained or our Union preserved by invasions of the rights and powers of the several States. In thus attempting to make our General Government strong we make it weak. Its true strength consists in leaving individuals and States as much as possible to themselves. . . .

. . . Many of our rich men have not been content with equal protection and equal benefits, but have besought us to make them richer by act of Congress. By attempting to gratify their desires we have in the results of our legislation arrayed section against section, interest against interest, and man against man, in a fearful commotion with threatens to shake the foundations of our Union. . . . If we can not at once, in justice to interests vested under improvident legislation, make our Government what it ought to be, we can at least take a stand against all new grants of monopolies and exclusive privileges, against any prostitution of our Government to the advancement of the few at the expense of the many, and in favor of compromise and gradual reform in our code of laws and system of political economy.

Andrew Jackson: Farewell Address

On the last day of his presidency, in March 1837, Jackson issued a Farewell Address, a valedictory message summarizing his mature political philosophy. The address urged Americans to avoid sectional contention and cherish the Union. But it also warned of a conspiratorial "money power" that threatened to destroy the liberties of the citizens and subvert republican government. Hitherto Jackson had come out on different occasions against internal improvement subsidies, protective tariffs, and bank charters. Here he linked them all together, in the most radical of his political pronouncements. Excerpted from A Compilation of the Messages and Papers of the Presidents, *ed. James D. Richardson (Washington, 1896), 3:298-303, 305-6.*

It is well known that there have always been those amongst us who wish to enlarge the powers of the General Government, and experience would seem to indicate that there is a tendency on the part of this Government to overstep the boundaries marked out for it by the Constitution. Its legitimate authority is abundantly sufficient for all the purposes for which it was created, and its powers being expressly enumerated, there can be no justification for claiming anything beyond them. Every attempt to exercise power beyond these limits should be promptly and firmly opposed. . . .

Plain as these principles appear to be, you will yet find there is a constant effort to induce the General Government to go beyond the limits of its taxing power and to impose unnecessary burdens upon the people. Many powerful interests are continually at work to procure heavy duties on commerce and to swell the revenue beyond the real necessities of the public service, and the country has already felt the injurious effects of their combined influence. They succeeded in obtaining a tariff of duties bearing most oppressively on the agricultural and laboring classes of society and producing a revenue that could not be usefully employed within the range of the powers conferred upon Congress, and in order to fasten upon the people this unjust and unequal system of taxation extravagant schemes of internal improvement were got up in various quarters to squander the money and to purchase support. Thus one unconstitutional measure was intended to be upheld by another, and the abuse of the power of taxation was to be maintained by usurping the power of expending the money in internal improvements. . . .

. . . Do not allow yourselves, my fellow-citizens, to be misled on this subject. The Federal Government can not collect a surplus for such purposes without violating the principles of the Constitution and assuming powers which have not been granted. It is, moreover, a system of injustice, and if persisted in will inevitably lead to corruption, and must end in ruin. The surplus revenue will be drawn from the pockets of the people—from the farmer, the mechanic, and the laboring classes of society; but who will receive it when distributed among the States, where it is to be disposed of by leading State politicians, who have friends to favor and political partisans to gratify? It will certainly not be returned to those who paid it and who have most need of it and are honestly entitled to it. There is but one safe rule, and that is to confine the General Government rigidly within the sphere of its appropriate duties. It has no power to raise a revenue or impose taxes except for the purposes enumerated in the Constitution, and if its income is found to exceed these wants it should be forthwith reduced and the burden of the people so far lightened.

In reviewing the conflicts which have taken place between different interests in the United States and the policy pursued since the adoption of our present form of Government, we find nothing that has produced such deep-seated evil as the course of legislation in relation to the currency. The Constitution of the United States unquestionably intended to secure to the people a circulating medium of gold and silver. But the establishment of a national bank by Congress, with the privilege of issuing paper money receivable in the payment of the public dues, and the unfortunate course of legislation in the several States upon the same subject, drove from general circulation the constitutional currency and substituted one of paper in its place. . . .

Recent events have proved that the paper-money system of this country may be used as an engine to undermine your free institutions, and that those who desire to engross all power in the hands of the few and to govern by corruption or force are aware of its power and prepared to employ it. Your banks now furnish your only circulating medium, and money is plenty or scarce according to the quantity of notes issued by them. While they have capitals not greatly disproportioned to each other, they are competitors in business, and no one of them can exercise dominion over the rest; and although in the present state of the currency these banks may and do operate injuriously upon the habits of business, the pecuniary concerns, and the moral tone of society, yet, from their number and dispersed situation, they can not combine for the purposes of political influence, and whatever may be the dispositions of some of them their power of mischief must necessarily be confined to a narrow space and felt only in their immediate neighborhoods.

But when the charter for the Bank of the United States was obtained from Congress it perfected the schemes of the paper system and gave to its advocates the position they have struggled to obtain from the commencement of the Federal Government to the present hour. The immense capital and peculiar privileges bestowed upon it enabled it to exercise despotic sway over the other banks in every part of the country. . . . The other banking institutions were sensible of its strength, and they soon generally became its obedient instruments, ready at all times to execute its mandates. . . . The result of the ill-advised legislation which established this great monopoly was to concentrate the whole moneyed power of the Union, with its boundless means of corruption and its numerous dependents, under the direction and command of one acknowleged head. . . . In the hands of this formidable power, thus perfectly organized, was also placed unlimited dominion over the amount of the circulating medium, giving it the power to regulate the value of property and the fruits of labor in every quarter of the Union, and to bestow prosperity or bring ruin upon any city or section of the country as might best comport with its own interest or policy. . . .

It is one of the serious evils of our present system of banking that it enables one class of society—and that by no means a numerous one—by its control over the currency, to act injuriously upon the interests of all the others and to exercise more than its just proportion of influence in political affairs. The agricultural, the mechanical, and the laboring classes have little or no share in the direction of the great moneyed corporations, and from their habits and the nature of their pursuits they are incapable of forming extensive combinations to act together with united force. . . . The planter, the farmer, the mechanic, and the laborer all know that their success depends upon their own industry and economy, and that they must not expect to become suddenly rich by the fruits of their toil. Yet these classes of society form the great body of the people of the United States; they are the bone and sinew of the country—men who love liberty and desire nothing but equal rights and equal laws, and who, moreover, hold the great mass of our national wealth, although it is distributed in moderate amounts among the millions of freemen who possess it. But with overwhelming numbers and wealth on their side they are in constant danger of losing their fair influence in the Government, and with difficulty maintain their just rights against the incessant efforts daily made to encroach upon them. The mischief springs from the power which the moneyed interest derives from a paper currency which they are able to control, from the multitude of corporations with exclusive privileges which they have succeeded in obtaining in the different States, and which are employed altogether for their benefit; and unless you become more watchful in your States and check this spirit of monopoly and thirst for exclusive privileges you will in the end find that the most important powers of Government have been given or bartered away, and the control over your dearest interests has passed into the hands of these corporations.

The paper-money system and its natural associations—monopoly and exclusive privileges—have already struck their roots too deep in the soil, and it will require all your efforts to check its further growth and to eradicate the evil. The men who profit by the abuses and desire to perpetuate them will continue to besiege the halls of legislation in the General Government as well as in the States, and will seek by every artifice to mislead and deceive the public servants. It is to yourselves that you must look for safety and the means of guarding and perpetuating your free institutions. In your hands is rightfully placed the sovereignty of the country, and to you everyone placed in authority is ultimately responsible.... [W]hile the people remain, as I trust they ever will, uncorrupted and incorruptible, and continue watchful and jealous of their rights, the Government is safe, and the cause of freedom will continue to triumph over all its enemies.

Henry Clay: The Whig Response

Henry Clay of Kentucky personified the Whigs as Jackson did the Democrats. He was their most popular figure as well as their chief framer of policy. In Senate speeches defending the protective tariff in 1833 and the banking system in 1837, he presented the Whig alternative to Jackson's view of economic relationships. Excerpted from The Speeches of Henry Clay, *ed. Calvin Colton (New York, 1857), 1:442-43, 464, 2:71-75.*

If the system of protection be founded on principles erroneous in theory, pernicious in practice, above all, if it be unconstitu-

A portrait of Henry Clay, Jackson's chief political adversary. (Courtesy of the National Portrait Gallery/Art Resource.)

tional, as is alleged, it ought to be forthwith abolished, and not a vestige of it suffered to remain. But before we sanction this sweeping denunciation, let us look a little at this system, its magnitude, its ramifications, its duration, and the high authorities which have sustained it. . . . Why, sir, there is scarcely an interest, scarcely a vocation in society, which is not embraced by the beneficence of this system.

It comprehends our coasting tonnage and trade, from which all foreign tonnage is absolutely excluded. . . .

It embraces our fisheries, and all our hardy and enterprising fishermen.

It extends to almost every mechanic art—to tanners, cord-wainers, tailors, cabinet-makers, hatters, tinners, brass-workers, clock-makers, coach-makers, tallow-chandlers, trace-makers, rope-makers, cork-cutters, tobacconists, whip-makers, paper-makers, umbrella-makers, glass-blowers, stocking-weavers, button-makers, saddle and harness-makers, cutlers, brush-makers, bookbinders, dairymen, milk-farmers, blacksmiths, typefounders, musical-instrument-makers, basket-makers, milliners, potters, chocolate-makers, floor-cloth-makers, bonnet-makers, hair-cloth-makers, copper-smiths, pencil-makers, bellows-makers, pocket-book-makers, card-makers, glue-makers, mustard-makers, lumber-sawyers, saw-makers, scale-beam-makers, scythe-makers, wood-saw-makers, and many others. . . .

I regret, Mr. President, that one topic has, I think, unnecessarily been introduced into this debate. I allude to the charge brought against the manufacturing system, as favoring the growth of aristocracy. . . . The joint-stock companies of the North, as I understand them, are nothing more than associations, sometimes of hundreds, by means of which the small earnings of many are brought into a common stock, and the associates, obtaining corporate privileges, are enabled to prosecute, under one superintending head, their business to better advantage. Nothing can be more essentially democratic or better devised to counterpoise the influence of individual wealth. In Kentucky, almost every manufactory known to me, is in the hands of enterprising and self-made men, who have acquired whatever wealth they possess by patient and diligent labor.

The professed object of the administration is, to establish what it terms the currency of the Constitution, which it proposes to accomplish by restricting the federal government, in all receipts and payments, to the exclusive use of specie, and by refusing all bank paper, whether convertible or not. . . .

Is it desirable to banish a convertible paper medium, and to substitute the precious metals as the sole currency to be used in all the vast extent of varied business of this entire country? I think not. The quantity of precious metals in the world, looking to our fair distributive share of them, is wholly insufficient. A convertible paper is a great time-saving and labor-saving instrument, independent of its superior advantages in transfers and remittances. . . . A young, growing, and enterprising people, like those of the United States, more than any other, need the use of those credits which are incident to a sound paper system. Credit is the friend of indigent merit. . . . We must cease to be a commercial people; we must separate, divorce ourselves from the commercial world, and throw ourselves back for centuries, if we restrict our business to the exclusive use of specie. . . .

. . . What are these banks, now so decried and denounced? Intruders, aliens, enemies, that have found their way into the bosom of our country against our will? Reduced to their elements, and the analysis shows that they consist, first of stockholders; secondly, debtors; and, thirdly, bill-holders and other creditors. In some one of these three relations, a large majority of the people of the United States stand. In making war upon the banks, therefore, you wage war upon the people of the United States. It is not a mere abstraction that you would kick and cuff, bankrupt and destroy; but a sensitive, generous, confiding people. . . .

We are told, that it is necessary to separate, divorce the government from the banks. Let us not be deluded by sounds. Senators might as well talk of separating the government from the States, or from the people, or from the country. We are all—people, States, Union, banks — bound up and interwoven together, united in fortune and destiny, and all, all entitled to the protecting care of a parental government. . . .

. . . The people of the United States have been always a paper-money people. It was paper money that carried us through the Revolution, established our liberties, and made us a free and independent people. And if the experience of the revolutionary war convinced our ancestors, as we are convinced, of the evils of an irredeemable paper medium, it was put aside only to give place to that convertible paper, which has so powerfully contributed to our rapid advancement, prosperity, and greatness.

Questions

1. *What are the central points of agreement or contrast between Tocqueville's view of American democracy, Jackson's, and Clay's?*
2. *Who, according to Jackson, are "the people," and who are their enemies? How does Clay respond?*
3. *How do Jackson and Clay differ in their views of economic relationships? Do they see the interests of different groups in America as being harmonious or antagonistic?*
4. *How do Jackson and Clay differ in their views of the proper role of government? What policies do they advocate, and what, if anything, makes either of them "democratic?"*
5. *Jackson and Tocqueville speak of equality. What do they mean by it? What is the relationship between equality and democracy?*

FURTHER READING

Arthur M. Schlesinger, Jr.'s classic The Age of Jackson *(Boston, 1945) remains the essential work on Jacksonian Democracy and the Jacksonian era. Other comprehensive treatments with strong interpretive thrusts include Edward Pessen,* Jacksonian America: Society, Personality, and Politics, *(Urbana, Illinois, 1978), and Charles Sellers,* The Market Revolution: Jacksonian America, 1815-1846 *(New York, 1991). For a briefer, more balanced overview, see Harry L. Watson,* Liberty and Power: The Politics of Jacksonian America *(New York, 1990), or Daniel Feller,* The Jacksonian Promise: America, 1815-1840 *(Baltimore, 1995). On Jackson himself, see John William's brief and suggestive* Andrew Jackson: Symbol for an Age *(New York, 1955) or Robert V. Remini's definitive* The Life of Andrew Jackson *(New York, 1988). Alexis de Tocqueville's* Democracy in America, *available in many editions and translations, is the most influential contemporary portrait of the age.*

John C. Calhoun's Remarks in the Senate
by John C. Calhoun

John C. Calhoun, "On Nullification and the Force Bill."
U.S. Senate, 15 February 1833

Mr. President:

At the last session of Congress, it was avowed on all sides that
the public debt, as to all practical purposes, was in fact paid,
the small surplus remaining being nearly covered by the money in
the Treasury and the bonds for duties which had already accrued;
but with the arrival of this event our last hope was doomed to be
disappointed. After a long session of many months, and the most
earnest effort on the part of South Carolina and the other
Southern States to obtain relief, all that could be effected was
a small reduction of such a character that, while it diminished
the amount of burden, it distributed that burden more unequally
than even the obnoxious Act of 1828; reversing the principle
adopted by the Bill of 1816, of laying higher duties on the
unprotected than the protected articles, by repealing almost
entirely the duties laid upon the former, and imposing the burden
almost entirely on the latter. It was thus that, instead of
relief-- instead of an equal distribution of burdens and benefits
of the government, on the payment of the debt, as had been fondly
anticipated--the duties were so arranged as to be, in fact,
bounties on one side and taxation on the other; thus placing the
two great sections of the country in direct conflict in reference
to its fiscal action, and thereby letting in that flood of
political corruption which threatens to sweep away our
Constitution and our liberty.

This unequal and unjust arrangement was pronounced, both by the
administration, through its proper organ, the Secretary of the
Treasury, and by the opposition, to be a *permanent* adjustment;
and it was thus that all hope of relief through the action of the
general government terminated; and the crisis so long apprehended
at length arrived, at which the State was compelled to choose
between absolute acquiescence in a ruinous system of oppression,
or a resort to her reserved powers--powers of which she alone was

the rightful judge, and which only, in this momentous juncture, could save her. She determined on the latter.

The consent of two-thirds of her Legislature was necessary for the call of a convention, which was considered the only legitimate organ through which the people, in their sovereignty, could speak. After an arduous struggle the States-rights party succeeded; more than two-thirds of both branches of the Legislature favorable to a convention were elected; a convention was called--the ordinance adopted. The convention was succeeded by a meeting of the Legislature, when the laws to carry the ordinance into execution were enacted--all of which have been communicated by the President, have been referred to the Committee on the Judiciary, and this bill is the result of their labor.

Having now corrected some of the prominent misrepresentations as to the nature of this controversy, and given a rapid sketch of the movement of the State in reference to it, I will next proceed to notice some objections connected with the ordinance and the proceedings under it.

The first and most prominent of these is directed against what is called the test oath, which an effort has been made to render odious. So far from deserving the denunciation that has been levelled against it, I view this provision of the ordinance as but the natural result of the doctrines entertained by the State, and the position which she occupies. The people of Carolina believe that the Union is a union of States, and not of individuals; that it was formed by the States, and that the citizens of the several States were bound to it through the acts of their several States; that each State ratified the Constitution for itself, and that it was only by such ratification of a State that any obligation was imposed upon its citizens. Thus believing, it is the opinion of the people of Carolina that it belongs to the State which has imposed the obligation to declare, in the last resort, the extent of this obligation, as far as her citizens are concerned; and this upon the plain principles which exist in all analogous cases of compact between sovereign bodies. On this principle the people of the State, acting in their sovereign capacity in convention, precisely as they did in the adoption of their own and the

Federal Constitution, have declared, by the ordinance, that the acts of Congress which imposed duties under the authority to lay imposts, were acts not for revenue, as intended by the Constitution, but for protection, and therefore null and void. The ordinance thus enacted by the people of the State themselves, acting as a sovereign community, is as obligatory on the citizens of the State as any portion of the Constitution. In prescribing, then, the oath to obey the ordinance, no more was done than to prescribe an oath to obey the Constitution. It is, in fact, but a particular oath of allegiance, and in every respect similar to that which is prescribed, under the Constitution of the United States, to be administered to all the officers of the State and Federal governments; and is no more deserving the harsh and bitter epithets which have been heaped upon it than that or any similar oath. It ought to be borne in mind that, according to the opinion which prevails in Carolina, the right of resistance to the unconstitutional acts of Congress belongs to the State, and not to her individual citizens; and that, though the latter may, in a mere question of *meum* and *tuum,* resist through the courts an unconstitutional encroachment upon their rights, yet the final stand against usurpation rests not with them, but with the State of which they are members; and such act of resistance by a State binds the conscience and allegiance of the citizen. But there appears to be a general misapprehension as to the extent to which the State has acted under this part of the ordinance. Instead of sweeping every officer by a general proscription of the minority, as has been represented in debate, as far as my knowledge extends, not a single individual has been removed. The State has, in fact, acted with the greatest tenderness, all circumstances considered, toward citizens who differed from the majority; and, in that spirit, has directed the oath to be administered only in the case of some official act directed to be performed in which obedience to the ordinance is involved....

It is next objected that the enforcing acts have legislated the United States out of South Carolina. I have already replied to this objection on another occasion, and will now but repeat what I then said: that they have been legislated out only to the extent that they had no right to enter. The Constitution has admitted the jurisdiction of the United States within the limits of the several States only so far as the delegated powers authorize; beyond that they are intruders, and may rightfully be expelled; and that they have been efficiently expelled by the legislation of the State through her civil process, as has been acknowledged on all sides in the debate, is only a confirmation of the truth of the doctrine for which the majority in Carolina have contended.

The very point at issue between the two parties there is, whether nullification is a peaceful and an efficient remedy against an unconstitutional act of the general government, and may be asserted, as such, through the State tribunals. Both parties agree that the acts against which it is directed are unconstitutional and oppressive. The controversy is only as to the means by which our citizens may be protected against the acknowledged encroachments on their rights. This being the point at issue between the parties, and the very object of the majority being an efficient protection of the citizens through the State tribunals, the measures adopted to enforce the ordinance, of course, received the most decisive character. We were not children, to act by halves. Yet for acting thus efficiently the State is denounced, and this bill reported, to overrule, by military force, the civil tribunal and civil process of the State! Sir, I consider this bill, and the arguments which have been urged on this floor in its support, as the most triumphant acknowledgment that nullification is peaceful and efficient, and so deeply intrenched in the principles of our system, that it cannot be assailed but by prostrating the Constitution, and substituting the supremacy of military force in lieu of the supremacy of the laws. In fact, the advocates of this bill refute their own argument. They tell us that the ordinance is unconstitutional; that it infracts the Constitution of South Carolina, although, to me, the objection appears absurd, as it was adopted by the very authority which adopted the Constitution itself. They also tell us that the Supreme Court is the appointed arbiter of all controversies between a State and the general government. Why, then, do they not leave this controversy to that tribunal? Why do they not confide to them the abrogation of the ordinance, and the laws made in pursuance of it, and the assertion of that supremacy which they claim for the laws of Congress? The State stands pledged to resist no process of the court. Why, then, confer on the President the extensive and unlimited powers provided in this bill? Why authorize him to use military force to arrest the civil process of the State? But one answer can be given: That, in a contest between the State and the general government, if the resistance be limited on both sides to the civil process, the State, by its inherent sovereignty, standing upon its reserved powers, will prove too powerful in such a controversy, and must triumph over the Federal government, sustained by its delegated and limited authority; and in this answer we have an acknowledgment of the truth of those great principles for which the State has so firmly and nobly contended....

Notwithstanding all that has been said, I may say that neither the Senator from Delaware (Mr. Clayton), nor any other who has spoken on the same side, has directly and fairly met the great question at issue: Is this a Federal Union? a union of States, as distinct from that of individuals? Is the sovereignty in the several States, or in the American people in the aggregate? The very language which we are compelled to use when speaking of our political institutions affords proof conclusive as to its real character. The terms union, federal, united, all imply a combination of sovereignties, a confederation of States. They never apply to an association of individuals. Who ever heard of the United State of New York, of Massachusetts, or of Virginia? Who ever heard the term federal or union applied to the aggregation of individuals into one community? Nor is the other point less clear--that the sovereignty is in the several States, and that our system is a union of twenty-four sovereign powers, under a constitutional compact, and not of a divided sovereignty between the States severally and the United States? In spite of all that has been said, I maintain that sovereignty is in its nature indivisible. It is the supreme power in a State, and we might just as well speak of half a square, or half of a triangle, as of half a sovereignty. It is a gross error to confound the *exercise* of sovereign powers with *sovereignty* itself, or the *delegation* of such powers with the *surrender* of them. A sovereign may delegate his powers to be exercised by as many agents as he may think proper, under such conditions and with such limitations as he may impose; but to surrender any portion of his sovereignty to another is to annihilate the whole. The

Senator from Delaware (Mr. Clayton) calls this metaphysical reasoning, which he says he cannot comprehend. If by metaphysics he means that scholastic refinement which makes distinctions without difference, no one can hold it in more utter contempt than I do; but if, on the contrary, he means the power of analysis and combination--that power which reduces the most complex idea into its elements, which traces causes to their first principle, and, by the power of generalization and combination, unites the whole in one harmonious system--then, so far from deserving contempt, it is the highest attribute of the human mind. It is the power which raises man above the brute--which distinguishes his faculties from mere sagacity, which he holds in common with inferior animals. It is this power which has raised the astronomer from being a mere gazer at the stars to the high intellectual eminence of a Newton or a Laplace, and astronomy itself from a mere observation of isolated facts into that noble science which displays to our admiration the system of the universe. And shall this high power of the mind, which has effected such wonders when directed to the laws which control the material world, be forever prohibited, under a senseless cry of metaphysics, from being applied to the high purposes of political science and legislation? I hold them to be subject to laws as fixed as matter itself, and to be as fit a subject for the application of the highest intellectual power. Denunciation may, indeed, fall upon the philosophical inquirer into these first principles, as it did upon Galileo and Bacon, when they first unfolded the great discoveries which have immortalized their names; but the time will come when truth will prevail in spite of prejudice and denunciation, and when politics and legislation will be considered as much a science as astronomy and chemistry.

In connection with this part of the subject, I understood the Senator from Virginia (Mr. Rives) to say that sovereignty was divided, and that a portion remained with the States severally, and that the residue was vested in the Union. By Union, I suppose, the Senator meant the United States. If such be his meaning--if he intended to affirm that the sovereignty was in the twenty-four States, in whatever light he may view them, our opinions will not disagree; but according to my conception, the whole sovereignty is in the several States, while the exercise of sovereign power is divided--a part being exercised under compact, through this general government, and the residue through the separate State governments. But if the Senator from Virginia (Mr. Rives) means to assert that the twenty-four States form but one community, with a single sovereign power as to the objects of the Union, it will be but the revival of the old question, of whether the Union is a union between States, as distinct communities, or a mere aggregate of the American people, as a mass of individuals; and in this light his opinions would lead directly to consolidation....

Disguise it as you may, the controversy is one between power and liberty; and I tell the gentlemen who are opposed to me, that, as strong as may be the love of power on their side, the love of liberty is still stronger on ours. History furnishes many instances of similar struggles, where the love of liberty has prevailed against power under every disadvantage, and among them few more striking than that of our own Revolution; where, as strong as was the parent country, and feeble as were the Colonies, yet, under the impulse of liberty, and the blessing of God, they gloriously triumphed in the contest. There are, indeed, many striking analogies between that and the present controversy. They both originated substantially in the same cause--with this difference--in the present case, the power of taxation is converted into that of regulating industry; in the other the power of regulating industry, by the regulation of commerce, was attempted to be converted into the power of taxation. Were I to trace the analogy further, we should find that the perversion of the taxing power, in the one case, has given precisely the same control to the northern section over the industry of the southern section of the Union, which the power to regulate commerce gave to Great Britain over the industry of the Colonies in the other; and that the very articles in which the Colonies were permitted to have a free trade, and those in which the mother-country had a monopoly, are almost identically the same as those in which the Southern States are permitted to have a free trade by the Act of 1832, and in which the Northern States have, by the same act, secured a monopoly. The only difference is in the means. In the former, the Colonies were permitted to have a free trade with all countries south of Cape Finisterre, a cape in the northern part of Spain; while north of that, the trade of the Colonies was prohibited, except through the mother-country, by means of her commercial regulations. If we compare the products of the country north and south of Cape Finisterre, we shall find them almost identical with the list of last year. Nor does the analogy terminate here. The very arguments resorted to at the commencement of the American Revolution, and the measures adopted, and the motives assigned to bring on that contest (to enforce the law), are almost identically the same.

But to return from this digression to the consideration of the bill. Whatever difference of opinion may exist upon other points, there is one on which I should suppose there can be none; that this bill rests upon principles which, if carried out, will ride over State sovereignties, and that it will be idle for any advocates hereafter to talk of State rights. The Senator from Virginia (Mr. Rives) says that he is the advocate of State rights; but he must permit me to tell him that, although he may differ in premises from the other gentlemen with whom he acts on this occasion, yet, in supporting this bill, he obliterates every vestige of distinction between him and them, saving only that, professing the principles of '98, his example will be more pernicious than that of the most open and bitter opponent of the rights of the States. I will also add, what I am compelled to say, that I must consider him (Mr. Rives) as less consistent than our old opponents, whose conclusions were fairly drawn from their premises, while his premises ought to have led him to opposite conclusions. The gentleman has told us that the new-fangled doctrines, as he chooses to call them, have brought State rights into disrepute. I must tell him, in reply, that what he calls new- fangled are but the doctrines of '98; and that it is he (Mr. Rives), and others with him, who, professing these doctrines, have degraded them by explaining away their meaning and efficacy. He (Mr. R.) has disclaimed, in behalf of Virginia, the authorship of nullification. I will not dispute that point. If Virginia chooses to throw away one of her brightest ornaments, she must not hereafter complain that it has become the property of another. But while I have, as a representatives of Carolina, no right to complain of the disavowal of the Senator from Virginia, I must believe that he (Mr. R.) has done his native State great injustice by declaring on this floor, that when she gravely resolved, in '98, that "in cases of deliberate and dangerous infractions of the Constitution, the States, as parties to the compact, have the right, and are in duty bound, to interpose to arrest the progress of the evil, and to maintain within their respective limits the authorities, rights, and liberties appertaining to them," she meant no more than to proclaim the right to protest and to remonstrate. To suppose that, in putting forth so solemn a declaration, which she afterward sustained by so able and elaborate an argument, she meant no more than to assert what no one had ever denied, would be to suppose that the State had been guilty of the most egregious trifling that ever was exhibited on so solemn an occasion.

The First Women's
Rights Movement

Susan M. Hartmann

INTRODUCTION

Examining women's history in the 1830s and 1840s demonstrates the inaccuracy of the term "Jacksonian Democracy" to characterize that era. At a time when white men achieved full rights of citizenship, women were just beginning their own movement to secure equality. As early as 1642, the New England poet Anne Bradstreet chafed at being denied the full use of her talents, writing, "I am obnoxious to each carping tongue, who sayes, my hand a needle better fits." During the next two centuries, other women expressed their dissatisfaction at being deemed inferior to men, legally subordinated to their fathers and husbands, and barred from intellectual and public pursuits. In the 1840s, these isolated protests swelled into a concerted movement for women's rights.

Feminist activism grew out of women's increasing participation in church-related benevolent societies and in social reform, which claimed substantial numbers of white and free black women in the North. Susan B. Anthony's feminist consciousness originated with her work in the temperance movement, but most women's rights leaders, including Sarah and Angelina Grimké, Elizabeth Cady Stanton, Lucretia Mott, and Lucy Stone, came to women's rights through abolitionism. Although white women dominated the women's rights movement, prominent black abolitionists, such as Frederick Douglass and Sojourner Truth, also championed the cause. Women inaugurated their bold and radical movement in 1848 at Seneca Falls, New York, where three hundred women and men approved a sweeping list of grievances and demands. Ministers, journalists, and other spokesmen viewed these demands as a radical challenge to the social order and dismissed their advocates as "old maids, whose personal charms were

*never very attractive," "women who have been badly married,"
and "hen-pecked husbands." In the face of intense opposition and
hostility, the women's rights movement gained converts slowly.
Women made piecemeal progress in the North, winning state laws
expanding the rights of married women and gaining access to
some colleges. But it took seventy-two years to achieve their most
controversial demand, the right to vote. Although succeeding
waves of feminism have introduced new issues, the women's
rights movement of the nineteenth century established goals and
arguments that continue to shape the debate over gender roles
today.*

WOMEN MAKE THE
CASE FOR WOMEN'S RIGHTS

*In the 1830s women increasingly wrote and spoke about their condition
as women and called on Americans to work against the ideas, laws, and
practices that made them second-class citizens. The following documents
provide a sampling of the issues that engaged activist women and the
arguments they used in their efforts to transform society.*

Maria Stewart Claims
the Right of Women to Speak in Public

*Maria W. Stewart was born in Connecticut in 1803 and orphaned at the
age of five. Although, like most free blacks, she had little opportunity for
formal education, she became an eloquent champion of the rights of blacks
and women. In fact, she was the first American-born woman to address
public audiences. In this selection, an address given in 1833, she challenges the nearly universal opposition to women speaking in public.
Taken from "Mrs. Stewart's Farewell Address to Her Friends In the City
of Boston," in* Black Women in Nineteenth-Century American Life:
Their Words, Their Thoughts, Their Feelings, *ed. Bert James
Loewenberg and Ruth Bogin (University Park, Pennsylvania, 1976),
198–200.*

I felt that I had a great work to perform; and was in haste to
make a profession of my faith in Christ, that I might be about my
Father's business. Soon after I made this profession, the Spirit of
God came before me, and I spake before many. When going home,

reflecting on what I had said, I felt ashamed, and knew not where I should hide myself. A something said within my breast, "press forward, I will be with thee." And my heart made this reply, Lord, if thou wilt be with me, then will I speak for thee so long as I live. And thus far I have every reason to believe that it is the divine influence of the Holy Spirit operating upon my heart. . . .

What if I am a woman; is not the God of ancient times the God of these modern days? Did he not raise up Deborah, to be a mother, and a judge in Israel? Did not queen Esther save the lives of the Jews? And Mary Magdalene first declare the resurrection of Christ from the dead? . . . St. Paul declared that it was a shame for a woman to speak in public, yet our great High Priest and Advocate did not condemn the woman for a more notorious offence than this; neither will he condemn this worthless worm. . . . Did St. Paul but know of our wrongs and deprivations, I presume he would make no objections to our pleading in public for our rights. Again; holy women ministered unto Christ and the apostles; and women of refinement in all ages, more or less, have had a voice in moral, religious and political subjects. . . .

. . . Among the Greeks, women delivered the Oracles; the respect the Romans paid to the Sybils, is well known. The Jews had their prophetesses. The prediction of the Egyptian women obtained much credit at Rome, even under the Emperors. And in the most barbarous nations, all things that have the appearance of being supernatural, the mysteries of religion, the secrets of physic, and the rites of magic, were in the possession of women.

If such women as are here described have once existed, be no longer astonished then, my brethren and friends, that God at this eventful period should raise up your own females to strive, by their example both in public and private, to assist those who are endeavoring to stop the strong current of prejudice that flows so profusely against us at present. No longer ridicule their efforts, it will be counted for sin. For God makes use of feeble means sometimes, to bring about his most exalted purposes. . . .

What if such women as are here described should rise among our sable race? And it is not impossible. For it is not the color of the skin that makes the man or the woman, but the principle formed in the soul. Brilliant wit will shine, come from whence it will; and genius and talent will not hide the brightness of its lustre.

Black Women's Activism

Although Northern black and white women sometimes cooperated in abolitionist activities, they had different priorities. Whereas white women focused singularly on abolition, black women activists pursued a much broader agenda for the elimination of racial injustice. Maria Stewart calls for women to work for the development of the black community in this selection from her pamphlet, "Religion and the Pure Principles of Morality . . . " issued in 1831 and reprinted in Black Women in Nineteenth-Century American Life: Their Words, Their Thoughts, Their Feelings, *ed. Bert James Loewenberg and Ruth Bogin (University Park, Pennsylvania, 1976), 189–90.*

Shall it any longer be said of the daughters of Africa, they have no ambition, they have no force? By no means. Let every female heart become united, and let us raise a fund ourselves; and at the end of one year and a half, we might be able to lay the corner-stone for the building of a High School, that the higher branches of knowledge might be enjoyed by us; and God would raise us up, and enough to aid us in our laudable designs. Let each one strive to excel in good house-wifery, knowing that prudence and economy are the road to wealth. Let us not say, we know this, or, we know that, and practise nothing; but let us practise what we do know.

How long shall the fair daughters of Africa be compelled to bury their minds and talents beneath a load of iron pots and kettles? Until union, knowledge and love begin to flow among us. How long shall a mean set of men flatter us with their smiles, and enrich themselves with our hard earnings; their wives' fingers sparkling with rings, and they themselves laughing at our folly? Until we begin to promote and patronize each other. . . . Do you ask, what can we do? Unite and build a store of your own, if you cannot procure a license. Fill one side with dry goods, and the other with groceries. . . . We have never had an opportunity of displaying our talents; therefore the world thinks we know nothing. . . . Do you ask the disposition I would have you possess? Possess the spirit of independence. The Americans do, and why should not you? Possess the spirit of men, bold and enterprising, fearless and undaunted. Sue for your rights and privileges. Know the reason that you cannot attain them. Weary them with your importunities. You can but die, if you make the attempt; and we shall certainly die if you do not. The Americans have practised nothing but head-work these 200 years, and we have done their drudgery. And is it not high time for us to imitate their examples, and practise head-work too, and keep what we have got, and get what we can? We need never to think that any body is going to feel interested for us, if we do not feel interested for ourselves.

Sarah Grimké Challenges the Clergy

Sarah Grimké and her sister Angelina, daughters of a prominent Charleston, South Carolina slaveholder, were the first American-born white women to give public speeches. Their hatred of slavery had driven them from the South to Philadelphia, where they became Quakers and leading abolitionists. In this selection, Sarah Grimké responds with sarcasm and wit to the "Pastoral Letter," a denunciation of women's public speaking promulgated by a group of clergymen in the Congregational General Association. Taken from The Liberator, *6 October 1837.*

DEAR FRIEND,— . . . [T]he Pastoral Letter of the General Association . . . is . . . so extraordinary a document, that when the minds of men and women become emancipated from the thraldom of superstition, and 'traditions of men,' it will be recurred to with as much astonishment as the opinions of Cotton Mather and other distinguished men of his day, on the subject of witchcraft; nor will it be deemed less wonderful, that a body of divines should gravely assemble and endeavor to prove that woman has no right to 'open her mouth for the dumb,' than it now is that judges should have sat on the trials of witches, and solemnly condemned nineteen persons and one dog to death for witchcraft.

But to the letter: it says, 'we invite your attention to the dangers which at present seem to threaten the FEMALE CHARACTER with wide-spread and permanent injury.' I rejoice that they have called the attention of my sex to this subject, because I believe if woman investigates it, she will soon discover that danger is impending, though from a totally different source from that which the Association apprehends,—danger from those who, having long held the reins of *usurped* authority, are unwilling to permit us to fill that sphere which God created us to move in, and who have entered into league to crush the immortal mind of woman. I rejoice, because I am persuaded that the rights of woman, like the rights of slaves, need only be examined, to be understood and asserted, even by some of those who are now endeavoring to smother the irrepressible desire for mental and spiritual freedom which glows in the breast of many who hardly dare to speak their sentiments. . . .

No one can desire more earnestly than I do, that woman may move exactly in the sphere which her Creator has assigned her; and I believe her having been displaced from that sphere, has introduced confusion into the world. It is therefore of vast importance to herself, and to all the rational creation, that she should ascertain what are her duties and her privileges as a responsible and immortal being. The New Testament has been referred to, and I am willing to abide by its decisions, and must enter my protest against the false translations of some passages by the MEN who did that work, and against the perverted interpretation by the MEN who undertook to write commentaries thereon. I am inclined to think, when we are admitted to the honor of studying Greek and Hebrew, we shall produce some various readings of the Bible, a little different from those we now have.

I find the Lord Jesus defining the duties of his followers in his sermon on the Mount. . . . giving the same directions to women as to men, never even referring to the distinction now so strenuously insisted upon between masculine and feminine virtues: this is one of the anti-christian 'traditions of men' which are taught instead of the 'commandments of God.' Men and women were CREATED EQUAL: they are both moral and accountable beings, and whatever is right for man to do, is right for woman to do.

But the influence of woman, says the Association, is to be private and unobtrusive; her light is not to shine before man like that of her brethren; but she is passively to let the lords of the creation, as they call themselves, put the bushel over it . . . 'Her influence is the source of mighty power.' This has ever been the language of man since he laid aside the whip as a means to keep woman in subjection. He spares her body, but the war he has waged against her mind, her heart, and her soul, has been no less destructive to her as a moral being. How monstrous is the doctrine that woman is to be dependent on man! Where in all the sacred scriptures is this taught? But, alas, she has too well learned the lesson which he has labored to teach her. She has surrendered her dearest RIGHTS, and been satisfied with the privileges which man has assumed to grant her; whilst he has amused her with the show of power, and absorbed all the reality into himself. He has adorned the creature, whom God gave him as a companion, with baubles and gewgaws, turned her attention to personal attractions, offered incense to her vanity, and made her the instrument of his selfish gratification, a plaything to please his eye, and amuse his hours of leisure. . . . This doctrine of dependence upon man is utterly at variance with the doctrine of the Bible. In that book I find nothing like the softness of woman, nor the sternness of man; both are equally commanded to bring forth the fruits of the Spirit—Love, meekness, gentleness.

. . . [O]ur powers of mind have been crushed, as far as man could do it, our sense of morality has been impaired by his interpretation of our duties, but no where does God say that he made any distinction between us as moral and intelligent beings. . . .

The General Association say that 'when woman assumes the place and tone of man as a public reformer, our care and protection of her seem unnecessary; we put ourselves in self-defence against her, and her character becomes unnatural.' . . . The motto of woman, when she is engaged in the great work of public reformation, should be.—'The Lord is my light and my salvation; whom shall I fear? The Lord is the strength of my life; of whom shall I be afraid?' She must feel, if she feels rightly, that she is fulfilling one of the important duties laid upon her as an accountable being, and that her character, instead of being 'unnatural,' is in exact accordance with the will of Him to whom and to no other, she is responsible for the talents and the gifts confided to her. . . .

And my sex now feel in the dominion so unrighteously exercised over them, under the gentle appellation of protection, that what they have leaned upon has proved a broken reed at best, and oft a spear.

Birth of the Women's Rights Movement: The Seneca Falls Convention

The conflict over women's public participation in the abolitionist movement simmered for a decade and helped to split the antislavery movement itself. In 1848, two women who still felt the humiliation of their exclusion from the World Antislavery Convention in 1840, Lucretia Mott and Elizabeth Cady Stanton, called a meeting to discuss women's rights. Some three hundred people, including about forty men, gathered in Seneca Falls, New York, on 19 and 20 July 1848. The assembly issued a broad declaration of grievances and list of demands, drafted primarily by Stanton and modeled after the Declaration of Independence. The "Declaration of Sentiments" is abridged from History of Woman Suffrage, *ed. Elizabeth Cady Stanton, Susan B. Anthony, and Matilda Joslyn Gage (Rochester, New York, 1889), 1:70–73.*

When, in the course of human events, it becomes necessary for one portion of the family of man to assume among the people of the earth a position different from that which they have hitherto occupied, but one to which the laws of nature and of nature's God entitle them, a decent respect to the opinions of mankind requires that they should declare the causes that impel them to such a course.

We hold these truths to be self-evident: that all men and women are created equal. . . . [The rest of this paragraph follows almost exactly the second paragraph of the Declaration of Independence, up to the final sentence.] Such has been the patient sufferance of the women under this government, and such is now the necessity which constrains them to demand the equal station to which they are entitled.

The history of mankind is a history of repeated injuries and usurpations on the part of man toward woman, having in direct object the establishment of an absolute tyranny over her. To prove this, let facts be submitted to a candid world.

He has never permitted her to exercise her inalienable right to the elective franchise.

He has compelled her to submit to laws, in the formation of which she had no voice.

He has withheld from her rights which are given to the most ignorant and degraded men—both natives and foreigners.

Having deprived her of this first right of a citizen, the elective franchise, thereby leaving her without representation in the halls of legislation, he has oppressed her on all sides.

He has made her, if married, in the eye of the law, civilly dead.

He has taken from her all right in property, even to the wages she earns.

He has made her, morally, an irresponsible being, as she can commit many crimes with impunity, provided they be done in the presence of her husband. In the covenant of marriage, she is compelled to promise obedience to her husband, he becoming, to all intents and purposes, her master—the law giving him power to deprive her of her liberty, and to administer chastisement.

He has so framed the laws of divorce, as to what shall be the proper causes, and in case of separation, to whom the guardianship of the children shall be given, as to be wholly regardless of the happiness of women—the law, in all cases, going upon a false supposition of the supremacy of man, and giving all power into his hands.

After depriving her of all rights as a married woman, if single, and the owner of property, he has taxed her to support a government which recognizes her only when her property can be made profitable to it.

He has monopolized nearly all the profitable employments, and from those she is permitted to follow, she receives but a scanty remuneration. He closes against her all the avenues to wealth and distinction which he considers most honorable to himself. As a teacher of theology, medicine, or law, she is not known.

He has denied her the facilities for obtaining a thorough education, all colleges being closed against her.

He allows her in Church, as well as State, but a subordinate position, claiming Apostolic authority for her exclusion from the ministry, and, with some exceptions, from any public participation in the affairs of the Church.

He has created a false public sentiment by giving to the world a different code of morals for men and women, by which moral delinquencies which exclude women from society, are not only tolerated, but deemed of little account in man.

He has usurped the prerogative of Jehovah himself, claiming it as his right to assign for her a sphere of action, when that belongs to her conscience and to her God.

He has endeavored, in every way that he could, to destroy her confidence in her own powers, to lessen her self-respect, and to make her willing to lead a dependent and abject life.

Now, in view of this entire disfranchisement of one-half the people of this country, their social and religious degradation—in view of the unjust laws above mentioned, and because women do feel themselves aggrieved, oppressed, and fraudulently deprived of their most sacred rights, we insist that they have immediate admission to all the rights and privileges which belong to them as citizens of the United States.

In entering upon the great work before us, we anticipate no small amount of misconception, misrepresentation, and ridicule; but we shall use every instrumentality within our power to effect our object. We shall employ agents, circulate tracts, petition the State and National legislatures, and endeavor to enlist the pulpit and the press in our behalf. We hope this Convention will be followed by a series of Conventions embracing every part of the country.

The following resolutions were . . . adopted:

WHEREAS, The great precept of nature is conceded to be, that "man shall pursue his own true and substantial happiness." Blackstone in his Commentaries remarks, that this law of Nature being coeval with mankind, and dictated by God himself, is of course superior in obligation to any other. It is binding over all the globe, in all countries and at all times; no human laws are of any validity if contrary to this, and such of them as are valid, derive all their force, and all their validity, and all their authority, mediately and immediately, from this original; therefore,

Resolved, That such laws as conflict, in any way, with the true and substantial happiness of woman, are contrary to the great precept of nature and of no validity. . . .

Resolved, That all laws which prevent woman from occupying such a station in society as her conscience shall dictate, or which place her in a position inferior to that of man, are contrary to the great precept of nature, and therefore of no force or authority.

Resolved, That woman is man's equal—was intended to be so by the Creator, and the highest good of the race demands that she should be recognized as such.

Resolved, That the women of this country ought to be enlightened in regard to the laws under which they live, that they may no longer publish their degradation by declaring themselves satisfied with their present position, nor their ignorance, by asserting that they have all the rights they want.

Resolved, That inasmuch as man, while claiming for himself intellectual superiority, does accord to woman moral superiority, it is pre-eminently his duty to encourage her to speak and teach, as she has an opportunity, in all religious assemblies.

Resolved, That the same amount of virtue, delicacy, and refinement of behavior that is required of woman in the social state, should also be required of man, and the same transgressions should be visited with equal severity on both man and woman.

Resolved, That the objection of indelicacy and impropriety, which is so often brought against woman when she addresses a public audience, comes with a very ill-grace from those who encourage, by their attendance, her appearance on the stage, in the concert, or in feats of the circus.

Resolved, That woman has too long rested satisfied in the circumscribed limits which corrupt customs and a perverted application of the Scriptures have marked out for her, and that it is time she should move in the enlarged sphere which her great Creator has assigned her.

Resolved, That it is the duty of the women of this country to secure to themselves their sacred right to the elective franchise.

Resolved, That the equality of human rights results necessarily from the fact of the identity of the race in capabilities and responsibilities.

Resolved, therefore, That, being invested by the Creator with the same capabilities, and the same consciousness of responsibility for their exercise, it is demonstrably the right and duty of woman, equally with man, to promote every righteous cause by every righteous means; and especially in regard to the great subjects of morals and religion, it is self-evidently her right to participate with her brother in teaching them, both in private and in public, by writing and by speaking, by any instrumentalities proper to be used, and in any assemblies proper to be held; and this being a self-evident truth growing out of the divinely implanted principles of human nature, any custom or authority adverse to it, whether modern or wearing the hoary sanction of antiquity, is to be regarded as a self-evident falsehood, and at war with mankind. . . .

Resolved, That the speedy success of our cause depends upon the zealous and untiring efforts of both men and women, for the overthrow of the monopoly of the pulpit, and for the securing to woman an equal participation with men in the various trades, professions, and commerce.

The Stanton-Anthony Partnership

Elizabeth Cady Stanton and Susan B. Anthony became the most prominent women's rights leaders in the nineteenth century. Married and the mother of seven children, Stanton grew discontented with women's status through her abolitionist work, where she was deeply influenced by the Quaker, Lucretia Mott. Anthony, who never married, was first active in the temperance movement. After the two met in 1851, they forged a personal friendship and public partnership that gave direction to women's rights ideology and agitation throughout the nineteenth century. The following correspondence reflects the nature of their relationship and the burden that women's traditional domestic responsibilities placed on their public work. Taken from Elizabeth Cady Stanton As Revealed in Her Letters, Diary and Reminiscences, *ed. Theodore Stanton and Harriot Stanton Blatch (New York, 1922), 2:41–42, 54–55, 59–60, 64–67, 70–71.*

Stanton to Anthony, April 2, 1852

Men and angels give me patience! I am at the boiling point! If I do not find some day the use of my tongue on this question, I

"Correspondence Between Elizabeth Cady Stanton and Susan B. Anthony," reprinted from *Elizabeth Cady Stanton as Revealed in Her Letters, Diary and Reminiscences* edited by Theodore Stanton and Harriet Stanton Blatch. Published by Harper and Brothers, 1922. Copyright © 1922 by Harper & Brothers.

shall die of an intellectual repression, a woman's rights convulsion! Oh, Susan! Susan! Susan! You must manage to spend a week with me before the Rochester convention, for I am afraid that I cannot attend it; I have so much care with all these boys on my hands. But I will write a letter. How much I do long to be free from housekeeping and children, so as to have some time to read, and think, and write. But it may be well for me to understand all the trials of woman's lot, that I may more eloquently proclaim them when the time comes.

Stanton to Anthony, Dec. 1, 1853

Can you get any acute lawyer . . . sufficiently interested in our movement to look up just eight laws concerning us—the very worst in all the code? I can generalize and philosophize easily enough of myself; but the details of the particular laws I need, I have not time to look up. You see, while I am about the house, surrounded by my children, washing dishes, baking, sewing, etc., I can think up many points, but I cannot search books, for my hands as well as my brains would be necessary for that work. . . . I seldom have one hour undisturbed in which to sit down and write. Men who can, when they wish to write a document, shut themselves up for days with their thoughts and their books, know little of

The great suffrage team, Susan B. Anthony and Elizabeth Cady Stanton, pose together in 1870, the year they founded the National Woman Suffrage Association (Courtesy of The Schlesinger Library.)

what difficulties a woman must surmount to get off a tolerable production.

Stanton to Anthony, September 10, 1855

I wish that I were as free as you and I would stump the state in a twinkling. But I am not, and what is more, I passed through a terrible scourging when last at my father's. I cannot tell you how deep the iron entered my soul. I never felt more keenly the degradation of my sex. To think that all in me of which my father would have felt a proper pride had I been a man, is deeply mortifying to him because I am a woman. That thought has stung me to a fierce decision—to speak as soon as I can do myself credit. But the pressure on me just now is too great. Henry sides with my friends, who oppose me in all that is dearest to my heart. They are not willing that I should write even on the woman question. But I will both write and speak.

Anthony to Stanton, June 5, 1856

And, Mrs. Stanton, not a word on that Address for the Teachers' Convention. This week was to be leisure to me, and the Mercy only knows when I can get a moment; and what is worse, as the Lord knows full well, if I get all the time the world has, I can't get up a decent document. Oh, dear, dear! There is so much to say and I am so without constructive power to put in symmetrical order. So, for the love of me and for the saving of the reputation of womanhood, I beg you, with one baby on your knee and another at your feet, and four boys whistling, buzzing, hallooing "Ma, Ma," set yourself about the work. It is of but small moment who writes the Address, but of vast moment that it be well done. Ah! Mrs. Stanton, don't say No, nor don't delay it a moment; for I must have it all done and almost commit to memory. . . . Don't delay one mail to tell me what you will do, for I must not and will not allow these schoolmasters to say: "See, these women can't or won't do anything when we do give them a chance." . . . Now do, I pray you, give heed to my prayer. Those of you who have the talent to do honor to poor—oh! how poor—womanhood, have all given yourself over to baby-making; and left poor brainless me to do battle alone. It is a shame. Such a body as I might be spared to rock cradles. But it is a crime for you and Lucy Stone and

Antoinette Brown to be doing it. I have just engaged to attend a progressive meeting in Erie County, the first of September, just because there is no other woman to be had, but not because I feel in the least competent.

Stanton to Anthony, June 10, 1856

Your servant is not dead but liveth. Imagine me, day in and day out, watching, bathing, dressing, nursing, and promenading the precious contents of a little crib in the corner of the room. I pace up and down these two chambers of mine like a caged lioness, longing to bring to a close nursing and housekeeping cares. . . . Is your speech to be exclusively on the point of educating the sexes together, or as to the best manner of educating women? I will do what I can to help you with your lecture. Let Lucy and Antoinette rest awhile in peace and quietness and think great thoughts for the future. It is not well to be in the excitement of public life all the time; do not keep stirring them up or mourning over their repose. You need rest too, Susan. Let the world alone awhile. We cannot bring about a moral revolution in a day or year. Now that I have two daughters, I feel fresh strength to work. It is not in vain that in myself I have experienced all the wearisome cares to which woman in her best estate is subject.

Stanton to Anthony, July 20, 1857

A man in marrying gives up no right; but a woman, every right, even the most sacred of all—the right to her own person. There will be no response among women to our demands until we have first aroused in them a sense of personal dignity and independence; and so long as our present false marriage relation continues, which in most cases is nothing more nor less than legalized prostitution, woman can have no self-respect, and of course man will have none for her; for the world estimates us according to the value we put upon ourselves. Personal freedom is the first right to be proclaimed, and that does not and cannot now belong to the relation of wife, to the mistress of the isolated home, to the financial dependent.

Stanton to Anthony, August 20, 1857

DEAR SUSAN,—I did indeed see by the papers that you had once more stirred that part of intellectual stagnation, the educational convention. The *Times* was really quite complimentary. Henry brought me every item he could see about you. "Well," he would say, "another notice about Susan. You stir up Susan, and she stirs the world." What a set of fools those schoolmarms must be! Well, if in order to please men they wish to live on air, let them. I was glad you went to torment them. I will do anything to help you on. If I do nothing else this fall I am bound to aid you to get up an antislavery address. You must come here for a week or two and we will accomplish wonders. You and I have a prospect of a good long life. We shall not be in our prime before fifty, and after that we shall be good for twenty years at least.

Questions

---

1. *Why did women use religious arguments to claim their rights? What arguments did they use? What claims did they make based on republican ideas?*
2. *Did women's rights advocates emphasize sex differences or did they stress what men and women had in common? What differences and commonalities did they acknowledge?*
3. *How might the Seneca Falls Declaration of Sentiments have differed if Maria Stewart or other black women had helped write it?*
4. *If Elizabeth Cady Stanton were alive today, how might she assess the results of the movement she helped found? Have all the grievances been redressed and all the demands been achieved? What ideas or arguments of the nineteenth-century women's rights movement are still relevant today?*

FURTHER READING

The classic history of women's activism remains Eleanor Flexner, Century of Struggle: The Woman's Movement in the United States *(1959; rev. ed., Cambridge, Massachusetts, 1975). Shirley Yee,* Black Women Abolitionists: A Study in Activism, 1828–1860 *(Knoxville, 1992), tells the story of African American women's work for their race and their sex. Gerda Lerner,* The Grimké Sisters from South Carolina: Pioneers for Woman's Rights and Abolition *(New York, 1971), places these two women in the context of antebellum reform. Details of the lives and work of Anthony and Stanton can be found in* The Elizabeth Cady Stanton-Susan B. Anthony Reader: Correspondence, Writings, Speeches, *ed. Ellen Carol DuBois, rev. ed. (Boston, 1992).*

The Mexican-American War: America's First Foreign War

James M. McCaffrey

INTRODUCTION

Spanish explorers arrived in what is now Mexico in 1519 and for the next three hundred years worked hard to establish and maintain it as a viable colony. Spain grew very wealthy on the vast mineral riches it extracted therefrom, and Spanish missionaries brought Christianity to the native peoples. By the early years of the nineteenth century colonists in most of Spain's colonies had grown restive to the point of rebellion. In Mexico, that rebellion began in 1810 and finally succeeded eleven years later in achieving an independent Mexico.

Concurrent with independence, settlers from the United States began moving to the sparsely settled Mexican province of Texas in the 1820s. Mexican officials welcomed them, expecting their presence to provide a buffer zone with the neighboring United States and to serve as a lure for Mexican settlers. In 1835, however, the Americans, dissatisfied with Mexican rule, rose up in a successful revolution. From 1836 to 1845 Texas existed as a sovereign, independent nation, although Mexico never officially acknowledged this status. Not only did Mexico refuse to recognize the loss of Texas, but it resented Texan claims to lands between the Rio Grande and Nueces rivers that had traditionally been part of the Mexican state of Tamaulipas. In 1845, the United States annexed Texas into the Union, something Mexico regarded as an act of war, and actual hostilities commenced on the lower Rio Grande River in April 1846.

Militarily, the war was an almost unbroken string of American victories. Brigadier General Zachary Taylor ("Old Rough and Ready" to his men) twice led his force to victory over Mexican troops near Matamoros in May, forcing them to retreat toward

Monterrey. In the meantime, a second American force occupied Santa Fe, New Mexico, without a struggle and continued on to Mexican California.

When peace still seemed elusive following Taylor's victory at Monterrey in September, a third force was organized under the command of Major General Winfield Scott. Scott landed his men at Veracruz in early March 1847, and proceeded to fight his way all the way to Mexico City. Scott occupied the Mexican capital in September, and peace soon followed.

To arrive at a good understanding of any conflict such as that between the United States and Mexico one must study it from a myriad of perspectives—diplomatic, political, military, and social. The selections that follow seek to introduce some of these important viewpoints.

Contemporaries Discuss the Mexican-American War

Primary sources, documents created by participants in historic events, are often excellent windows into the minds of the writers. Even among primary sources, however, there are gradations. The following section, for example, presents documents created by President James K. Polk and Congressman Abraham Lincoln. These men undoubtedly spent considerable time preparing these writings. They may have added some passages, deleted others, and rewritten still others before reaching the final version. The results of these efforts reflect the considered opinions of their writers, men who likely were aware that these documents would be scrutinized not only by their contemporaries but by later readers all the way down to the present.

This section also contains excerpts from the letters of two volunteer soldiers. Letters and diaries leave us a more immediate record of events. These men were writing home to family members not for posterity. They had little reason to believe that anyone outside of their families would ever read them. Unlike government officials they can give vent to their feelings about commanding officers, for example, without worrying about how their comments could affect their careers. Documents such as these are especially valuable for understanding how the common soldiers perceived the war.

Whose Land Is It Anyway?

In President James K. Polk's message to Congress on May 11, 1846, asking it to declare war on Mexico, he emphasizes that Mexican forces brought on the war by their invasion of American territory—the area north of the Rio Grande. Excerpted from House Executive Document, 29th Congress, 1st session, No. 196, contained in Origins of the Mexican War: A Documentary Source Book, *ed. Ward McAfee and J. Cordell Robinson (Salisbury, North Carolina, 1982), 2:146-49.*

In my message at the commencement of the present session, I informed you that, upon the earnest appeal both of the Congress and convention of Texas, I had ordered an efficient military force to take a position "between the Nueces and the Del Norte [Rio Grande]." This had become necessary to meet a threatened invasion of Texas by the Mexican forces, for which extensive military preparations had been made. The invasion was threatened solely because Texas had determined, in accordance with a solemn resolution of the Congress of the United States, to annex herself to our Union; and, under these circumstances, it was plainly our duty to extend our protection over her citizens and soil. . . .

Meantime, Texas, by the final action of our Congress, had become an integral part of our Union. The Congress of Texas, by its act of December 19, 1836, had declared the Rio del Norte [Rio Grande] to be the boundary of that republic. Its jurisdiction had been extended and exercised beyond the Nueces. The country between that river and the Del Norte had been represented in the [Texas] Congress and in the convention of Texas [and] had thus taken part in the act of annexation itself; and is now included within one of our Congressional districts. . . . It became, therefore, of urgent necessity to provide for the defense of that portion of our country. Accordingly, on the 13th of January last instructions were issued to the general in command of these troops to occupy the left bank of the Del Norte. This river, which is the southwestern boundary of the State of Texas, is an exposed frontier; from

Excerpts reprinted from *Origins of the Mexican War: A Documentary Source Book*, by Ward McAfee and J. Cordell Robinson, 1982, Documentary Publications.

A portrait of President James K. Polk, who declared war on Mexico in May 1846. (Courtesy of Corbis Images.)

this quarter invasion was threatened; upon it, and in its immediate vicinity, in the judgement of high military experience, are the proper stations for the protecting forces of the government. . . .

The Mexican forces at Matamoros assumed a belligerent attitude, and, on the 12th of April [1846] General [Pedro de] Ampudia, then in command, notified General [Zachary] Taylor to break up his camp within twenty-four hours and to retire beyond the Nueces River, and in the event of his failure to comply with these demands, announced that arms, and arms alone, must decide the question. But no open act of hostility was committed until the 24th of April. On that day, General [Mariano] Arista, who had succeeded to the command of the Mexican forces, communicated to General Taylor that "he considered hostilities commenced, and should prosecute them." A party of dragoons, of 63 men and officers, were on the same day dispatched from the American camp up the Rio del Norte, on its left bank, to ascertain whether the Mexican troops had crossed, or were preparing to cross, the river; [it] "became engaged with a large body of these troops, and, after a short affair, in which some 16 were killed and wounded, appear to have been surrounded and compelled to surrender.". . .

[W]e have been exerting our best efforts to propitiate her [Mexico's] good will. Upon the pretext that Texas, a nation as independent as herself, thought proper to unite its destinies with our own, she has affected to believe that we have severed her rightful territory, and in official proclamations and manifestoes has repeatedly threatened to make war upon us for the purpose of reconquering Texas. In the meantime, we have tried every effort at reconciliation. The cup of forbearance had been exhausted, even before the recent information from the frontier of the Del Norte. But now, after reiterated menaces, Mexico has passed the boundary of the United States, has invaded our territory, and shed American blood upon the American soil. She has proclaimed that hostilities have commenced and that the two nations are now at war.

As war exists, and, notwithstanding all our efforts to avoid it, exists by the act of Mexico herself, we are called upon by every consideration of duty and patriotism to vindicate with decision the honor, the rights, and the interests of our country. . . .

Lincoln Questions Polk

Freshman Whig Congressman Abraham Lincoln, from Illinois, disagreed with the president's characterization of "American soil" when he offered the following resolution on December 22, 1847. Excerpted from Journal of the House of Representatives of the United States: Being the First Session of the Thirtieth Congress; Begun and Held at the City of Washington, December 6, 1847, in the Seventy-Second Year of the Independence of the United States *(Washington, 1847-48), 149-51.*

Whereas the President of the United States, in his message of May 11, 1846, has declared that "the Mexican government not only refused to receive him" (the envoy of the United States) "or listen to his propositions, but, after a long continued series of menaces, have at last invaded *our territory*, and shed the blood of our fellow *citizens* on *our own soil*:"

And again, in his message of December 8, 1846, that "we had ample cause of war against Mexico, long before the breaking out of hostilities; but even then we forbore to take redress into our own hands, until Mexico herself became the aggressor, by invading *our soil* in hostile array, and shedding the blood of our *citizens*:["]

And yet again, in his message of December 7, 1847, that "the Mexican government refused even to hear the terms of adjustment which he" (our minister of peace) "was authorized to propose; and finally, under wholly unjustifiable pretexts, involved the two countries in war, by invading the territory of the State of Texas, striking the first blow, and shedding the blood of our *citizens* on *our own soil*."

And whereas this House desires to obtain a full knowledge of all the facts which go to establish whether the particular spot of soil on which the blood of our *citizens* was so shed was, or was not, *our own soil*, at that time: therefore,

Resolved, by the House of Representatives, That the President of the United States be respectfully requested to inform this House,

First. Whether the spot of soil on which the blood of our *citizens* was shed, as in his messages declared, was, or was not, within the territories of Spain, at least from the treaty of 1819 until the Mexican revolution.

Second. Whether that spot is, or is not, within the territory which was wrested from Spain by the Mexican revolution.

Third. Whether that spot is, or is not, within a settlement of people, which settlement had existed ever since long before the Texas revolution, until its inhabitants fled from the approach of the United States army.

Fourth. Whether that settlement is, or is not, isolated from any and all other settlements, by the Gulf of Mexico and the Rio Grande on the south and west, and by wide uninhabited regions on the north and east.

Fifth. Whether the *people* of that settlement, or a *majority* of them, or *any* of them, had ever, previous to the bloodshed mentioned in his message, submitted themselves to the government or laws of Texas, or of the United States, by *consent*, or by *compulsion*, either by accepting office, or voting at elections, or paying taxes, or serving on juries, or having process served upon them, or in *any other way*.

Sixth. Whether the people of that settlement did, or did not, flee from the approach of the United States army, leaving unprotected their homes and their growing crops, *before* the blood was shed, as in message stated; and whether the first blood so shed was, or was not, shed within the *inclosure* of the people, or some of them, who had thus fled from it.

Seventh. Whether our *citizens*, whose blood was shed, as in his messages declared, were, or were not, at that time, *armed* officers and *soldiers*, sent into that settlement by the military order of the President, through the Secretary of War; and,

Eighth. Whether the military force of the United States, including those *citizens*, was, or was not, so sent into that settlement after General Taylor had, more than once, intimated to the War Department that, in his opinion, no such movement was necessary to the defence or protection of Texas.

Soldiers' Letters Home

Excerpt from a letter from Lieutenant Will Wallace (near Monclova, Mexico), to his father, November 6, 1846, Wallace-Dickey Collection, Illinois State Historical Library, Springfield, Illinois.

My dear Father

I believe I wrote to you while on the march from San Antonio but in the hurry & bustle of recent events I have no distinct recollection of what I wrote or from what precise point. These letters seem to me like firing at the moon, the distance is so great & the means of communication so uncertain. Yet I cannot resist the inclination I feel to write whenever I have time or anything like an opportunity of sending. We are now lying in camp on the edge of the town of Monclova, a place of some 8000 inhabitants, situated at the foot of a lofty & barren chain of Mountains, a spur of the Bolson Massimi Range. In whatever direction you look from our camp the bold or indistinct outlines of these mountains as they are near or more remote, rise like mighty barriers to oppose our progress or our retreat. A stream some larger than Pine Creek comes down from the Mountains & rushes past the town, supplying innumerable ducts & hydrants that water every part of the town. A broad valley of fine land borders this stream & is dotted here and there with Ranchos & Hasiendas (cattle & grain farms) in some of them in a fine state of cultivation, covered with luxurious crops of corn, cotton & sugar cane. All the cultivated lands here require to be irrigated, & for this purpose their fields & farms are intersected with numerous ditches running in every direction. For the same reason lands are never cultivated except near some running stream that can afford sufficient water for irrigation. The farms or Ranchos are generally miserable affairs, with little or no fencing & mud Huts; though occasionally we passed one of superior order. Two days before we reached here we encamped at the Hot Springs where was the finest Hacienda I have seen. The main building & out houses, including a sugar house, & stables were enclosed by a heavy stone wall 12 feet high, the whole covering a space of about 7 acres. The place is owned by two brothers Sanchez, one of whom lives in Saltillo & the other in the city of Mexico. They own all the country from San Fernando to this place & on to near Saltillo, a scope of country some 250 miles in extent. The Hacienda is now occupied by Senor Miguel Blanco, a nephew of Sanchez. He works 160 servants. I visited every part of the establishment in company with a Texan who speaks Spanish. The quarters of the working people were far inferior to those of the slaves on the Mississippi, but they appeared neat & clean as far as could be. A system of slavery exists here which is a vast improvement on the Slavery in our southern states. Whenever a man is in debt, his creditor sues him, gets a judgement, & if the debtor has not the means to satisfy it, the creditor may take him as his servant, & compel him to work out the debt at the rate of $3.00 per month, finding his own clothing. I am told that hunderds of men here enter this Kind of service to avoid being drafted into the Army. Before they can discharge the original debt they have necessarily contracted others, & thus they continue for years in slavery, until old age & hard labor have rendered them unfit for farther service, & then they are released to the wretched liberty of a penniless old age. The differences in the classes are as distinctly marked here as in the slave states. The *peans* [peons] or servants are generally a dark swarthy shaggy haired race—evidently a mixture of Indian & Negro with occasionally a touch of the Spanish blood. The leading men & men of wealth are much whiter & more intelligent in appearance, & some of the women of the upper class are decidedly beautiful. It is difficult to tell their true feelings towards us—some of them profess to be greatly dissatisfied with the rapacity & imbecility of the Central [Mexican] Government, &

are very willing to sell us corn & other commodities at about three prices. On the other hand, I have concluded from what I have seen in Monclova that there is a deep feeling of hostility toward us; & I know that Senor Blanco at the Hot Springs had assembled a considerable force at his Hasienda to oppose our progress, & only disbanded it a few days before our arrival. I am also informed by a young Spaniard, a resident of Monclova, who speaks English, that the priests exerted their utmost influence to raise the people against us, representing us as a plundering band, with whom their property & families would be ruined. Thus far they have nothing to complain of, & indeed they say themselves that we are not half so great a terror to them as their own armies. From the policy that Gen. [John] Wool has adopted I think we will not give them any reason to complain for we pay them their own price for every thing we get from them—the war thus far is more injury to us than to Mexico. Gen. Shield[s] thinks all these northern provinces are ripe for a revolution. He came up from Matamoros & Camargo to Presidio, & was very kindly received by the authorities of all the frontier towns, & the feeling he found there is what he bases his presumption upon. But I've no doubt he overestimates the extent of this feeling, & if we should meet with any reverses these very fellows who are now so kind & so full of professions of friendship would be the first to cut our throats. Treachery is a characteristic of the Race, & after getting all our money I've no doubt they would shoot us for the sake of our clothes. I don't think they will ever fight us with anything like equal numbers. Taylors victory at Monterey over a superior force & that force entrenched has frightened them. It is said that Santa Anna is now fortifying San Luis Potosi, & if peace is not concluded before the expiration of the armistice, Gen. Taylor will push on to that point, & our greatest hope is to join him. Wool is very unpopular with his command—he has quarrelled with every field officer in it. . . . Gen. Wool is a very old & a very vain man; I do not blame, tho I pity him. The Management of our army in the field is "above his hair" & the Government & the Department is culpably & criminally foolish for putting him in command of a division. I have a matter to settle after the war is over—he cussed me—charges will be preferred against him & I hope to see him relieved from his command. . . .

Excerpt from a letter from Henry Smith Lane (Matamoros) to his brother, November 5, 1846, Henry Smith Lane Collection, Filson Club, Louisville, Kentucky.

My dear Brother:

Since I last wrote to you I have seen & suffered much. You are no doubt apprized of my position in the Army. I am at present stationed with a part of our Regiment at Palo Altotucks, miles below this city. On the 22d of July we arrived upon the Rio Grande, since which time our Regiment has been stationed at the mouth of the River in a very sickly & unpleasant location. We have suffered a vast deal from fevers, there have been over sixty deaths in the regiment & about two hundred discharged on account of ill health, but we hope that this sickly season has passed by. My own health is now good but I have had fever & a constant bow[e]l complaint a great part of the time since I landed. We are now daily expecting orders to march into the interior of the country towards Tampico. Our position did not enable us to participate in the glory of the fight at Monterey but we are confident that we shall have a chance at Saltillo or Tampico to show what we are made of; the boys are exceedingly anxious for a free fight & I think the Mexicans will gratify them for we shall have no peace with the copper skinned rascals until they are soundly thrashed and that will be whenever they stand long enough before Old Rough & Ready & his boys to take it. . . . The country so far as I have seen of it along the Rio Grande is very fertile but miserably cultivated; the people are lazy, ignorant & perfidious with no patriotism, no public spirit, no enterprise and it would be a great mercy to them to take their country & give them a settled form of free government & Americanize their Republic; it is known to you that I have always been opposed to the Annexation of Texas & that I said that a war with Mexico would grow out of it, but the deed is done. Texas is a part of the United States & I feel as much bound to fight for her as I would for Indiana, or even old Kentucky.

The people here are ignorant & bigotted Roman Catholics & are more than One Hundred years behind the improvement & the spirit of the age & it requires no gift of prophecy to foretell their doom, they are destined soon to fall before the all grasping & all conquering genius of genuine Americanism. We have a singular climate here at least it seems to a Northern man, there is now in market here green corn, peas, beans, water melons, musk melons, onions, radishes & every variety of vegetables which we have in the Spring at the North, besides a great many more which are peculiar to this climate. In a word God has done as much to bless & man to curse this country as any region on earth.

I shall be home about next July, if I live until that time. I got a letter a short time since from my dear Joan. She was well but rather gloomy on account of my absence. I sometimes reproach myself for leaving her, for she is all the time anxious & uneasy about me, but if she will forgive me I promise to do so no more. . . . Brother Higgins wrote to me in Sept. He & his family were all well then, he was very anxious to come out with me to Mexico but I persuaded him not to think of it & he very reluctantly yielded. Major Hazelrigg wrote to me about the same time, they are all well.

My pay as Major is $130 per month & I like the service very well if we could get into a battle & have some chance for distinction. I am on excellent terms so far as I know or believe with every officer & private in our Brigade & shall take pains to remain so.

Give my love to Father & Mother & to Sister Sally & the dear children & to all the relatives & friends & tell them that tho far removed from them I still think of them very often & very kindly & that I love them as much as ever.

Farewell, may God bless & preserve you and yours, I am

> Your affectionate brother,
> Henry S. Lane

Questions

1. *Compare Polk's and Lincoln's characterizations of the land and inhabitants between the Nueces and the Rio Grande. Who do you think makes the stronger case?*
2. *Lincoln suggests that the residents of the area between the Nueces and the Rio Grande were not truly governed by Texas, but he does not assert that they were governed by Mexico. Why not?*
3. *Why does Lincoln appear to differentiate between the deaths of our citizens and the deaths of our soldiers?*
4. *Lane's descriptions of Mexican civilization reveals a lot about himself. What can we surmise about the background—religion, occupation, etc.—of Henry Lane from these descriptions?*
5. *Having been unable to experience "the glory" of the battle at Monterey, what possible reasons might Lane have for discouraging his brother from joining him?*

FURTHER READING

The standard treatment of this conflict from the American viewpoint is still The Mexican War, 1846-1848 *by K. Jack Bauer (New York, 1974), although John S. D. Eisenhower's very readable* So Far From God: The U.S. War With Mexico, 1846-1848 *(New York, 1989) is also good. An early Mexican account is Ramon Alcaraz et al.,* The Other Side; or, Notes for the History of the War Between Mexico and the United States, *trans. and ed. by Albert C. Ramsey (New York, 1850). Robert W. Johannsen's* To the Halls of the Montezumas: The Mexican War in the American Imagination *(New York, 1985) examines the impact the war had on American culture. The two best studies of the American army during the war are Richard Bruce Winder's* Mr. Polk's Army: The American Military Experience in the Mexican War *(College Station, Texas, 1997) and James M. McCaffrey's* Army of Manifest Destiny: The American Soldier in the Mexican War, 1846-1848 *(New York, 1992), while the Mexican Army is examined by Pedro Santoni in* Mexicans at Arms: Pyro Federalists and the Politics of War, 1845-1848 *(Fort Worth, Texas, 1996) and William A. DePalo, Jr. in* The Mexican National Army, 1822-1852 *(College Station, Texas, 1997). For a video treatment of the war see Public Broadcasting's* The U.S.-Mexican War *(Dallas, 1998).*

Manifest Destiny

Peter L. Hahn and Michael J. Hogan

INTRODUCTION

During the 1840s, the United States acquired control over vast tracts of land in Texas, the southwest, including California, and the Oregon Territory. Some of the land was acquired by diplomacy and some by force; all of it has remained an integral part of the country. Some Americans advocated and celebrated such enormous territorial growth by rallying behind a sense of national mission and exceptionalism called "Manifest Destiny" and supporting war against Mexico as a means to continental empire. Others opposed this expansionism on political, economic, strategic, and moral grounds. Such controversy over expansionism has persisted since the 1840s.

THE CONTEMPORARY DEBATE OVER CONTINENTAL EXPANSION

The following documents reveal many aspects of the debate on expansionism that began in the 1830s and persisted into the 1840s. The first two documents offer contrasting views of the general question of expansionism. The remaining documents reveal the parameters of debate as it focused on specific issues: whether to annex Texas in 1844, whether to wage war on Mexico in 1846–1848, and whether to permit slavery to spread into the territories acquired. Collectively, these records demonstrate that the American people reached no consensus either in favor of, or in opposition to, the expansionism that occurred.

John L. O'Sullivan
Advocates Manifest Destiny

An intellectual atmosphere conducive to expansionism stood behind the United States's drive across the continent in the 1840s. Some of the strongest advocates of expansion and conquest were writers of editorials in the popular press, and of these perhaps the most famous was John L. O'Sullivan, editor of The United States Magazine and Democratic Review. *The selection printed below, comprised of parts of two O'Sullivan editorials published in 1839 and 1845, conveys the themes and tone of O'Sullivan's advocacy. The editorials originally appeared in* The United States Magazine and Democratic Review, *6 (November 1839):426–27, 429–30; and 17 (July 1845):5, 7–8.*

[1839]

The American people having derived their origin from many other nations, and the Declaration of National Independence being entirely based on the great principle of human equality, these facts demonstrate at once our disconnected position as regards any other nation; that we have, in reality, but little connection with the past history of any of them, and still less with all antiquity, its glories, or its crimes. On the contrary, our national birth was the beginning of a new history, the formation and progress of an untried political system, which separates us from the past and connects us with the future only; and so far as regards the entire development of the natural rights of man, in moral, political, and national life, we may confidently assume that our country is destined to be *the great nation* of futurity. . . .

We have no interest in the scenes of antiquity, only as lessons of avoidance of nearly all their examples. The expansive future is our arena, and for our history. We are entering on its untrodden space, with the truths of God in our minds, beneficent objects in our hearts, and with a clear conscience unsullied by the past. We are the nation of human progress, and who will, what can, set limits to our onward march? Providence is with us, and no earthly power can. We point to the everlasting truth on the first page of our national declaration, and we proclaim to the millions of other lands, that "the gates of hell"—the powers of aristocracy and monarchy—"shall not prevail against it."

The far-reaching, the boundless future will be the era of American greatness. In its magnificent domain of space and time, the nation of many nations is destined to manifest to mankind the excellence of divine principles; to establish on earth the noblest temple ever dedicated to the worship of the Most High—the Sacred and the True. Its floor shall be a hemisphere—its roof the firmament of the star-studded heavens, and its congregation an Union of many Republics, comprising hundreds of happy millions, calling, owning no man master, but governed by God's natural and moral law of equality, the law of brotherhood—of "peace and good will amongst men." . . .

Yes, we are the nation of progress, of individual freedom, of universal enfranchisement. Equality of rights is the cynosure of our union of States, the grand exemplar of the correlative equality of individuals; and while truth sheds its effulgence, we cannot retrograde, without dissolving the one and subverting the other.

We must onward to the fulfilment of our mission—to the entire development of the principle of our organization—freedom of conscience, freedom of person, freedom of trade and business pursuits, universality of freedom and equality. This is our high destiny, and in nature's eternal, inevitable decree of cause and effect we must accomplish it. All this will be our future history, to establish on earth the moral dignity and salvation of man—the immutable truth and beneficence of God. For this blessed mission to the nations of the world, which are shut out from the life-giving light of truth, has America been chosen; and her high example shall smite unto death the tyranny of kings, hierarchs, and oligarchs, and carry the glad tidings of peace and good will where myriads now endure an existence scarcely more enviable than that of beasts of the field. Who, then, can doubt that our country is destined to be *the great nation* of futurity?

[1845]

It is time now for opposition to the Annexation of Texas to cease, all further agitation of the waters of bitterness and strife, at least in connexion with this question,—even though it may perhaps be required of us as a necessary condition of the freedom of our institutions, that we must live on for ever in a state of unpausing struggle and excitement upon some subject of party division or other. But, in regard to Texas, enough has now been given to Party. It is time for the common duty of Patriotism to the Country to succeed;—or if this claim will not be recognized, it is at least time for common sense to acquiesce with decent grace in the inevitable and the irrevocable.

Texas is now ours. Already, before these words are written, her Convention has undoubtedly ratified the acceptance, by her Congress, of our proffered invitation into the Union; and made the requisite changes in her already republican form of constitution to adopt it to its future federal relations. Her star and her stripe may already be said to have taken their place in the glorious blazon of our common nationality; and the sweep of our eagle's wing already includes within its circuit the wide extent of her fair and fertile land. She is no longer to us a mere geographical space—a certain combination of coast, plain, mountain, valley, forest and stream. She is no longer to us a mere country on the map. She comes within the dear and sacred designation of Our Country; no longer a *"pays,"* [country] she is part of *"la patrie;"*

[the nation] and that which is at once a sentiment and a virtue, Patriotism, already begins to thrill for her too within the national heart. . . .

Why, were other reasoning wanting, in favor of now elevating this question of the reception of Texas into the Union, out of the lower region of our past party dissensions, up to its proper level of a high and broad nationality, it surely is to be found, found abundantly, in the manner in which other nations have undertaken to intrude themselves into it, between us and the proper parties to the case, in a spirit of hostile interference against us, for the avowed object of thwarting our policy and hampering our power, limiting our greatness and checking the fulfilment of our manifest destiny to overspread the continent allotted by Providence for the free development of our yearly multiplying millions. This we have seen done by England, our old rival and enemy; and by France. . . .

. . . Texas has been absorbed into the Union in the inevitable fulfilment of the general law which is rolling our population westward; the connexion of which with that ratio of growth in population which is destined within a hundred years to swell our numbers to the enormous population of *two hundred and fifty millions* (if not more), is too evident to leave us in doubt of the manifest design of Providence in regard to the occupation of this continent. It was disintegrated from Mexico in the natural course of events, by a process perfectly legitimate on its own part, blameless on ours; and in which all the censures due to wrong, perfidy and folly, rest on Mexico alone. And possessed as it was by a population which was in truth but a colonial detachment from our own, and which was still bound by myriad ties of the very heartstrings to its old relations, domestic and political, their incorporation into the Union was not only inevitable, but the most natural, right and proper thing in the world—and it is only astonishing that there should be any among ourselves to say it nay.

W. E. Channing Denounces Expansion

Of course, not all Americans endorsed the annexation of Texas or the general pattern of continental expansion. Many Americans opposed this territorial growth on the grounds that it would undermine democratic institutions at home, estrange relations with foreign states, encourage the spread of slavery, and violate the country's deepest values, such as peace and the rule of law. Boston minister William Ellery Channing emerged as a leading anti-expansionist spokesman during the national debate on the Republic of Texas's request for annexation in 1837, a request that, at first, was denied. The selection below is taken from Channing's letter of August 1837 to Henry Clay. Excerpted from The Works of William E. Channing, D.D., *6th edition, (Boston, 1846), 2:183–87, 204–8, 210, 217–18, 220, 231–32, 240.*

MY DEAR SIR,

. . . It is with great reluctance that I enter on the topic of this letter. . . . I desire nothing so much as to devote what remains of life to the study and exposition of great principles and universal truths. But the subject of Texas weighs heavily on my mind, and I cannot shake it off. To me, it is more than a political question. It belongs eminently to morals and religion. . . . Should Texas be annexed to our country, I feel that I could not forgive myself, if, with my deep, solemn impressions, I should do nothing to avert the evil. I cannot easily believe, that this disastrous measure is to be adopted, especially at the present moment. The annexation of Texas, under existing circumstances, would be more than rashness; it would be madness. That opposition to it must exist at the South, as well as at the North, I cannot doubt. Still, there is a general impression, that great efforts will be made to accomplish this object at the approaching session of Congress, and that nothing but strenuous resistance can prevent their success. I must write, therefore, as if the danger were real and imminent; and if any should think that I am betrayed into undue earnestness by a false alarm, they will remember that there are circumstances, in which excess of vigilance is a virtue. . . .

We have a strong argument against annexing Texas to the United States, in the Criminality of the revolt which threatens to sever that country from Mexico. On this point our citizens need light. The Texan insurrection is seriously regarded by many among us as a struggle of the oppressed for freedom. The Texan revolution is thought to resemble our own. Our own is contaminated by being brought into such relationship, and we owe to our fathers and ourselves a disclaimer of affinity with this new republic. The Texan revolt, if regarded in its causes and its means of success, is criminal; and we ought in no way to become partakers in its guilt. . . .

Having unfolded the argument against the annexation of Texas from the criminality of the revolt, I proceed to a second very solemn consideration, namely, that by this act our country will enter on a career of encroachment, war, and crime, and will merit and incur the punishment and woe of aggravated wrong-doing. The seizure of Texas will not stand alone. It will darken our future history. It will be linked by an iron necessity to long-continued deeds of rapine and blood. Ages may not see the catastrophe of the tragedy, the first scene of which we are so ready to enact. It is strange that nations should be so much more rash than individuals; and this, in the face of experience, which has been teaching, from the beginning of society, that, of all precipitate and criminal deeds, those perpetrated by nations are the most fruitful of misery.

Did this country know itself, or were it disposed to profit by self-knowledge, it would feel the necessity of laying an immediate curb on its passion for extended territory. It would not trust itself to new acquisitions. It would shrink from the temptation to conquest. We are a restless people, prone to encroachment, impatient of the ordinary laws of progress, less anxious to consolidate and perfect than to extend our institutions, more ambitious of spreading ourselves over a wide space than of diffusing beauty and fruitfulness over a narrower field. We boast of our rapid growth, forgetting that, throughout nature, noble growths are slow. Our people throw themselves beyond the bounds of civilization, and expose themselves to relapses into a semi-barbarous state, under the impulse of wild imagination, and for the name of great possessions. . . .

It is full time, that we should lay on ourselves serious, resolute restraint. Possessed of a domain, vast enough for the growth of ages, it is time for us to stop in the career of acquisition and conquest. Already endangered by our greatness, we cannot advance without imminent peril to our institutions, union, prosperity, virtue, and peace. . . .

Even were the dispositions of our government most pacific and opposed to encroachment, the annexation of Texas would almost certainly embroil us with Mexico. This territory would be overrun by adventurers; and the most unprincipled of these, the proscribed, the disgraced, the outcasts of society, would, of course, keep always in advance of the better population. These would represent our republic on the borders of the Mexican States. The history of the connexion of such men with the Indians, forewarns us of the outrages which would attend their contact with the border inhabitants of our southern neighbour. . . .

Hitherto I have spoken of the annexation of Texas as embroiling us with Mexico; but it will not stop here. It will bring us into collision with other states. It will, almost of necessity, involve us in hostility with European powers. . . .

I proceed now to a consideration of what is to me the strongest argument against annexing Texas to the United States. . . . The annexation of Texas, I have said, will extend and perpetuate slavery. It is fitted, and, still more, intended to do so. On this point there can be no doubt. . . .

I now ask, whether, as a people, we are prepared to seize on a neighbouring territory for the end of extending slavery? I ask, whether, as a people, we can stand forth in the sight of God, in the sight of the nations, and adopt this atrocious policy? Sooner perish! Sooner be our name blotted out from the record of nations! . . .

I now proceed to another important argument against the annexation of Texas to our country, the argument drawn from the bearings of the measure on our National Union. Next to liberty, union is our great political interest, and this cannot but be loosened, it may be dissolved, by the proposed extension of our territory. . . .

I proceed now to the last head of this communication. I observe, that the cause of Liberty, of free institutions, a cause more sacred than union, forbids the annexation of Texas. It is plain from the whole preceding discussion, that this measure will exert a disastrous influence on the moral sentiments and principles of this country, by sanctioning plunder, by inflaming cupidity, by encouraging lawless speculation, by bringing into the confederacy a community whose whole history and circumstances are adverse to moral order and wholesome restraint, by violating national faith, by proposing immoral and inhuman ends, by placing us as a people in opposition to the efforts of philanthropy, and the advancing movements of the civilized world. It will spread a moral corruption, already too rife among us, and, in so doing, it will shake the foundations of freedom at home, and bring reproach on it abroad. It will be treachery to the great cause which has been confided to this above all nations.

Polk Asks for War on Mexico

Nine months after the Senate rejected the annexation treaty, lame-duck President John Tyler pushed through Congress a joint resolution authorizing the admission of Texas into the Union. That move provoked tension between the United States and Mexico, a country that felt cheated by the annexation of Texas and that contested American claims regarding Texas's border. Perhaps eager to provoke a war of conquest, President James K. Polk ordered the U.S. Army deep into the contested land. Fighting erupted between U.S. and Mexican soldiers in April 1846, and in early May, Polk asked Congress, in the message printed below, to issue a declaration of war. The message is taken from A Compilation of the Messages and Papers of the Presidents. . ., *ed.* James D. Richardson *(New York, 1897), 6:2287, 2291–93.*

WASHINGTON, May 11, 1846.
To the Senate and House of Representatives:

The existing state of the relations between the United States and Mexico renders it proper that I should bring the subject to the consideration of Congress. . . .

The Army moved from Corpus Christi on the 11th of March, and on the 28th of that month arrived on the left bank of the Del Norte opposite to Matamoras, where it encamped on a commanding position, which has since been strengthened by the erection of field works. . . .

The Mexican forces at Matamoras assumed a belligerent attitude, and on the 12th of April General Ampudia, then in command, notified General Taylor to break up his camp within twenty-four hours and to retire beyond the Nueces River, and in the event of his failure to comply with these demands announced that arms, and arms alone, must decide the question. . . .

The grievous wrongs perpetrated by Mexico upon our citizens throughout a long period of years remain unredressed, and solemn treaties pledging her public faith for this redress have been disregarded. A government either unable or unwilling to enforce the execution of such treaties fails to perform one of its plainest duties.

. . . Our forbearance has gone to such an extreme as to be mistaken in its character. Had we acted with vigor in repelling the insults and redressing the injuries inflicted by Mexico at the commencement, we should doubtless have escaped all the difficulties in which we are now involved.

Instead of this, however, we have been exerting our best efforts to propitiate her good will. Upon the pretext that Texas, a nation as independent as herself, thought proper to unite its destinies with our own, she has affected to believe that we have severed her rightful territory, and in official proclamations and manifestoes has repeatedly threatened to make war upon us for the purpose of reconquering Texas. In the meantime we have tried every effort at reconciliation. The cup of forbearance had been exhausted even before the recent information from the frontier of the Del Norte. But now, after reiterated menaces, Mexico has passed the boundary of the United States, has invaded our territory and shed American blood upon the American soil. She has proclaimed that hostilities have commenced, and that the two nations are now at war.

As war exists, and, notwithstanding all our efforts to avoid it, exists by the act of Mexico herself, we are called upon by every consideration of duty and patriotism to vindicate with decision the honor, the rights, and the interests of our country. . . .

In further vindication of our rights and defense of our territory, I invoke the prompt action of Congress to recognize the existence of the war, and to place at the disposition of the Executive the means of prosecuting the war with vigor, and thus hastening the restoration of peace.

JAMES K. POLK

Abraham Lincoln
Challenges Polk's Justification for War

The war against Mexico went well for the United States, which eventually occupied Mexico City and forced Mexico to cede approximately one-third of its land. Yet from the earliest days of fighting, many in the United States questioned the legal and moral grounds for conducting what they viewed as an aggressive war of conquest. The following address, delivered by Representative Abraham Lincoln, Whig of Illinois, in Congress on 12 January 1848, raised such concerns. The speech is reprinted from Complete Works of Abraham Lincoln, *ed. John G. Nicolay and John Hay (New York, 1905), 1:329–30, 338–41.*

[T]aking for true all the President states as facts, he falls far short of proving his justification. . . . The President, in his first war message of May, 1846, declares that the soil was ours on which hostilities were commenced by Mexico, and he repeats that declaration almost in the same language in each successive annual message, thus showing that he deems that point a highly essential one. In the importance of that point I entirely agree with the President. To my judgment it is the very point upon which he should be justified, or condemned. . . .

. . . I propose to state my understanding of the true rule for ascertaining the boundary between Texas and Mexico. It is that wherever Texas was exercising jurisdiction was hers; and wherever Mexico was exercising jurisdiction was hers; and that whatever separated the actual exercise of jurisdiction of the one from that of the other was the true boundary between them. . . . The extent of our territory in that region depended not on any treaty-fixed boundary (for no treaty had attempted it), but on revolution. . . .

. . . In my view, just so far as she carried her resolution by obtaining the actual, willing or unwilling, submission of the people, so far the country was hers, and no farther. Now, sir, for the purpose of obtaining the very best evidence as to whether Texas had actually carried her revolution to the place where the hostilities of the present war commenced, let the President answer the interrogatories I proposed, as before mentioned, or some other similar ones. Let him answer fully, fairly, and candidly. . . . And if, so answering, he can show that the soil was ours where the first blood of the war was shed,—that it was not within an inhabited country, or, if within such, that the inhabitants had submitted themselves to the civil authority of Texas or of the United States, and that the same is true of the site of Fort Brown,—then I am with him for his justification. . . . But if he can not or will not do this,— if on any pretense or no pretense he shall refuse or omit it—then I shall be fully convinced of what I more than suspect already—that he is deeply conscious of being in the wrong; that he feels the blood of this war, like the blood of Abel, is crying to Heaven against him; that originally having some strong motive—what, I will not stop now to give my opinion concerning—to involve the two countries in a war, and trusting to escape scrutiny by fixing the public gaze upon the exceeding brightness of military glory,—that attractive rainbow that arises in showers of blood—that serpent's eye that charms to destroy,—he plunged into it, and has swept on and on till, disappointed in his calculation of the ease with which Mexico might be subdued, he now finds himself he knows not where. How like the half-insane mumbling of a fever dream is the whole war part of his late message!

The Expansion of Slavery Justified

The acquisition of vast territory in the southwest raised the question of whether slavery would be permitted to expand there. Representative David Wilmot, a Pennsylvania Democrat, provoked furious debate by proposing in August 1846 a prohibition against slavery in lands acquired in the war. The so-called Wilmot Proviso repeatedly passed the House, where northerners enjoyed a majority, but died in the Senate, where southerners and other Democrats blocked it. The document that follows, an editorial condemning the Wilmot Proviso, first appeared in The United States Magazine and Democratic Review *(October 1847), 21:292.*

All the territory of the Union is the common property of all the states—every member, new or old, of the Union, admitted to partnership under the constitution, has a perfect right to enjoy the territory, which is the common property of all. Some of the territory was acquired by treaty from England—much of it by cession from the older states; yet more by treaties with Indians, and still greater quantities by purchase from Spain and France;—large tracts again by the annexation of Texas—and the present war will add still more to the quantity yet to be entered by citizens of the United States, or of those of any of the countries of Europe that choose to migrate thither. All this land, no matter whence it was derived, belongs to all the states jointly. . . . [N]o citizen of the United States can be debarred from moving thither with his property, and enjoying the liberties guaranteed by the constitution. . . .

Any law or regulation which interrupts, limits, delays or postpones the rights of the owner to the immediate command of his service or labor, operates a discharge of the slave from service, and is a violation of the constitution. . . . To set up therefore a pretence that if they adhere to the property they possess, they shall be deprived of their rights in the states to be formed in any acquired territory, is an unprincipled violation of a solemn treaty, an attack upon the constitution, and a gross injustice to the rights of neighboring states. If the constitution is respected, then the rights of no member in the common property can be impaired, because it is possessed of other property distasteful to other members.

The Expansion of Slavery Condemned

Among the most strident supporters of the Wilmot Proviso stood the noted abolitionist Charles Sumner of Massachusetts. In this treatise, written for the Massachusetts legislature in April 1847, Sumner criticizes the war against Mexico on anti-slavery and other grounds. Taken from "Report on the War with Mexico," in Old South Leaflets, *no. 132 (Boston, n.d.), 150–53, 155–56 [separately paginated as 14–17, 19–20].*

It can no longer be doubted that this is a war of conquest. . . .

A war of conquest is bad; but the present war has darker shadows. It is a war for the extension of slavery over a territory which has already been purged, by Mexican authority, from this stain and curse. Fresh markets of human beings are to be established; further opportunities for this hateful traffic are to be opened; the lash of the overseer is to be quickened in new regions; and the wretched slave is to be hurried to unaccustomed fields of toil. It can hardly be believed that now, more than eighteen hundred years since the dawn of the Christian era, a government, professing the law of charity and justice, should be employed in war to extend an institution which exists in defiance of these sacred principles.

It has already been shown that the annexation of Texas was consummated for this purpose. The Mexican war is a continuance, a prolongation, of the same efforts; and the success which crowned the first emboldens the partisans of the latter, who now, as before, profess to extend the area of freedom, while they are establishing a new sphere for slavery. . . . But it is not merely proposed to open new markets for slavery: it is also designed to confirm and fortify the "Slave Power.". . . Regarding it as a war to strengthen the "Slave Power," we are conducted to a natural conclusion, that it is virtually, and in its consequences, a war against the free States of the Union. . . . Nor should we be indifferent to the enormous expenditures which have already been lavished upon the war, and the accumulating debt which will hold in mortgage the future resources of the country. It is impossible to estimate the exact amount of these. At this moment the cost of the war cannot be less than seventy millions. It may be a hundred millions.

This sum is so vast as to be beyond easy comprehension. It may be estimated, partly, by reference to the cost of other objects of interest. It is far more than all the funds for common schools throughout the United States. It is ample for the endowment of three or more institutions like Harvard College in every State. It would plant churches in all the neglected valleys of the land. It would bind and interlace every part of the country by new railroads. It would make our broad and rude soil blossom like a garden. . . .

. . . The war is a crime, and all who have partaken in the blood of its well-fought fields have aided in its perpetration. It is a principle of military law that the soldier shall not question the orders of his superior. If this shall exonerate the army from blame, it will be only to press with accumulated weight upon the government, which has set in motion this terrible and irresponsible machine.

Questions

1. *On what grounds did some Americans advocate expansion into Texas, Oregon, and other regions? Why did other Americans oppose such steps? In your judgment, which side made the most compelling arguments on political, legal, and moral grounds?*
2. *Was the U.S. war against Mexico justified?*
3. *How did slavery and the emerging sectional dispute influence the debate over expansion? How did the acquisition of territory, in turn, aggravate the sectional conflict?*

FURTHER READING

Scholarship has diversified remarkably since Justin H. Smith published The War With Mexico *(New York, 1919), a patriotic account of U.S. expansionism in the 1840s. Norman A.* Graebner, Empire on the Pacific: A Study in American Continental Expansion *(New York, 1955), and David M.* Pletcher, The Diplomacy of Annexation: Texas, Oregon, and the Mexican War *(Columbia, Missouri, 1973), chronicle and critically analyze the westward surge of the American domain. Reginald Horsman,* Race and Manifest Destiny: The Origins of American Racial Anglo-Saxonism *(Cambridge, Massachusetts, 1981), probes the racism underlying expansionism, while Gene Brack,* Mexico Views Manifest Destiny, 1821–1845: An Essay on the Origins of the Mexican War *(Albuquerque, 1975), offers a view from south of the border.*

Nat Turner and Slave Resistance

Merton L. Dillon

INTRODUCTION

Africans, who were forcefully brought to North America, did not willingly accept enslavement. They used every opportunity to prove to their "owners" that, even though the law considered them slaves, they still were human beings with wills of their own and that there were limits beyond which they would not allow themselves to be pushed. Most slaveowners accepted these limits as the price they had to pay for getting an acceptable amount of work from their labor force and for maintaining order on the plantation. Most slaves, in turn, learned that there also were limits to the degree of resistance that their owners—or the state—would tolerate. Outright defiance of authority or overt rebellion risked such severe punishment that only the bravest or most aggrieved dared undertake them. Thus life on every plantation was marked by tension between the slaves, who were trying to gain advantage in order to create a tolerable life for themselves, and the owners and overseers, who were trying to maintain strict control in order to run a profitable plantation. On rare occasions, this uneasy accommodation broke down, and violence, even revolt, was the result.

Slaves in the West Indies and in South America, like slaves in ancient Greece and Rome, carried out extensive uprisings. In contrast, only three such outbreaks occurred in North America: the Stono revolt in South Carolina (1739), the revolt in Louisiana (1811), and Nat Turner's revolt in Virginia (1831). Of these, Nat Turner's was the costliest in human life, for both races, and the most momentous in its impact on official policy and public opinion. It was also the most difficult for the white population to understand, first, because its leader apparently had been subjected to no unusually cruel treatment and, second, because the revolt was characterized by a messianic quality foreign to the experience of many, if not most, white people at the time.

SLAVE REVOLT AND
SLAVE VIOLENCE:
THEIR CAUSES AND CONSEQUENCE

Resistance to slavery, common throughout its existence, took various forms, each of them annoying and costly to the owners. Feigning illness, breaking or losing tools, slow or shoddy work, insolence, running away—these were only a few of the many unspectacular ways slaves exerted their independence and countered their owners' power.

Every slaveowner and every plantation experienced such resistance to some degree at one time or another. It apparently was inseparable from the institution itself. Rarer than any of these mundane forms of resistance, but more to be feared, was slave violence directed against whites. Most incidents of assault and murder resulted from identifiable grievances experienced by individual slaves; the motive appeared limited to personal revenge and retribution. In rare instances, however, slaves joined together in overt action calculated to damage, or even destroy, the institution of slavery itself and to free themselves from it. On those occasions when slaves organized revolts, they used violence to achieve a political rather than a personal end. North American slaves made only a few such attempts, and their success was nil, especially when compared with the more frequent, extensive, and long lasting revolts undertaken by slaves in the West Indies and in South America. The Stono Revolt in South Carolina (1739), the revolt in Louisiana (1811), and Nat Turner's revolt in Virginia (1831) practically exhaust the list. Each was limited in scope and readily put down. Nevertheless, each of them had important consequences for the slave community and for white southerners as well as for the future of slavery itself and of opposition to it. Of the three North American revolts, the one led by Nat Turner (sometimes called the Southampton revolt) is by far the best known and the most extensively documented. That revolt, like its predecessors, led to vicious reprisals

215

against black people and to intensified efforts by slaveholders to make slavery more secure. In the North it contributed to the growth of an antislavery movement.

A Virginia State Official
Explains Nat Turner's Revolt

John Floyd, governor of Virginia, pondering the causes of Turner's revolt, concluded that it resulted from influences other than those inherent in slavery itself. Here Floyd tells James Hamilton, Jr., the governor of South Carolina, his explanation of the revolt and the plan he will propose to prevent its repetition. Excerpted from The Southampton Slave Revolt of 1831, *ed. Henry Irving Tragle (Amherst, 1971), 275–76.*

Richmond
November 19, 1831
Sir:

I received your letter yesterday and with great pleasure will give you my impressions freely—

I will notice this affair in my annual message, but here only give a very careless history of it, as it appeared to the public—

Nat Turner's revolt dramatized in a popular woodcut.

I am fully persuaded, the spirit of insubordination which has, and still manifests itself in Virginia, had its origin among, and eminated . . . from, the Yankee population, upon their *first* arrival amongst us, but mostly especially the Yankee pedlers and traders.

The course has been by no means a direct one—they began first, by making them religious—their conversations were of that character—telling the blacks God was no respecter of persons—the black man was as good as the white—that all men were born free and equal—that they cannot serve two masters—that the white people rebelled against England to obtain freedom, so have the blacks a right to do.

In the mean time, I am sure without any purpose of this kind, the preachers, principally Northern—were very assidious in operating upon our population, day and night, they were at work—and religion became, and is, the fashion of the time—finally our females and of the most respectable were persuaded that it was piety to teach negroes to read and write, to the end that they might read the Scriptures—many of them became tutoress in Sunday schools and, pious distributors of tracts, from the New York Tract Society.

At this point, more active operations commenced—our magistrates and laws became more inactive—large assemblages of negroes were suffered to take place for religious purposes—Then commenced the efforts of the black preachers, often from the pulpits these pamphlets and papers were read—followed by the incendiary publications of Walker, Garrison and Knapp of Boston, these too with songs and hymns of a similar character were circulated, read and commented upon—We resting in apathetic security until the Southampton affair.

From all that has come to my knowledge during and since this affair—I am fully convinced that every black preacher in the whole country east of the Blue Ridge was in [on] the secret, that the plans as published by those Northern presses were adopted and acted upon by them—that their congregations, as they were called knew nothing of this intended rebellion, except a few leading and intelligent men, who may have been head men in the

---

Reprinted from *The Southampton Slave Revolt of 1831,* Henry I. Tragle, Editor. Amherst: The University of Massachusetts Press, 1971. Copyright © 1971 by Henry I. Tragle.

Church—*the mass* were prepared by making them aspire to an equal station by such conversations as I have related as the first step.

I am informed that they had settled the form of government to be that of white people, whom they intended to cut off to a man—with the difference that the preachers were to be their Governors, Generals and Judges. I feel fully justified to myself, in believing the Northern incendiaries, tracts, Sunday Schools, religion and reading and writing has accomplished this end.

I shall in my annual message recommend that laws be passed—To confine the Slaves to the estates of their masters—prohibit negroes from preaching—absolutely to drive from this State all free negroes—and to substitute the surplus revenue in our Treasury annually for slaves, to work for a time upon our Rail Roads etc etc and these sent out of the country, preparatory, or rather as the first step to emancipation—This last point will of course be tenderly and cautiously managed and will be urged or delayed as your State and Georgia may be disposed to co-operate.

In relation to the extent of this insurrection I think it greater than will ever appear. . . .

I am Sir,
with consideration and respect
your obt Sevnt
[obedient servant,]
s/John Floyd/

Religion as a Bulwark of Slavery

As Governor Floyd suggests, slaveowners generally did not object to their slaves being exposed to religious teachings. In fact, some viewed such instruction as one of their responsibilities, but, like Governor Floyd, they believed that in the "wrong" hands (as in Turner's), religion could be a subversive or revolutionary force. The following excerpt was written in 1842 by Lunsford Lane, a North Carolina slave. This memoir illustrates the use of religion for conservative ends. Excerpted from Five Slave Narratives: A Compendium *(New York, 1968), 20–21, with some minor grammatical corrections.*

I had never been permitted to learn to read; but I used to attend church, and there I received instruction which I trust was of some benefit to me. . . .

I often heard select portions of the scriptures read. And on the Sabbath there was one sermon preached expressly for the colored people which it was generally my privilege to hear. I became quite familiar with the texts, "Servants be obedient to your masters."— "Not with eye service as men pleasers."—"He that knoweth his master's will and doeth it not, shall be beaten with many stripes," and others of this class: for they formed the basis of most of these public instructions to us. The first commandment impressed upon our minds was to obey our masters, and the second was like unto it, namely, to do as much work when they or the overseers were not watching us as when they were. But connected with these instructions there was more or less that was truly excellent; though mixed up with much that would sound strangely in the ears of freedom. There was one very kind hearted Episcopal minister whom I often used to hear; he was very popular with the colored people. But after he had preached a sermon to us in which he argued from the Bible that it was the will of heaven from all eternity we should be slaves, and our masters be our owners, most of us left him; for like some of the faint hearted disciples in early times we said,—"This is a hard saying, who can bear it?"

Popular Reaction to Nat Turner's Revolt

Following revolts, retribution against African Americans, slave or free, guilty or innocent, was severe and indiscriminate and may help to account for the rarity of such revolts. The following newspaper report describes the aftermath of Nat Turner's revolt and the part that armed forces played in halting the reprisals. From the Constitutional Whig, *Richmond, Virginia, 3 September 1831, reprinted in* The Southampton Slave Revolt of 1831, *ed. Henry Irving Tragle (Boston, 1971), 69–70.*

It is with pain we speak of another feature of the Southampton Rebellion; for we have been most unwilling to have our sympathies for the sufferers diminished or affected by their misconduct. We allude to the slaughter of many blacks, without trial, and under circumstances of great barbarity. How many have thus been put into death (generally by decapitation or shooting) reports vary; probably however some five and twenty and from that to 40; possibly a yet larger number. To the great honor of General Eppes, he used every precaution in his power, and we hope and believe with success, to put a stop to the disgraceful procedure.—We met with one individual of intelligence, who stated that he himself had killed between 10 and 15. He justified himself on the grounds of the barbarities committed on the whites; and that he thought himself right is certain from the fact that he narrowly escaped losing his own life in an attempt to save a negro woman whom he thought innocent but who was shot by the multitude in despite of his exertions. We (the Richmond Troop) witnessed with surprise the sanguinary temper of the population who evinced a strong disposition to inflict immediate death on every prisoner. Not having witnessed the horrors committed by the blacks, or seen the unburied and disfigured remains of their wives and children, we were unprepared to understand their feelings, and could not at first admit of their extenuation, which a closer observation of the atrocities of the insurgents suggested. Now, however, we feel individually compelled to offer an apology for the people of Southampton, while we deeply deplore that human nature urged them to such extremities. Let the fact not be doubted by those whom it most concerns, that another such insurrection will be the signal for the extirmination of the whole black population in the quarter of the state where it occurs. . . .

The presence of the troops from Norfolk and Richmond alone prevented retaliation from being carried much farther.

Popular Reaction to a Rumored Revolt in Louisiana

Solomon Northup, a slave in Louisiana during the 1840s, describes an abortive attempt by slaves to organize a mass escape to Mexico and the retaliation that followed. Note the apparent absence of a religious im-

pulse for the revolt and the similarities with the aftermath of Nat Turner's revolt. Note, too, that the violence against slaves came to an end in a similar way. Abridged from Solomon Northup, Twelve Years a Slave: Narrative of Solomon Northup . . . *(Auburn, 1853), 246–49.*

The year before my arrival in the country there was a concerted movement among a number of slaves on Bayou Boeuf, that terminated tragically indeed. It was, I presume, a matter of newspaper notoriety at the time, but all the knowledge I have of it, has been derived from the relation of those living at that period in the immediate vicinity of the excitement. It has become a subject of general and unfailing interest in every slave-hut on the bayou, and will doubtless go down to succeeding generations as their chief tradition. Lew Cheney, with whom I became acquainted—a shrewd, cunning negro, more intelligent than the generality of his race, but unscrupulous and full of treachery—conceived the project of organizing a company sufficiently strong to fight their way against all opposition, to the neighboring territory of Mexico.

A remote spot, far within the depths of the swamp back of Hawkins' plantation, was selected as the rallying point. Lew flitted from one plantation to another, in the dead of night, preaching a crusade to Mexico, and, like Peter the Hermit, creating a furor of excitement wherever he appeared. At length a large number of runaways were assembled; stolen mules, and corn gathered from the fields, and bacon filched from smoke-houses, had been conveyed into the woods. The expedition was about ready to proceed, when their hiding place was discovered. Lew Cheney, becoming convinced of the ultimate failure of his project, in order to curry favor with his master, and avoid the consequences which he foresaw would follow, deliberately determined to sacrifice all his companions. Departing secretly from the encampment, he proclaimed among the planters the number collected in the swamp, and, instead of stating truly the object they had in view, asserted their intention was to emerge from their seclusion the first favorable opportunity, and murder every white person along the bayou.

Such an announcement, exaggerated as it passed from mouth to mouth, filled the whole country with terror. The fugitives were surrounded and taken prisoners, carried in chains to Alexandria, and hung by the populace. Not only those, but many who were suspected, though entirely innocent, were taken from the field and from the cabin, and without the shadow of process or form of trial, hurried to the scaffold. The planters on Bayou Boeuf finally rebelled against such reckless destruction of property, but it was not until a regiment of soldiers had arrived from some fort on the Texan frontier, demolished the gallows, and opened the doors of the Alexandria prison, that the indiscriminate slaughter was stayed. Lew Cheney escaped, and was even rewarded for his treachery. He is still living, but his name is despised and execrated by all his race throughout the parishes of Rapides and Avoyelles.

Such an idea as insurrection, however, is not new among the enslaved population of Bayou Boeuf. More than once I have joined in serious consultation, when the subject has been discussed, and there have been times when a word from me would have placed hundreds of my fellow-bondsmen in an attitude of defiance. Without arms or ammunition, or even with them, I saw such a step would result in certain defeat, disaster and death, and always raised my voice against it.

During the Mexican war I well remember the extravagant hopes that were excited. The news of victory filled the great house with rejoicing, but produced only sorrow and disappointment in the cabin. In my opinion—and I have had opportunity to know something of the feeling of which I speak—there are not fifty slaves on the shores of Bayou Boeuf, but would hail with unmeasured delight the approach of an invading army.

A Northern Editor Reacts to Nat Turner's Revolt

Slave unrest obviously was primarily a southern problem, but Nat Turner's revolt led even northerners who were not abolitionists to worry about its probable effects on the nation at large. Here, a northern newspaper editor speculates on possible solutions to the "problem" of slave revolts. From the Ohio State Journal and Columbus Gazette, *October 20, 1831, 3.*

Since the suppression of the late Negro insurrection in Southampton county, Va. it appears that similar outrages have been attempted by the slaves and free colored people in different parts of North and South Carolina, Louisiana, Delaware, and the Eastern Shore of Maryland; and although the designs of the poor wretches concerned therein have been for the most part discovered and frustrated before much actual mischief had been done, yet the frequency of their late attempts has occasioned no little alarm in those parts of the union which have most to fear from a servile war. Whether these almost simultaneous movements in sections of the country so remote from each other be the result of accident, or of something like a preconcerted plan for a general insurrection among the slaves about this time does not fully appear. The latter supposition, however, is not altogether improbable; and although every man possessed of common sense will at once see that an attempt of this kind, however well matured, must ultimately result in the total extermination of at least all those engaged in it, if not of the entire colored population, yet, it is evident that it would inevitably occasion the loss of many valuable lives, and be productive of a vast amount of misery, before it could be suppressed.

A southern paper, speaking of these movements, and of the probability of their frequent recurrence so long as slavery shall be tolerated among us, suggests, whether it would not be right and expedient, after the National Debt shall have been paid, to apply the surplus revenue to the general emancipation of the slaves, and their removal beyond our territorial limits; and without intending to express an opinion, either as to the expediency or the feasibility of such a measure, we must say that it appears to us to be worthy of serious consideration. We believe that the people of these United States ought no longer to shut their eyes to the dreadful evils of slavery, and the consequences which, sooner or later, must inevitably result from it; and that the time has fully arrived when some plan should be devised for the removal of this curse from among us. We shall probably recur to the subject in a future number.

An Abolitionist Reacts to Nat Turner's Revolt

For many years before 1831, opponents of slavery had warned that slaves in the South would someday follow the example of the slaves in Saint-

Domingue who successfully rebelled in the 1790s. In this selection, William Lloyd Garrison, the best known of the abolitionists, interprets Nat Turner's revolt as a fulfillment of that prophecy, calling for immediate emancipation as the only means to prevent a catastrophic race war for liberation. Abridged from William Lloyd Garrison, "The Insurrection," Liberator, *Boston, September 3, 1831, 143.*

What we have so long predicted,—at the peril of being stigmatized as an alarmist and declaimer,—has commenced its fulfilment. The first step of the earthquake, which is ultimately to shake down the fabric of oppression, leaving not one stone upon another, has been made. The first drops of blood, which are but the prelude to a deluge from the gathering clouds, have fallen. The first flash of the lightning, which is to smite and consume, has been felt. The first wailings of a bereavement, which is to clothe the earth in sackcloth, have broken upon our ears. . . .

True, the rebellion is quelled. Those of the slaves who were not killed in combat, have been secured, and the prison is crowded with victims destined for the gallows!

'Yet laugh not in your carnival of crime
Too proudly, ye oppressors!'

You have seen, it is to be feared, but the beginning of sorrows. All the blood which has been shed will be required at your hands. At your hands alone? No—but at the hands of the people of New-England and of all the free states. The crime of oppression is national. The south is only the agent in this guilty traffic. But, remember! the same causes are at work which must inevitably produce the same effects; and when the contest shall have again begun, it must be again a war of extermination. In the present instance, no quarters have been asked or given.

[Garrison now attempts to voice the slaveholders' justification for revenge against Nat Turner's band:]

But we have killed and routed them [the slaves] now. . . We have the power to kill *all*—let us, therefore, continue to apply the whip and forge new fetters! . . . They were black—brutes, pretending to be men—legions of curses upon their memories! They were black—God made them to serve us! . . .

[Garrison, as an abolitionist, now addresses the slaveholders:]

Ye accuse the pacific friends of emancipation of instigating the slaves to revolt. Take back the charge as a foul slander. The slaves need no incentives at our hands. They will find them in their stripes—in their emaciated bodies—in their ceaseless toil— in their ignorant minds—in every field, in every valley, on every hill-top and mountain, wherever you and your fathers have fought for liberty—in your speeches, your conversations, your celebrations, your pamphlets, your newspapers—voices in the air, sounds from across the ocean, invitations to resistance above, below, around them! What more do they need? Surrounded by such influences, and smarting under their newly made wounds, is it wonderful that they should rise to contend—as other 'heroes' have contended—for their lost rights? It is *not* wonderful.

In all that we have written, is there aught to justify the excesses of the slaves? No. Nevertheless, they deserve no more censure than the Greeks in destroying the Turks, or the Poles in exterminating the Russians, or our fathers in slaughtering the British. Dreadful, indeed, is the standard erected by worldly patriotism!

For ourselves, we are horror-struck at the late tidings. We have exerted our utmost efforts to avert the calamity. We have warned our countrymen of the danger of persisting in their unrighteous conduct. We have preached to the slaves the pacific precepts of Jesus Christ. We have appealed to christians, philanthropists and patriots, for their assistance to accomplish the great work of national redemption through the agency of moral power—of public opinion—of individual duty. How have we been received? We have been threatened, proscribed, vilified and imprisoned—a laughing-stock and a reproach. Do we falter, in view of these things? Let time answer. If we have been hitherto urgent, and bold, and denunciatory in our efforts,—hereafter we shall grow vehement and active with the increase of danger. We shall cry, in trumpet tones, night and day,—Wo to this guilty land, unless she speedily repent of her evil doings! The blood of millions of her sons cries aloud for redress! IMMEDIATE EMANCIPATION can alone save her from the vengeance of Heaven, and cancel the debt of ages!

Slave Violence Directed against Individual Owners

Instances of slaves murdering their masters were frequent enough to cause concern even though slaveowners usually insisted that their own slaves could be trusted. Here, Mary Chesnut of South Carolina recounts the fate of two white women, one her acquaintance, the other her relative, who met their deaths at the hands of aggrieved slaves. Note that in each instance, the cause of the murders, as Mrs. Chesnut understands it, was not too much, but too little, discipline. How might the slaves' explanation for the murders differ from that given by Mrs. Chesnut? Excerpted from Mary Chesnut's Civil War, *ed. C. Vann Woodward (New Haven, 1981), 209–12.*

And now comes back on us that bloody story that haunts me night and day, Mrs. Witherspoon's murder.

The man William, who was the master spirit of the gang, once ran away and was brought back from somewhere west. And then his master and himself had a reconciliation, and the master henceforth made a pet of him.

The night preceding the murder, John Witherspoon went over to his mother's to tell her of some of William and Rhody's misdeeds. While their mistress was away from home, they had given a ball fifteen miles away from Society Hill. To that place they had taken their mistress's china, silver, house linen, &c&c. After his conversation with his mother, as he rode out of the gate, he shook his whip at William and said, "Tomorrow I mean to come here and give every one of you a thrashing."

That night Mrs. Witherspoon was talking it all over with her grandson, a half-grown boy who lived with her—slept, indeed, in a room opening into hers.

"I do not intend John to punish these negroes. It is too late to begin discipline now. It is all nonsense. I have indulged them past bearing, they all say. I ought to have tried to control them. It is all my fault. That's the end of it."

Mrs. Edwards, who was a sister of Mrs. Witherspoon, was found dead in her bed. It is thought this suggested their plan of action to the negroes. What more likely than she should die as her sister had done.

They were all in great trouble when John went off. William said, "Listen to me, and there will be no punishment here tomorrow." They made their plan, and then all of them *went to sleep,* William remaining awake to stir up the others at the proper hour.

What first attracted the attention of the family was the appearance of black and blue spots about the face and neck of the body of their mother. Then someone in moving the candle from the table at her bedside found blood upon their fingers. . . .

. . . [T]hey began to scent mischief and foul play in earnest, and they sent for the detective. Before he came they searched all houses and found bloody rags.

The detective dropped in from the skies quite unexpectedly. He saw that one of the young understrappers of the gang looked frightened and uncomfortable. This one he fastened upon and got up quite an intimacy with him. Finally he told this boy that he knew all about it. William had confessed privately to him to save himself and hang the others. But as the detective had taken a fancy to this boy, if he would confess everything, he would take him as state's evidence instead of William. The young man was utterly confounded at first but fell in the trap laid for him and told every particular from beginning to end.

Then they were all put in jail, the youth who had confessed among them, as he did not wish them to know of his *treachery* to them.

This was his story. "After John went away that night, Rhody and William made a great fuss—were furious at Mars John threatening them after all these years—to talk to them that away."

William said: "Mars John more than apt to do what he say he will do. You-all follow what I say and he'll have something else to think of beside stealing and breaking glass and china and tablecloths. If ole Marster was alive now, what would he say? Talk of whipping us at this time of day, &c&c."

Rhody kept the key of the house to let herself in every morning. So they arranged to go in at twelve. And then William watched, and they slept the sleep of the righteous.

Before that, however, they had a "rale fine supper and a heap of laughing at the way dey's all look tomorrow."

They smothered her with a counterpane [quilt] from a bed in the entry. He had no trouble the first time because they found her asleep and "done it all 'fore she waked." But after Rhody took her keys and went into the trunk and got a clean nightgown—for they had spoiled the one she had on—and fixed everything, candle, medicine, and all—she came to! Then she begged them hard for life. She asked them what she had ever done that they should want to kill her? She promised them before God never to tell on them. Nobody should ever know. But Rhody stopped her mouth by the counterpane. William held her head and hands down. And the other two sat on her legs. Rhody had a thrifty mind and wished to save the sheets and nightgown. She did not destroy them—they were found behind her mantelpiece. There the money was also, all in a hole made among the bricks behind the wooden mantelpiece.

A grandson of Rhody's slept in her house. Him she locked up in his room. She did not want him to know anything of this fearful night.

That innocent old lady and her gray hairs moved them not a jot.

Fancy how we feel. I am sure I will never sleep again without this nightmare of horror haunting me.

Mrs. Chesnut [Mary Chesnut's mother-in-law], who is their good angel, is and has always been afraid of negroes. In her youth the St. Domingo stories were indelibly printed on her mind.

She shows her dread now by treating everyone as if they were a black Prince Albert or Queen Victoria.

We were beginning to forget Mrs. Cunningham, the only other woman we ever heard of murdered by her negroes.

Poor Cousin Betsey was goodness itself. After years of freedom and indulgence and tender kindness, it was an awful mistake to threaten them like children. It was only threats. Everybody knew she would never do anything.

How about Mrs. Cunningham? He [Mr. Cunningham] was an old bachelor, and the negroes had it all their own way till he married. And then they hated her. They took her from her room, just over one in which her son-in-law and her daughter slept. They smothered her, dressed her, and carried her out—all without the slightest noise—and hung her by the neck to an apple tree, as if she had committed suicide. Waked nobody in the house by all this. If they want to kill us, they can do it when they please—they are noiseless as panthers.

They were discovered—first, because dressing her in the dark, her tippet [nightcap] was put on hind part before. And she was supposed to have walked out and hung herself in a pair of brand-new shoes whose soles evidently had never touched the ground.

We ought to be grateful that any one of us is alive. But nobody is afraid of their own negroes. These are horrid brutes—savages, monsters—but I find everyone like myself, ready to trust their own yard. I would go down on the plantation tomorrow and stay there, if there were no white person in twenty miles. My Molly and half a dozen others that *I know*—and all the rest I believe— would keep me as safe as I should be in the Tower of London.

Questions

1. *How do you account for the indiscriminate fury directed against African Americans in the wake of Nat Turner's revolt and the abortive revolt in Louisiana? Why do you think the armed forces quelled that fury instead of supporting it?*
2. *Both Governor John Floyd and William Lloyd Garrison agreed that outside influences were partly responsible for slave unrest, but their understanding of those influences varied greatly. Explain.*
3. *Religion is sometimes assumed to be a conservative force. Yet, it appears to have been a prime influence in the Nat Turner revolt. How do you account for this discrepancy? Can you think of other situations in which religion has been employed in support of radical causes?*

Further Reading

Nearly all the surviving sources for studying Nat Turner's revolt can be found in The Southampton Slave Revolt of 1831: A Compilation of Source Material Including the Full Text of the Confessions of Nat Turner, *ed.* Henry Irving Tragle (Boston, 1971). *For two good accounts of the revolt based on the documents in Tragle's book, see Stephen B. Oates,* The Fires of Jubilee: Nat Turner's Fierce Rebellion *(New York, 1975); and Herbert Aptheker,* Nat Turner's Slave Rebellion *(New York, 1966). Herbert Aptheker,* American Negro Slave Revolts *(New York, 1943), provides extensive information about various forms of African American resistance to slavery. For a discussion of the relation of slave discontent to American political and diplomatic history and to American wars see Merton L. Dillon,* Slavery Attacked: Southern Slaves and Their Allies, 1619–1865 *(Baton Rouge, 1990).*

THE
CONFESSIONS
OF
NAT TURNER, THE LEADER OF THE LATE
INSURRECTION IN SOUTH HAMPTON, VA.

As fully and voluntarily made to
THOMAS R. GRAY
In the prison where he was confined, and acknowledged by
him to be such when read before the Court of Southampton;
with the certificate, under seal of
the Court convened at Jerusalem,
Nov. 5, 1831, for his trial.
ALSO, AN AUTHENTIC
ACCOUNT OF THE WHOLE INSURRECTION,
WITH LISTS OF THE WHITES WHO WERE MURDERED,
AND OF THE NEGROES BROUGHT BEFORE THE COURT OF
SOUTHHAMPTON, AND THERE SENTENCED, &c.

Baltimore:
PUBLISHED BY THOMAS R. GRAY.
Lucas & Deaver, print.
1831.

Page verso

DISTRICT OF COLUMBIA, TO WIT:

Be it remembered, That on this tenth day of November, Anno Domini, eighteen hundred and thirty-one, Thomas R. Gray of the said District, deposited in this office the title of a book, which is in the words as following:

"The Confessions of Nat Turner, the leader of the late insurrection in Southampton, Virginia, as fully and voluntarily made to Thomas R. Gray, in the prison where he was confined, and acknowledged by him to be such when read before the Court of Southampton; with the certificate, under seal, of the Court convened at Jerusalem, November 5, 1831, for his trial. Also, an authentic account of the whole insurrection, with lists of the whites who were murdered, and of the negroes brought before the Court of Southampton, and there sentenced, &c. the right whereof he claims as proprietor, in conformity with an Act of Congress, entitled "An act to amend the several acts respecting Copy Rights."

EDMUND J. LEE, Clerk of the District.

In testimony that the above is a true copy
from the record of the District Court for
the District of Columbia, I, Edmund I.
Lee, the Clerk thereof, have hereunto
set my hand and affixed the seal of my

office, this 10th day of November, 1831.
EDMUND J. LEE, C. D. C.
(Seal.)

TO THE PUBLIC.

The late insurrection in Southampton has greatly excited the public mind, and led to a thousand idle, exaggerated and mischievous reports. It is the first instance in our history of an open rebellion of the slaves, and attended with such atrocious circumstances of cruelty and destruction, as could not fail to leave a deep impression, not only upon the minds of the community where this fearful tragedy was wrought, but throughout every portion of our country, in which this population is to be found. Public curiosity has been on the stretch to understand the origin and progress of this dreadful conspiracy, and the motives which influences its diabolical actors. The insurgent slaves had all been destroyed, or apprehended, tried and executed, (with the exception of the leader,) without revealing any thing at all satisfactory, as to the motives which governed them, or the means by which they expected to accomplish their object. Every thing connected with this sad affair was wrapt in mystery, until Nat Turner, the leader of this ferocious band, whose name has resounded throughout our widely extended empire, was captured. This "great Bandit" was taken by a single individual, in a cave near the residence of his late owner, on Sunday, the thirtieth of October, without attempting to make the slightest resistance, and on the following day safely lodged in the jail of the County. His captor was Benjamin Phipps, armed with a shot gun well charged. Nat's only weapon was a small light sword which he immediately surrendered, and begged that his life might be spared. Since his confinement, by permission of the Jailor, I have had ready access to him, and finding that he was willing to make a full and free confession of the origin, progress and consummation of the insurrectory movements of the slaves of which he was the contriver and head; I determined for the gratification of public curiosity to commit his

statements to writing, and publish them, with little or no variation, from his own words. That this is a faithful record of his confessions, the annexed certificate of the County Court of Southampton, will attest. They certainly bear one stamp of truth and sincerity. He makes no attempt (as all the other insurgents who were examined did,) to exculpate himself, but frankly acknowledges his full participation in all the guilt of the transaction. He was not only the contriver of the conspiracy, but gave the first blow towards its execution.

It will thus appear, that whilst every thing upon the surface of society wore a calm and peaceful aspect; whilst not one note of preparation was heard to warn the devoted inhabitants of woe and death, a gloomy fanatic was revolving in the recesses of his own dark, bewildered, and overwrought mind, schemes of indiscriminate massacre to the whites. Schemes too fearfully executed as far as his fiendish band proceeded in their desolating march. No cry for mercy penetrated their flinty bosoms. No acts of remembered kindness made the least impression upon these remorseless murderers. Men, women and children, from hoary age to helpless infancy were involved in the same cruel fate. Never did a band of savages do their work of death more unsparingly. Apprehension for their own personal safety seems to have been the only principle of restraint in the whole course of their bloody proceedings. And it is not the least remarkable feature in this horrid transaction, that a band actuated by such hellish purposes, should have resisted so feebly, when met by the whites in arms. Desperation alone, one would think, might have led to greater efforts. More than twenty of them attacked Dr. Blunt's house on Tuesday morning, a little before day-break, defended by two men and three boys. They fled precipitately at the first fire; and their future plans of mischief, were entirely disconcerted and broken up.

232

Escaping thence, each individual sought his own safety either in concealment, or by returning home, with the hope that his participation might escape detection, and all were shot down in the course of a few days, or captured and brought to trial and punishment. Nat has survived all his followers, and the gallows will speedily close his career. His own account of the conspiracy is submitted to the public, without comment. It reads an awful, and it is hoped, a useful lesson, as to the operations of a mind like his, endeavoring to grapple with things beyond its reach. How it first became bewildered and confounded, and finally corrupted and led to

---

the conception and perpetration of the most atrocious and heart-rending deeds. It is calculated also to demonstrate the policy or our laws in restraint of this class of our population, and to induce all those entrusted with their execution, as well as our citizens generally, to see that they are strictly and rigidly enforced. Each particular community should look to its own safety, whilst the general guardians of the laws, keep a watchful eye over all. If Nat's statements can be relied on, the insurrection in this county was entirely local, and his designs confided but to a few, and these in his immediate vicinity. It was not instigated by motives of revenge or sudden anger, but the results of long deliberation, and a settled purpose of mind. The offspring of gloomy fanaticism, acting upon materials but too well prepared for such impressions. It will be long remembered in the annals of our country, and many a mother as she presses her infant darling to her bosom, will shudder at the recollection of Nat Turner, and his band of ferocious miscreants.

Believing the following narrative, by removing doubts and conjectures from the public mind which otherwise must have remained, would give general satisfaction, it is respectfully submitted to the public by their ob't serv't,

T. R. GRAY.

Jerusalem, Southampton, Va. Nov. 5, 1831.

We the undersigned, members of the Court convened at Jerusalem, on Saturday, the 5th day of Nov. 1831, for the trial of Nat, *alias* Nat Turner, a negro slave, late the property of Putnam Moore, deceased, do hereby certify, that the confessions of Nat, to Thomas R. Gray, was read to him in our presence, and that Nat acknowledged the same to be full, free, and voluntary; and that furthermore, when called upon by the presiding Magistrate of the Court, to state if he had any thing to say, why sentence of death should not be passed upon him, replied he had nothing further than he had communicated to Mr. Gray. Given under our hands and seals at Jerusalem, this 5th day of November, 1831.

JEREMIAH COBB, [*Seal.*]
THOMAS PRETLOW, [*Seal.*]
JAMES W. PARKER, [*Seal.*]
CARR BOWERS, [*Seal.*]
SAMUEL B. HINES, [*Seal.*]
ORRIS A. BROWNE, [*Seal.*]

State of Virginia, Southampton County, to wit:

I, James Rochelle, Clerk of the County Court of Southampton in the State of Virginia, do hereby certify, that Jeremiah Cobb, Thomas Pretlow, James W. Parker, Carr Bowers, Samuel B. Hines, and Orris A. Browne, esqr's are acting Justices of the Peace, in and for the County aforesaid, and were members of the Court which convened at Jerusalem, on Saturday the 5th day of November, 1831, for the trial of Nat *alias* Nat Turner, a negro slave, late the property of Putnam Moore, deceased, who was tried and convicted, as an insurgent in the late insurrection in the county of Southampton aforesaid, and that full faith and credit are due, and ought to be given to their acts as Justices of the peace aforesaid.

In testimony whereof, I have hereunto set my hand and caused the seal of the Court aforesaid, to be affixed this 5th day of November, 1831.

JAMES ROCHELLE, C. S. C. C.

[Seal.]

CONFESSION.

Agreeable to his own appointment, on the evening he was committed to prison, with permission of the jailer, I visited NAT on Tuesday the 1st November, when, without being questioned at all, commenced his narrative in the following words:--

SIR,--You have asked me to give a history of the motives which induced me to undertake the late insurrection, as you call it--To do so I must go back to the days of my infancy, and even before I was born. I was thirty-one years of age the 2d of October last, and born the property of Benj. Turner, of this county. In my childhood a circumstance occurred which made an indelible impression on my mind, and laid the ground work of that enthusiasm, which has terminated so fatally to many, both white and black, and for which I am about to atone at the gallows. It is here necessary to relate this circumstance--trifling as it may seem, it was the commencement of that belief which has grown with time, and even now, sir, in this dungeon, helpless and forsaken as I am, I cannot divest myself of. Being at play with other children, when three or four years old, I was telling them something, which my mother overhearing, said it had happened before I was born--I stuck to my story, however, and related somethings which went, in her opinion, to confirm it--others being called on were greatly astonished, knowing that these things had happened, and caused them to say in my hearing, I surely would be a prophet, as the Lord had shewn me things that had happened before my birth. And my father and mother strengthened me in this my first impression, saying in my presence, I was intended for some great purpose, which they had always thought from certain marks on my head and breast--[a parcel of excrescences which I believe are not at all uncommon, particularly among negroes, as I have seen several with the same. In this case he has either cut them off or they have nearly disappeared]--My grand mother, who was very religious, and to whom I was much attached

--my master, who belonged to the church, and other religious persons who visited the house, and whom I often saw at prayers, noticing the singularity of my manners, I suppose, and my uncommon intelligence for a child, remarked I had too much sense to be raised, and if I was, I would never be of any service to any one as a slave--To a mind like mine, restless, inquisitive and observant of every thing that was passing, it is easy to suppose that religion was the subject to which it would be directed, and although this subject principally occupied my thoughts--there was nothing that I saw or heard of to which my attention was not directed--The manner in which I learned to read and write, not only had great influence on my own mind, as I acquired it with the most perfect ease, so much so, that I have no recollection whatever of learning the alphabet--but to the astonishment of the family, one day, when a book was shewn me to keep me from crying, I began spelling the names of different objects--this was a source of wonder to all in the neighborhood, particularly the blacks--and this learning was constantly improved at all opportunities--when I got large enough to go to work, while employed, I was reflecting on many things that would present themselves to my imagination, and whenever an opportunity occurred of looking at a book, when the school children were getting their lessons, I would find many things that the fertility of my own imagination had depicted to me before; all my time, not devoted to my master's service, was spent either in prayer, or in making experiments in casting different things in moulds made of earth, in attempting to make paper, gunpowder, and many other experiments, that although I could not perfect, yet convinced me of its practicability if I had the means. ˙ I was not addicted to stealing in my youth, nor have ever been--Yet such was the confidence of the negroes in the neighborhood, even at this early period of my life, in my superior judgment, that they would often carry me with them when they were going on any roguery, to plan for them. Growing up among them, with this confidence in my superior judgment, and when this, in their opinions, was perfected by Divine inspiration, from the circumstances already alluded to in my infancy, and which belief was ever afterwards zealously inculcated by the austerity of my life and manners, which became the subject of remark by white and black.-- Having soon discovered to be great, I must appear so, and therefore studiously avoided mixing in society, and wrapped

* When questioned as to the manner of manufacturing those different articles, he was found well informed on the subject.

---

myself in mystery, devoting my time to fasting and prayer--By this time, having arrived to man's estate, and hearing the scriptures commented on at meetings, I was struck with that particular passage which says : "Seek ye the kingdom of Heaven and all things shall be added unto you." I reflected much on this passage, and prayed daily for light on this subject--As I was praying one day at my plough, the spirit spoke to me, saying "Seek ye the kingdom of Heaven and all things shall be added unto you." *Question*--what do you mean by the Spirit. *Ans.* The Spirit that spoke to the prophets in former days--and I was greatly astonished, and for two years prayed continually, whenever my duty would permit--and then again I had the same revelation, which fully confirmed me in the impression that I was ordained for some great purpose in the hands of the Almighty. Several years rolled round, in which many events occurred to strengthen me in this my belief. At this time I reverted in my mind to the remarks made of me in my childhood, and the things that had been shewn me--and as it had been said of me in my childhood by those by whom I had been taught to pray, both white and black, and in whom I had the greatest confidence, that I had too much sense to be raised, and if I was, I would never be of any use to any one as a slave. Now finding I had arrived to man's estate, and was a slave, and these revelations being made known to me, I began to direct my attention to this great object, to fulfil the purpose for which, by this time, I felt assured I was intended. Knowing the influence I had obtained over the minds of my fellow servants, (not by the means of conjuring and such like tricks--for to them I always spoke of such things with contempt) but by the communion of the Spirit whose revelations I often communicated to them, and they believed and said my wisdom came from God. I now began to prepare them for my purpose, by telling them something was about to happen that would terminate in fulfilling the great promise that had been made to me-- About this time I was placed under an overseer, from whom I ranaway - and after remaining in the woods thirty days, I returned, to the astonishment of the negroes on the plantation, who thought I had made my escape to some other part of the country, as my father had done before. But the reason of my return was, that the Spirit appeared to me and said I had my wishes directed to the things of this world, and not to the kingdom of Heaven, and that I should return to the service of my earthly master--"For he who knoweth his Master's will,

235

and doeth it not, shall be beaten with many stripes, and thus, have I chastened you." And the negroes found fault, and murmured against me, saying that if they had my sense they would not serve any master in the world. And about this time I had a vision--and I saw white spirits and black spirits engaged in battle, and the sun was darkened--the thunder rolled in the Heavens, and blood flowed in streams--and I heard a voice saying, "Such is your luck, such you are called to see, and let it come rough or smooth, you must surely bare it." I now withdrew myself as much as my situation would permit, from the intercourse of my fellow servants, for the avowed purpose of serving the Spirit more fully--and it appeared to me, and reminded me of the things it had already shown me, and that it would then reveal to me the knowledge of the elements, the revolution of the planets, the operation of tides, and changes of the seasons. After this revelation in the year 1825, and the knowledge of the elements being made known to me, I sought more than ever to obtain true holiness before the great day of judgment should appear, and then I began to receive the true knowledge of faith. And from the first steps of righteousness until the last, was I made perfect; and the Holy Ghost was with me, and said, "Behold me as I stand in the Heavens"--and I looked and saw the forms of men in different attitudes--and there were lights in the sky to which the children of darkness gave other names than what they really were--for they were the lights of the Saviour's hands, stretched forth from east to west, even as they were extended on the cross on Calvary for the redemption of sinners. And I wondered greatly at these miracles, and prayed to be informed of a certainty of the meaning thereof--and shortly afterwards, while laboring in the field, I discovered drops of blood on the corn as though it were dew from heaven-- and I communicated it to many, both white and black, in the neighborhood-- and I then found on the leaves in the woods hieroglyphic characters, and numbers, with the forms of men in different attitudes, portrayed in blood, and representing the figures I had seen before in the heavens. And now the Holy Ghost had revealed itself to me, and made plain the miracles it had shown me--For as the blood of Christ had been shed on this earth, and had ascended to heaven for the salvation of sinners, and was now returning to earth again in the form of dew--and as the leaves on the trees bore the impression of the figures I had seen in the heavens, it was plain to me that the Saviour was about to lay down the yoke he had borne for the sins of men, and the

great day of judgment was at band. About this time I told these things to a white man, (Etheldred T. Brantley) on whom it had a wonderful effect--and he ceased from his wickedness, and was attacked immediately with a cutaneous eruption, and blood ozed from the pores of his skin, and after praying and fasting nine days, he was healed, and the Spirit appeared to me again, and said, as the Saviour had been baptised so should we be also--and when the white people would not let us be baptised by the church, we went down into the water together, in the sight of many who reviled us, and were baptised by the Spirit--After this I rejoiced greatly, and gave thanks to God. And on the 12th of May, 1828, I heard a loud noise in the heavens, and the Spirit instantly appeared to me and said the Serpent was loosened, and Christ had laid down the yoke he had borne for the sins of men, and that I should take it on and fight against the Serpent, for the time was fast approaching when the first should be last and the last should be first. *Ques.* Do you not find yourself mistaken now? *Ans.* Was not Christ crucified. And by signs in the heavens that it would make known to me when I should commence the great work--and until the first sign appeared, I should conceal it from the knowledge of men--And on the appearance of the sign, (the eclipse of the sun last February) I should arise and prepare myself, and slay my enemies with their own weapons. And immediately on the sign appearing in the heavens, the seal was removed from my lips, and I communicated the great work laid out for me to do, to four in whom I had the greatest confidence, (Henry, Hark, Nelson, and Sam)--It was intended by us to have begun the work of death on the 4th July last--Many were the plans formed and rejected by us, and it affected my mind to such a degree, that I fell sick, and the time passed without our coming to any determination how to commence--Still forming new schemes and rejecting them, when the sign appeared again, which determined me not to wait longer.

Since the commencement of 1830, I had been living with Mr. Joseph Travis, who was to me a kind master, and placed the greatest confidence in me; in fact, I had no cause to complain of his treatment to me. On Saturday evening, the 20th of August, it was agreed between Henry, Hark and myself, to prepare a dinner the next day for the men we expected, and then to concert a plan, as we had not yet determined on any. Hark, on the following morning, brought a pig, and Henry brandy, and being joined by Sam, Nelson,

Page 12

Will and Jack, they prepared in the woods a dinner, where, about three o'clock, I joined them.

Q. Why were you so backward in joining them.

A. The same reason that had caused me not to mix with them for years before.

I saluted them on coming up, and asked Will how came he there, he answered, his life was worth no more than others, and his liberty as dear to him. I asked him if he thought to obtain it? He said he would, or loose his life. This was enough to put him in full confidence. Jack, I knew, was only a tool in the hands of Hark, it was quickly agreed we should commence at home (Mr. J. Travis') on that night, and until we had armed and equipped ourselves, and gathered sufficient force, neither age nor sex was to be spared, (which was invariably adhered to.) We remained at the feast until about two hours in the night, when we went to the house and found Austin; they all went to the cider press and drank, except myself. On returning to the house, Hark went to the door with an axe, for the purpose of breaking it open, as we knew we were strong enough to murder the family, if they were awaked by the noise; but reflecting that it might create an alarm in the neighborhood, we determined to enter the house secretly, and murder them whilst sleeping. Hark got a ladder and set it against the chimney, on which I ascended, and hoisting a window, entered and came down stairs, unbarred the door, and removed the guns from their places. It was then observed that I must spill the first blood. On which, armed with a hatchet, and accompanied by Will, I entered my master's chamber, it being dark, I could not give a death blow, the hatchet glanced from his head, and his liberty as dear to him, he sprang from the bed and called his wife, it was his last word, Will laid him dead, with a blow of his axe, and Mrs. Travis shared the same fate, as she lay in bed. The murder of this family, five in number, was the work of a moment, not one of them awoke; there was a little infant sleeping in a cradle, that was forgotten, until we had left the house and gone some distance, when Henry and Will returned and killed it; we got here, four guns that would shoot, and several old muskets, with a pound or two of powder. We remained some time at the barn, where we paraded; I formed them in a line as soldiers, and after carrying them through all the manoeuvres I was master of, marched them off to Mr. Salathul Francis', about six hundred yards distant. Sam and Will went to the door and knocked. Mr. Francis asked who was there, Sam replied, it was him, and he had a

Page 13

letter for him, on which he got up and came to the door, they immediately seized him, and dragging him out a little from the door, he was dispatched by repeated blows on the head; there was no other white person in the family. We started from there for Mrs. Reese's, maintaining the most perfect silence on our march, where finding the door unlocked, we entered, and murdered Mrs. Reese in her bed, while sleeping; her son awoke, but it was only to sleep the sleep of

237

death, he had only time to say who is that, and he was no more. From Mrs. Reese's we went to Mrs. Turner's, a mile distant, which we reached about sunrise, on Monday morning. Henry, Austin, and Sam, went to the still, where, finding Mr. Peebles, Austin shot him, and the rest of us went to the house; as we approached, the family discovered us, and shut the door. Vain hope! Will, with one stroke of his axe, opened it, and we entered and found Mrs. Turner and Mrs. Newsome in the middle of a room, almost frightened to death. Will immediately killed Mrs. Turner, with one blow of his axe. I took Mrs. Newsome by the hand, and with the sword I had when I was apprehended, I struck her several blows over the head, but not being able to kill her, as the sword was dull. Will turning around and discovering it, despatched her also. A general destruction of property and search for money and ammunition, always succeeded the murders. By this time my company amounted to fifteen, and nine men mounted, who started for Mrs. Whitehead's, (the other six were to go through a by way to Mr. Bryant's and rejoin us at Mrs. Whitehead's,) as we approached the house we discovered Mr. Richard Whitehead standing in the cotton patch, near the lane fence; we called him over into the lane, and Will, the executioner, was near at hand, with his fatal axe, to send him to an untimely grave. As we pushed on to the house, I discovered some one run round the garden, and thinking it was some of the white family, I pursued them, but finding it was a servant girl belonging to the house, I returned to commence the work of death, but they whom I left, had not been idle; all the family were already murdered, but Mrs. Whitehead and her daughter Margaret. As I came round to the door I saw Will pulling Mrs. Whitehead out of the house, and at the step he nearly severed her head from her body, with his broad axe. Miss Margaret, when I discovered her, had concealed herself in the corner, formed by the projection of the cellar cap from the house; on my approach she fled, but was soon overtaken, and after

---

repeated blows with a sword, I killed her by a blow on the head, with a fence rail. By this time, the six who had gone by Mr. Bryant's, rejoined us, and informed me they had done the work of death assigned them. We again divided, part going to Mr. Richard Porter's, and from thence to Nathaniel Francis', the others to Mr. Howell Harris', and Mr. T. Doyles. On my reaching Mr. Porter's, he had escaped with his family. I understood there, that the alarm had already spread, and I immediately returned to bring up those sent to Mr. Doyles, and Mr. Howell Harris'; the party I left going on to Mr. Francis', having told them I would join them in that neighborhood. I met these sent to Mr. Doyles' and Mr. Harris' returning, having met Mr. Doyle on the road and killed him; and learning from some who joined them, that Mr. Harris was from home, I immediately pursued the course taken by the party gone on before; but knowing they would complete the work of death and pillage, at Mr. Francis' before I could there, I went to Mr. Peter Edwards', expecting to find them there, but they had been here also. I then went to Mr. John T. Barrow's, they had been here and murdered him. I pursued on their track to Capt. Newit Harris', where I found the greater part mounted, and ready to start; the men now amounting to about forty, shouted and hurraed as I rode up, some were in the yard, loading their guns, others drinking. They said Captain Harris and his family had escaped, the property in the house they destroyed, robbing him of money and other valuables. I ordered them to mount and march instantly, this was about nine or ten o'clock, Monday morning. I proceeded to Mr. Levi Waller's, two or three miles distant. I took my station in the rear, and as it 'twas my object to carry terror and devastation wherever we went, I placed fifteen or twenty of the best armed and most to be relied on, in front, who generally approached the houses as fast as their horses could run; this was for two purposes, to prevent their escape and strike terror to the inhabitants--on this account I never got to the houses, after leaving Mrs. Whitehead's, until the murders were committed, except in one case. I sometimes got in sight in time to see the work of death completed, viewed the mangled bodies as they lay, in silent satisfaction, and immediately started in quest of other victims--Having murdered Mrs. Waller and ten children, we started for Mr. William Williams' -- having killed him and two little boys that were there; while engaged in this, Mrs. Williams fled and got some distance from the house, but she was pursued, overtaken, and compelled to get up behind one of the company, who brought her back, and after showing her the mangled body of her lifeless husband, she was told to get down and lay by his side, where she was shot dead. I then started for Mr. Jacob Williams, where the family were murdered--Here we found a young man named Drury, who had come on business with Mr. Williams--he was pursued, overtaken and shot. Mrs. Vaughan was the next place we visited--and after murdering the family here, I determined on starting for Jerusalem-- Our number amounted now to fifty or sixty, all mounted and armed with guns, axes, swords and clubs--On reaching Mr. James W. Parkers' gate, immediately on the road leading to Jerusalem, and about three miles distant, it was proposed to me to call there, but I objected, as I knew he was gone to Jerusalem, and my object was to reach there as soon as possible; but some of the men having relations at Mr. Parker's it was agreed that they might call and get his people. I remained at the gate on the road, with seven or eight; the others going across the field to the house, about half a mile off. After waiting some time for them, I became impatient, and started to the house for them, and on our return we were met by a party of white men, who had pursued our blood-stained track, and who had fired on those at the gate, and dispersed them, which I new nothing of, not having been at that time rejoined by any of them-- Immediately on discovering the whites, I ordered my men to halt and form, as they appeared to be alarmed--The white men, eighteen in number, approached us in about one hundred yards, when one of them fired, (this was against the positive orders of Captain Alexander P. Peete, who commanded, and who had directed the men to reserve their fire until within thirty paces) And I discovered about half of them retreating, I then ordered my men to fire and rush on them; the few remaining stood their ground until we approached within fifty yards, when they fired and retreated. We pursued and overtook some of them who we thought we left dead; (they were not killed) after pursuing them about two hundred yards, and rising a little hill, I discovered they were met by another party, and had haulted, and were re-loading their guns, (this was a small party from Jerusalem who knew the negroes were in the field, and had just tied their horses to await their return to the road, knowing that Mr. Parker aad family were in Jerusalem, but knew nothing of the party that had gone in with Captain

Peete; on hearing the firing they immediately rushed to the spot and arrived just in time to arrest the progress of these barbarous villians, and save the lives of their friends and fellow citizens.) Thinking that those who retreated first, and the party who fired on us at fifty or sixty yards distant, had all only fallen back to meet others with amunition. As I saw them re-loading their guns, and more coming up than I saw at first, and several of my bravest men being wounded, the others became panick struck and squandered over the field; the white men pursued and fired on us several times. Hark had his horse shot under him, and I caught another for him as it was running by me; five or six of my men were wounded, but none left on the field; finding myself defeated here I instantly determined to go through a private way, and cross the Nottoway river at the Cypress Bridge, three miles below Jerusalem, and attack that place in the rear, as I expected they would look for me on the other road, and I had a great desire to get there to procure arms and amunition. After going a short distance in this private way, accompanied by about twenty men, I overtook two or three who told me the others were dispersed in every direction. After trying in vain to collect a sufficient force to proceed to Jerusalem, I determined to return, as I was sure they would make back to their old neighborhood, where they would rejoin me, make new recruits, and come down again. On my way back, I called at Mrs. Thomas's, Mrs. Spencer's, and several other places, the white families having fled, we found no more victims to gratify our thirst for blood, we stopped at Majr. Ridley's quarter for the night, and being joined by four of his men, with the recruits made since my defeat, we mustered now about forty strong. After placing out sentinels, I laid down to sleep, but was quickly roused by a great racket; starting up, I found some mounted, and others in great confusion; one of the sentinels having given the alarm that we were about to be attacked, I ordered some to ride round and reconnoitre, and on their return the others being more alarmed, not knowing who they were, fled in different ways, so that I was reduced to about twenty again; with this I determined to attempt to recruit, and proceed on to rally in the neighborhood, I had left. Dr. Blunt's was the nearest house, which we reached just before day; on riding up the yard, Hark fired a gun. We expected Dr. Blunt and his family were at Maj. Ridley's, as I knew there was a company of men there; the gun was fired to ascertain if any of the family were at home; we were immediately fired upon and retreated,

---

leaving several of my men. I do not know what became of them, as I never saw them afterwards. Pursuing our course back and coming in sight of Captain Harris', where we had been the day before, we discovered a party of white men at the house, on which all deserted me but two, (Jacob and Nat,) we concealed ourselves in the woods until near night, when I sent them in search of Henry, Sam, Nelson, and Hark, and directed them to rally all they could, at the place we had had our dinner the Sunday before, where they would find me, and I accordingly returned there as soon as it was dark and remained until Wednesday evening, when discovering white men riding around the place as though they were looking for some one, and none of my men joining me, I concluded Jacob and Nat had been taken, and compelled to betray me. On this I gave up all hope for the present; and on Thursday night after having supplied myself with provisions from Mr. Travis's, I scratched a hole under a pile of fence rails in a field, where I concealed myself for six weeks, never leaving my hiding place but for a few minutes in the dead of night to get water which was very near; thinking by this time I could venture out, I began to go about in the night and eaves drop the houses in the neighborhood; pursuing this course for about a fortnight and gathering little or no intelligence, afraid of speaking to any human being, and returning every morning to my cave before the dawn of day. I know not how long I might have led this life, if accident had not betrayed me, a dog in the neighborhood passing by my hiding place one night while I was out, was attracted by some meat I had in my cave, and crawled in and stole it, and was coming out just as I returned. A few nights after, two negroes having started to go hunting with the same dog, and passed that way, the dog came again to the place, and having just gone out to walk about, discovered me and barked, on which thinking myself discovered, I spoke to them to beg concealment. On making myself known they fled from me. Knowing then they would betray me, I immediately left my hiding place, and was pursued almost incessantly until I was taken a fortnight afterwards by Mr. Benjamin Phipps, in a little hole I had dug out with my sword, for the purpose of concealment, under the top of a fallen tree. On Mr. Phipps' discovering the place of my concealment, he cocked his gun and aimed at me. I requested him not to shoot and I would give up, upon which he demanded my sword. I delivered it to him, and he brought me to prison. During the time I was

---

pursued, I had many hair breadth escapes, which your time will not permit you to relate. I am here loaded with chains, and willing to suffer the fate that awaits me.

I here proceeded to make some inquiries of him after assuring him of the certain death that awaited him, and that concealment would only bring destruction on the innocent as well as guilty, of his own color, if he knew of any extensive or concerted plan. His answer was, I do not. When I questioned him as to the insurrection in North Carolina happening about the same time, he denied any knowledge of it; and when I looked him in the face as though I would search his inmost thoughts, he replied, "I see sir, you doubt my word; but can you not think the same ideas, and strange appearances about this time in the heaven's might prompt others, as well as myself, to this undertaking." I now had much conversation with and asked him many questions, having

240

forborne to do so previously, except in the cases noted in parenthesis; but during his statement, I had, unnoticed by him, taken notes as to some particular circumstances, and having the advantage of his statement before me in writing, on the evening of the third day that I had been with him, I began a cross examination, and found his statement corroborated by every circumstance coming within my own knowledge or the confessions of others whom had been either killed or executed, and whom he had not seen nor had any knowledge since 22d of August last, he expressed himself fully satisfied as to the impracticability of his attempt. It has been said he was ignorant and cowardly, and that his object was to murder and rob for the purpose of obtaining money to make his escape. It is notorious, that he was never known to have a dollar in his life; to swear an oath, or drink a drop of spirits. As to his ignorance, he certainly never had the advantages of education, but he can read and write, (it was taught him by his parents,) and for natural intelligence and quickness of apprehension, is surpassed by few men I have ever seen. As to his being a coward, his reason as given for not resisting Mr. Phipps, shews the decision of his character. When he saw Mr. Phipps present his gun, he said he knew it was impossible for him to escape as the woods were full of men; he therefore thought it was better to surrender, and trust to fortune for his escape. He is a complete fanatic, or plays his part most admirably. On other subjects he possesses an uncommon share of intelligence, with a mind capable of attaining any thing; but warped and perverted by the influence of

early impressions. He is below the ordinary stature, though strong and active, having the true negro face, every feature of which is strongly marked. I shall not attempt to describe the effect of his narrative, as told and commented on by himself, in the condemned hole of the prison. The calm, deliberate composure with which he spoke of his late deeds and intentions, the expression of his fiend-like face when excited by enthusiasm, still bearing the stains of the blood of helpless innocence about him; clothed with rags and covered with chains; yet daring to raise his manacled hands to heaven, with a spirit soaring above the attributes of man; I looked on him and my blood curdled in my veins.

I will not shock the feelings of humanity, nor wound afresh the bosoms of the disconsolate sufferers in this unparalleled and inhuman massacre, by detailing the deeds of their fiend-like barbarity. There were two or three who were in the power of these wretches, had they known it, and who escaped in the most providential manner. There were two whom they thought they left dead on the field at Mr. Parker's, but who were only stunned by the blows of their guns, as they did not take time to re-load when they charged on them. The escape of a little girl who went to school at Mr. Waller's, and where the children were collecting for that purpose. excited general sympathy. As their teacher had not arrived, they were at play in the yard, and seeing the negroes approach, ran up on a dirt chimney (such as are common to log houses,) and remained there unnoticed during the massacre of the eleven that were killed at this place. She remained on her hiding place till just before the arrival of a party, who were in pursuit of the murderers, when she came down and fled to a swamp, where, a mere child as she was, with the horrors of the late scene before her, she lay concealed until the next day, when seeing a party go up to the house, she came up, and on being asked how she escaped, replied with the utmost simplicity, "The Lord helped her." She was taken up behind a gentleman of the party, and returned to the arms of her weeping mother Miss Whitehead concealed herself between the bed and the mat that supported it, while they murdered her sister in the same room, without discovering her. She was afterwards carried off, and concealed for protection by a slave of the family, who gave evidence against several of them on their trial. Mrs. Nathaniel Francis, while concealed in a closet heard their blows, and the shrieks of the victims of these ruthless savages; they then entered the closet where she was concealed, and went out without discovering her. While in this hiding place, she heard two of her women in a quarrel about the division of her clothes. Mr. John T. Baron, discovering them approaching his house, told his wife to make her escape, and scorning to fly, fell fighting on his own threshold. After firing his rifle, he discharged his gun at them, and then broke it over the villain who first approached him, but he was overpowered, and slain. His bravery, however, saved from the hands of these monsters, his lovely and amiable wife, who will long lament a husband so deserving of her love. As directed by him, she attempted to escape through the garden, when she was caught and held by one of her servant girls, but another coming to her rescue, she fled to the woods, and concealed herself. Few indeed, were those who escaped their work of death. But fortunate for society, the hand of retributive justice has overtaken them; and not one that was known to be concerned has escaped.

The Commonwealth,
vs.
Nat Turner.

Charged with making insurrection, and plotting to take away the lives of divers free white persons, &c. on the 22d of August, 1831.

The court composed of - , having met for the trial of Nat Turner, the prisoner was brought in and arraigned, and upon his arraignment pleaded *Not guilty*; saying to his counsel, that he did not feel so.

On the part of the Commonwealth, Levi Waller was introduced, who being sworn, deposed as follows: (*agreeably to Nat's own Confession.*) Col. Trezvant* was then introduced, who being Sworn, narrated Nat's Confession to him, as follows: (*his Confession as given to Mr. Gray.*) The prisoner introduced no evidence, and the case was submitted without argument to the court, who having found him guilty, Jeremiah Cobb, Esq. Chairman, pronounced the sentence of the court, in the following words: "Nat Turner! Stand up. Have you any thing to say why sentence of death should not be pronounced against you?"

Ans. I have not. I have made a full confession to Mr. Gray, and I have nothing more to say.

* The committing Magistrate.

Page 21

Attend then to the sentence of the Court. You have been arraigned and tried before this court, and convicted of one of the highest crimes in our criminal code. You have been convicted of plotting in cold blood, the indiscriminate destruction of men, of helpless women, and of infant children. The evidence before us leaves not a shadow of doubt, but that your hands were often imbrued in the blood of the innocent; and your own confession tells us that they were stained with the blood of a master; in your own language, "too indulgent." Could I stop here, your crime would be sufficiently aggravated. But the original contriver of a plan, deep and deadly, one that never can be effected, you managed so far to put it into execution, as to deprive us of many of our most valuable citizens; and this was done when they were asleep, and defenceless; under circumstances shocking to humanity. And while upon this part of the subject, I cannot but call your attention to the poor misguided wretches who have gone before you. They are not few in number--they were your bosom associates; and the blood of all cries aloud, and calls upon you, as the author of their misfortune. Yes! You forced them unprepared, from Time to Eternity. Borne down by this load of guilt, your only justification is, that you were led away by fanaticism. If this be true, from my soul I pity you; and while you have my sympathies, I am, nevertheless called upon to pass the sentence of the court. The time between this and your execution, will necessarily be very short; and your only hope must be in another world. The judgment of the court is, that you be taken hence to the jail from whence you came, thence to the place of execution, and on Friday next, between the hours of 10 A. M. and 2 P. M. be hung by the neck until you are dead! dead! dead and may the Lord have mercy upon your soul.

A list of persons murdered in the Insurrection, on the 21st and 22nd of August, 1831.

Joseph Travers and wife and three children, Mrs. Elizabeth Turner, Hartwell Prebles, Sarah Newsome, Mrs. P. Reese and son William, Trajan Doyle, Henry Bryant and wife and child, and wife's mother, Mrs. Catharine Whitehead, son Richard and four daughters and grand-child, Salathiel Francis, Nathaniel Francis' overseer and two children, John T. Barrow, George Vaughan, Mrs. Levi Waller and ten children, William Williams, wife and two boys, Mrs. Caswell Worrell and child, Mrs. Rebecca Vaughan, Ann Eliza Vaughan, and son Arthur, Mrs. John K. Williams and child, Mrs. Jacob Williams and three children, and Edwin Drury--amounting to fifty-five.

A List of Negroes brought before the Court of Southampton, with their owners' names, and sentence.

- Daniel,-- -- -- -- Richard Porter, Convicted.
- Moses, -- -- -- -- -- J. T. Barrow, Do.
- Tom, -- -- -- -- Caty Whitehead, Discharged.
- Jack and Andrew, -- -- -- -- Caty Whitehead, Con. and transported.
- Jacob, -- -- -- -- Geo. H. Charlton, Disch'd without trial.
- Isaac, -- -- -- -- Ditto, Convi. and transported.
- Jack, -- -- -- -- Everett Bryant, Discharged.
- Nathan, -- -- -- -- Benj. Blunt's estate, Convicted.
- Nathan, Tom, and Davy, (boys,) -- -- -- -- Nathaniel Francis, Convicted and transported.
- Davy, -- -- -- -- Elizabeth Turner, Convicted.
- Curtis, -- -- -- -- Thomas Ridley, Do.
- Stephen, -- -- -- -- Do. Do.
- Hardy and Isham, -- -- -- -- Benjamin Edwards, Convicted and transp'd.
- Sam, -- -- -- -- Nathaniel Francis, Convicted.
- Hark, -- -- -- -- Joseph Travis' estate, Do.
- Moses, (a boy,) -- -- -- -- Do. Do. and transported.
- Davy, -- -- -- -- Levi Waller, Convicted.
- Nelson, -- -- -- -- Jacob Williams, Do.
- Nat, -- -- -- -- Edm'd Turner's estate. Do.
- Jack, -- -- -- -- Wm. Reese's estate, Do.
- Dred, -- -- -- -- Nathaniel Francis, Do.
- Arnold, Artist, (free,) -- -- -- -- Discharged.
- Sam, -- -- -- -- J. W. Parker, Acquitted.
- Ferry and Archer, -- -- -- -- J. W. Parker, Disch'd without trial.
- Jim, -- -- -- -- William Vaughan, Acquitted.
- Bob, -- -- -- -- Temperance Parker, Do.

- Davy, -- -- -- -- Joseph Parker,
- Daniel, -- -- -- -- Solomon D. Parker, Disch'd without trial.
- Thomas Haithcock, (free,) -- -- -- -- Sent on for further trial.

- Joe, -- -- -- -- John C. Turner, Convicted.
- Lucy, -- -- -- -- John T. Barrow, Do.
- Matt, -- -- -- -- Thomas Ridley, Acquitted.
- Jim, -- -- -- -- Richard Porter, Do.
- Exum Artes, (free,) Richard Porter, Sent on or further trial.
- Joe, -- -- -- -- Richard P. Briggs, Disch'd without trial.
- Bury Newsome, (free,) -- -- -- -- Sent on for further trial.
- Stephen, -- -- -- -- James Bell, Acquitted.
- Jim and Isaac, -- -- -- -- Samuel Champion, Convicted and trans'd.
- Preston, -- -- -- -- Hannah Williamson, Acquitted.
- Frank, -- -- -- -- Solomon D. Parker, Convi'd and transp'd.
- Jack and Shadrach, -- -- -- -- Nathaniel Simmons, Acquitted.
- Nelson, -- -- -- -- Benj. Blunt's estate, Do.
- Sam, -- -- -- -- Peter Edwards, Convicted.
- Archer, -- -- -- -- Arthur G. Reese, Acquitted.
- Isham Turner, (free,) -- -- -- -- Sent on for further trial.
- Nat Turner, -- -- -- --Putnam Moore, dec'd, Convicted.

Abolitionism

Merton L. Dillon

INTRODUCTION

Opposition to slavery in North America was as old as the institution itself. Africans—after being transported forcibly from their homes—resisted their enslavement from the day they reached American shores. At an early date, a few sympathetic whites joined them in condemning bondage. A religiously inspired movement aimed at abolishing slavery began in the middle of the eighteenth century when Quakers made opposition to slavery a condition of membership in their sect. Soon after, during the revolutionary period, a new concern for Natural Rights helped end slavery in the northern states. Some southerners also freed their slaves at that time, but antislavery sentiment in the South never became general enough to lead any southern state to abolish the institution.

Most early opponents of slavery assumed that it would be ended gradually by state legislative action, and that abolition would be accompanied by colonization—the removal of at least some of the freed men and women from the United States. But around 1830 a younger, more determined, more spirited group of abolitionists rejected each of these assumptions. Their demand for the immediate end of slavery and the abandonment of all plans for the expatriation of African Americans ushered in a new, exceedingly contentious phase of the antislavery movement. African Americans heartily endorsed the new "immediatist" program and joined in promoting it. They focused on the plight of their race in the northern states more consistently than did most of their white colleagues and were more intent than were most whites on working against such evidences of prejudice as segregated schools and discriminatory laws. Nonetheless, from beginning to end, the antislavery movement was a partnership, albeit an unequal one, of white and African American abolitionists.

Abolitionists condemned slavery as a cruel and sinful institution that ought to be ended at once. They argued, first, that it violated the principles set forth in the Declaration of Independence upon which the nation was founded, and, second, that it conflicted with such fundamental biblical teachings as the Golden Rule.

The majority of Americans at the time, patriotic and religious though they may have been, did not find these arguments persuasive. Abolitionists always comprised only a minority in the northern population and typically were both scorned and feared as dangerous fanatics. Their campaign to end slavery aroused fierce opposition throughout the north as well as the south. Abolitionist lecturers were regularly mobbed, their printing presses were wrecked, and one abolitionist editor, Elijah P. Lovejoy, was murdered.

A later generation may find such resistance to a call for freedom, justice, and equality hard to understand because the abolitionists' program and their point of view now form part of the American consensus: They are taken for granted. But we should remember that this achievement came only at the cost of a horrendous civil war and, a century later, the painful social and political upheaval incident to the civil rights struggles of the1960s.

ABOLITIONISM:
ACTION AND RESPONSE

Abolitionists tried to publicize their program through lectures, newspapers, and pamphlets. Opposition to this effort by a resistant and sometimes enraged public (one abolitionist was mobbed two hundred times) inevitably raised the issue of civil rights for white Americans as well as for blacks and brought in to the open this important question: Should public opinion be allowed to stifle the rights of free speech, free assembly, and free press simply because a majority finds certain ideas or expressions objectionable or judges them dangerous? Abolitionist activism and rhetoric highlighted the debate on the proper limits of free speech, including the extent to which a community is obliged to tolerate speech that it deems offensive.

In order to consider these issues with respect to the abolitionists, it is necessary to examine their program, their rhetoric, and their mode of agitation, as well as the opposition to them.

The American Anti-Slavery
Society Declares its Sentiments

At its founding in 1833, the American Anti-Slavery Society adopted this Declaration of Sentiments. In his characteristically impassioned rhetoric, William Lloyd Garrison condemned slavery and set forth the new organization's principles and proposed activities. Excerpted from William Lloyd Garrison, Selections from the Writings and Speeches of William Lloyd Garrison *(Boston, 1852), 66-71.*

More than fifty-seven years have elapsed, since a band of patriots convened in this place, to devise measures for the deliverance of this country from a foreign yoke. The corner-stone upon which they founded the Temple of Freedom was broadly this—'that all men are created equal; that they are endowed by their Creator with certain inalienable rights; that among these are life, LIBERTY, and the pursuit of happiness.' At the sound of their trumpet-call, three millions of people rose up as from the sleep of death, and rushed to the strife of blood; deeming it more glorious to die instantly as freemen, than desirable to live one hour as slaves. They were few in number—poor in resources; but the honest conviction that Truth, Justice and Right were on their side, made them invincible.

We have met together for the achievement of an enterprise, without which that of our fathers is incomplete; and which, for its magnitude, solemnity, and probable results upon the destiny of the world, as far transcends theirs as moral truth does physical force. . . .

Their principles led them to wage war against their oppressors, and to spill human blood like water, in order to be free. Ours forbid the doing of evil that good may come, and lead us to reject, and to entreat the oppressed to reject, the use of all carnal weapons for deliverance from bondage; relying solely upon those which are spiritual, and mighty through God to the pulling down of strong holds.

Their measures were physical resistance—the marshalling in arms—the hostile array—the mortal encounter. Ours shall be such only as the opposition of moral purity to moral corruption—the destruction of error by the potency of truth—the overthrow of prejudice by the power of love—and the abolition of slavery by the spirit of repentance.

Their grievances, great as they were, were trifling in comparison with the wrongs and sufferings of those for whom we plead. Our fathers were never slaves—never bought and sold like cattle—never shut out from the light of knowledge and religion—never subjected to the lash of brutal taskmasters.

But those, for whose emancipation we are striving—constituting at the present time at least one-sixth part of our countrymen—are recognized by law, and treated by their fellow-beings, as marketable commodities, as goods and chattels, as brute beasts; are plundered daily of the fruits of their toil without redress;

really enjoy no constitutional nor legal protection from licentious and murderous outrages upon their persons; and are ruthlessly torn asunder—the tender babe from the arms of its frantic mother—the heart-broken wife from her weeping husband—at the caprice or pleasure of irresponsible tyrants. For the crime of having a dark complexion, they suffer the pangs of hunger, the infliction of stripes, the ignominy of brutal servitude. They are kept in heathenish darkness by laws expressly enacted to make their instruction a criminal offence.

These are the prominent circumstances in the condition of more than two millions of our people, the proof of which may be found in thousands of indisputable facts, and in the laws of the slaveholding States.

Hence we maintain—that, in view of the civil and religious privileges of this nation, the guilt of its oppression is unequalled by any other on the face of the earth; and, therefore, that it is bound to repent instantly, to undo the heavy burdens, and to let the oppressed go free.

We further maintain—that no man has a right to enslave or imbrute his brother—to hold or acknowledge him, for one moment, as a piece of merchandize—to keep back his hire by fraud—or to brutalize his mind, by denying him the means of intellectual, social and moral improvement.

The right to enjoy liberty is inalienable. To invade it is to usurp the prerogative of Jehovah. Every man has a right to his own body—to the products of his own labor—to the protection of law—and to the common advantages of society. It is piracy to buy or steal a native African, and subject him to servitude. Surely, the sin is as great to enslave an American as an African.

Therefore we believe and affirm—that there is no difference, in principle, between the African slave trade and American slavery:

That every American citizen, who detains a human being in involuntary bondage as his property, is, according to Scripture, (Ex. xxi. 16,) a man-stealer:

That the slaves ought instantly to be set free, and brought under the protection of law:

That if they had lived from the time of Pharaoh down to the present period, and had been entailed through successive generations, their right to be free could never have been alienated, but their claims would have constantly risen in solemnity:

That all those laws which are now in force, admitting the right of slavery, are therefore, before God, utterly null and void . . .

We further believe and affirm—that all persons of color, who possess the qualifications which are demanded of others, ought to be admitted forthwith to the enjoyment of the same privileges, and the exercise of the same prerogatives, as others; and that the paths of preferment, of wealth, and of intelligence, should be opened as widely to them as to persons of a white complexion.

We maintain that no compensation should be given to the planters emancipating their slaves:

Because it would be a surrender of the great fundamental principle, that man cannot hold property in man:

Because slavery is a crime, and therefore is not an article to be sold:

Because the holders of slaves are not the just proprietors of what they claim; freeing the slave is not depriving them of property, but restoring it to its rightful owner; it is not wronging the master, but righting the slave—restoring him to himself:

Because immediate and general emancipation would only destroy nominal, not real property; it would not amputate a limb or break a bone of the slaves, but by infusing motives into their breasts, would make them doubly valuable to the masters as free laborers; and

Because, if compensation is to be given at all, it should be given to the outraged and guiltless slaves, and not to those who have plundered and abused them.

We regard as delusive, cruel and dangerous, any scheme of expatriation which pretends to aid, either directly or indirectly, in the emancipation of the slaves or to be a substitute for the immediate and total abolition of slavery.

We fully and unanimously recognise the sovereignty of each State, to legislate exclusively on the subject of the slavery which is tolerated within its limits; we concede that Congress, under the present national compact, has no right to interfere with any of the slave States, in relation to this momentous subject:

But we maintain that Congress has a right, and is solemnly bound, to suppress the domestic slave trade between the several States, and to abolish slavery in those portions of our territory which the Constitution has placed under its exclusive jurisdiction. . . .

These are our views and principles—these our designs and measures. With entire confidence in the overruling justice of God, we plant ourselves upon the Declaration of our Independence and the truths of Divine Revelation, as upon the Everlasting Rock.

We shall organize Anti-Slavery Societies, if possible, in every city, town and village in our land.

We shall send forth agents to lift up the voice of remonstrance, of warning, of entreaty, and of rebuke.

We shall circulate, unsparingly and extensively, anti-slavery tracts and periodicals.

We shall enlist the pulpit and the press in the cause of the suffering and the dumb.

We shall aim at a purification of the churches from all participation in the guilt of slavery.

We shall encourage the labor of freemen [free African Americans] rather than that of slaves, by giving a preference to their productions: and

We shall spare no exertions nor means to bring the whole nation to speedy repentance.

Our trust for victory is solely in God. We may be personally defeated, but our principles never! Truth, Justice, Reason, Humanity, must and will gloriously triumph. Already a host is coming up to the help of the Lord against the mighty, and the prospect before us is full of encouragement.

The Influence of Slavery

In the following excerpt, Garrison claims that slaveholders virtually controlled national policy and politics and exerted a governing influence on ideas and institutions even in the North. According to this analysis, ending slavery would do much more than restore freedom to the slaves. It also would destroy the base of the slaveholders' power and thus bring revolutionary change to power relationships throughout the country. With this insight, Garrison accounted for the intense opposition that abolitionists encountered. Abridged from William Lloyd Garrison, Selections from the Writings and Speeches of William Lloyd Garrison *(Boston, 1852), 137-39.*

For more than two centuries, slavery has polluted the American soil. It has grown with the growth, and strengthened with the strength of the republic. Its victims have multiplied, from a single cargo of stolen Africans, to three millions of native-born inhabitants. In our colonial state, it was deemed compatible with loyalty to the mother country. In our revolutionary struggle for independence, it exchanged the sceptre of monarchy for the star-spangled banner of republicanism, under the folds of which it has found ample encouragement and protection. From the days of the Puritans down to the present time, it has been sanctified by the religion, and upheld by the patriotism of the nation. From the adoption of the American Constitution, it has declared war and made peace, instituted and destroyed national banks and tariffs, controlled the army and navy, prescribed the policy of the government, ruled in both houses of Congress, occupied the Presidential chair, governed the political parties, distributed offices of trust and emolument among its worshippers, fettered Northern industry and enterprise, and trampled liberty of speech and of conscience in the dust.

It has exercised absolute mastery over the American Church. In her skirts is found 'the blood of the souls of the poor innocents.' With the Bible in their hands, her priesthood have attempted to prove that slavery came down from God out of heaven. . . .

If slavery be thus entwined around the civil, social, and pecuniary interests of the republic—if the religious sects and political parties are banded together for its safety from internal revolt and external opposition—if the people, awed by its power and corrupted by its influence, are basely bending their knees at its foot-

The masthead of the abolitionist Liberator *newspaper from 1833 features an illustration of a slave auction alongside the name of editor William Lloyd Garrison. (Courtesy of The Library of Congress.)*

stool—is it wonderful that Church and State are shaken to their foundations by the rallying cry of Liberty? . . .

Slavery must be overthrown. No matter how numerous the difficulties, how formidable the obstacles, how strong the foes to be vanquished—slavery must cease to pollute the land. . . . No matter, though, to effect it, every party should be torn by dissensions, every sect dashed into fragments, the national compact dissolved, the land filled with the horrors of a civil and a servile war—still, slavery must be buried in the grave of infamy, beyond the possibility of a resurrection.

If the State cannot survive the anti-slavery agitation, then let the State perish. If the Church must be cast down . . . to be free, then let the Church fall. . . . If the American Union cannot be maintained . . . then let the American Union be consumed by a living thunderbolt, and no tear be shed over its ashes.

A Call for Women to Become Abolitionists

Women helped organize the American Anti-Slavery Society, held fundraising antislavery bazaars, circulated antislavery petitions, and otherwise promoted the abolitionist cause. This essay is one of the earliest appeals to women. It also shows that women's participation in the movement was sometimes opposed even by women themselves. This excerpt is a response to a woman who objected to other women publicly advocating emancipation. Taken from Elizabeth Margaret Chandler, The Poetical Works of Elizabeth Margaret Chandler *(Philadelphia, 1836), 21-23.*

We have been so long accustomed to consider the duty of the female sex, with regard to slavery, as entirely plain, that we had almost imagined it must be equally so to any unprejudiced thinker upon the subject. Not that we expected to find no difference of feeling, or contrariety of sentiment; apathy and prejudices we were prepared for; but we certainly had not thought that the interference of woman in behalf of suffering humanity, could be seriously objected to, as improper, and at variance with right principles. Yet this we are sorry to find is the light in which it is regarded by one of our own sex—a lady, whose talents and char-

The declaration of the American Anti-Slavery Society from its founding convention in Philadelphia, Pennsylvania in 1833. (Courtesy of The Library of Congress.)

acter we respect very highly, and whose approbation of the course we are pursuing, we should be proud to have obtained. But as this is withheld, and it is probable she may not be singular in her opinions, we have taken the liberty of quoting some of her sentiments, and appending to them a statement of our own ideas on the same subject.

"Should you inquire why I do not devote myself more sedulously to promote the cause of emancipation?—I would tell you, that I think it is a work which requires the energies of *men*."

And so it does; but it requires also the *influence of woman*. She was given to man 'to be a helpmeet [helpmate] for him;' and it is therefore her duty, whenever she can do so, to lend him her aid in every great work of philanthropy. In *this* her cooperation may be of essential service, without leading her one step beyond her own proper sphere. . . .

"It is a subject so connected with those of government, of law and politics, that I should fear the direct or even apparent interference of my own sex, would be a departure from that propriety of character which nature, as well as society, imposes on woman."

It is true that it is a question of government and politics, but it also rests upon the broader basis of humanity and justice; and it is on *this* ground only, that we advocate the interference of women. We have not the least desire to see our own sex transformed into a race of politicians; but we do not think that in this case such consequences are in the least to be apprehended. To plead for the miserable, to endeavour to alleviate the bitterness of their destiny, and to soften the stern bosoms of their oppressors into gentleness and mercy, can never be unfeminine or unbefitting the delicacy of woman! She does not advocate Emancipation because slavery is at variance with the political interests of the state, but because it is an outrage against *humanity* and *morality* and *religion;* because it is *criminal,* and because her own supineness makes her a *sharer in the crime;* and because a great number of *her own sex* are among its victims. It is therefore, that she should steadily and conscientiously rank among the number of its opponents, and refuse to be benefited by its advantages. She does not by this become a partizan of any system of policy—she seeks only to shield from outrage all that is most holy in her religion! She does not seek to direct, or share with men, the government of the state; but she entreats them to lift the iron foot of despotism from the neck of her sisterhood; and this we consider not only quite within the sphere of her privileges, but also of her positive duties.

A Northern Woman Condemns Prejudice

This passage was one of the most powerful early critiques of slavery and the prejudice that supported it. The author is nearly as critical of the racial prejudice exhibited by Northerners as she is of slavery itself. Excerpted from Lydia Maria Child, An Appeal in Favor of that Class of Americans Called Africans *(Boston, 1833), 208-9, 211, 232.*

While we bestow our earnest disapprobation on the system of slavery, let us not flatter ourselves that we are in reality any better than our brethren of the South. Thanks to our soil and climate, and the early exertions of the Quakers, the *form* of slavery does not exist among us; but the very *spirit* of the hateful and mischievous thing is here in all its strength. The manner in which we use what power we have, gives us ample reason to be grateful that the nature of our institutions does not intrust us with more. Our prejudices against colored people is [are] even more inveterate than it is at the South. The planter is often attached to his negroes, and lavishes caresses and kind words upon them, as he would on a favorite hound; but our cold-hearted, ignoble prejudice admits of no exception—no intermission.

The Southerners have long continued habit, apparent interest and dreaded danger, to palliate the wrong they do; but we stand without excuse. They tell us that Northern ships and Northern capital have been engaged in this wicked business; and the reproach is true. Several fortunes in this city [Boston] have been made by the sale of negro blood. If these criminal transactions are still carried on, they are done in silence and secrecy, because public opinion has made them disgraceful. But if the free States wished to cherish the system of slavery forever, they could not take a more direct course than they now do. Those who are kind and liberal on all other subjects, unite with the selfish and the proud in their unrelenting efforts to keep the colored population in the lowest state of degradation; and the influence they unconsciously exert over children early infuses into their innocent minds the same strong feelings of contempt.

The intelligent and well informed have the least share of this prejudice; and when their minds can be brought to reflect upon it, I have generally observed that they soon cease to have any at all. But such a general apathy prevails and the subject is so seldom brought into view, that few are really aware how oppressively the influence of society is made to bear upon this injured class of the community. . . .

. . . [A]n unjust law exists in this Commonwealth [Massachusetts], by which marriages between persons of different color is [are] pronounced illegal. I am perfectly aware of the gross ridicule to which I may subject myself by alluding to this particular; but I have lived too long, and observed too much, to be disturbed by the world's mockery. In the first place, the government ought not to be invested with power to control the affections, any more than the consciences of citizens. A man has at least as good a right to choose his wife, as he has to choose his religion. His taste may not suit his neighbors; but so long as his deportment is correct, they have no right to interfere with his concerns. . . .

There is among the colored people an increasing desire for information, and a laudable ambition to be respectable in manners and appearance. Are we not foolish as well as sinful, in trying to repress a tendency so salutary to themselves, and so beneficial to the community? Several individuals of this class are very desirous to have persons of their own color qualified to teach something more than mere reading and writing. But in the public schools, colored children are subject to many discouragements and difficulties; and into the private schools they cannot gain admission. A very sensible and well-informed colored woman in a neighboring town, whose family have been brought up in a manner that excited universal remark and approbation, has been extremely desirous to obtain for her eldest daughter the advantages of a private school; but she has been resolutely repulsed, on account of her complexion. . . .

By publishing this book I have put my mite into the treasury [expressed my thoughts]. The expectation of displeasing all classes has not been unaccompanied with pain. But it has been strongly impressed upon my mind that it was a duty to fulfil this task; and earthly considerations should never stifle the voice of conscience.

An Abolitionist Lecturer's Instructions

In 1834 the American Anti-Slavery Society commissioned Theodore Dwight Weld to serve as an abolitionist agent in Ohio. These are his instructions. Abridged from Letters of Theodore Dwight Weld, Angelina Grimké Weld and Sarah Grimké, 1822-1844, vol. 1, ed. Gilbert H. Barnes and Dwight L. Dumond *(New York, 1934), 125-27.*

Dear Sir—You have been appointed an Agent of the American Anti-Slavery Society; and will receive the following instructions from the Executive Committee. . . .

The general principles of the Society are set forth in the Declaration, signed by the members of the Convention which formed it at Philadelphia, Dec. 7, 1833. Our object is, the overthrow of American slavery, the most atrocious and oppressive system of bondage that has ever existed in any country. We expect to accomplish this, mainly by showing to the public its true character and legitimate fruits, its contrariety to the first principles of religion, morals, and humanity, and its special inconsistency with our pretensions, as a free, humane, and enlightened people. In this way, by the force of truth, we expect to correct the common errors that prevail respecting slavery, and to produce a just public sentiment, which shall appeal both to the conscience and love of character, of our slave-holding fellow-citizens, and convince them that both their duty and their welfare require the immediate abolition of slavery.

You will inculcate every where, the great fundamental principle of IMMEDIATE ABOLITION, as the duty of all masters, on the ground that slavery is both unjust and unprofitable. Insist principally on the SIN OF SLAVERY, because our main hope is in the consciences of men, and it requires little logic to prove that it is always safe to do right. To question this, is to impeach the superintending Providence of God.

We reprobate the idea of compensation to slave holders, because it implies the right of slavery. It is also unnecessary, because the abolition of slavery will be an advantage, as free labor is found to be more profitable than the labor of slaves. We also reprobate all plans of expatriation, by whatever specious pretences covered, as a remedy for slavery, for they all proceed from prejudice against color; and we hold that the duty of the whites in regard to this cruel prejudice is not to indulge it, but to repent and overcome it.

The people of color ought at once to be emancipated and recognized as citizens, and their rights secured as such, equal in all respects to others, according to the cardinal principle laid down in the American Declaration of Independence. . . .

Do not allow yourself to be drawn away from the main object, to exhibit a detailed PLAN of abolition; for men's consciences will be greatly relieved from the feeling of present duty, by any objections or difficulties which they can find or fancy in your plan. Let the *principle* be decided on, of immediate abolition, and the plans will easily present themselves. What ought to be done can be done. . . .

You will make yourself familiar with FACTS, for they chiefly influence reflecting minds. Be careful to use only facts that are well authenticated, and always state them with the precision of a witness under oath. You cannot do our cause a greater injury than by overstating facts. . . .

In traversing your field, you will generally find it wise to visit first several prominent places in it, particularly those where it is

known our cause has friends. In going to a place, you will naturally call upon those who are friendly to our objects, and take
advice from them. Also call on ministers of the gospel and other
leading characters, and labor specially to enlighten them and
secure their favor and influence. Ministers are the hinges of community, and ought to be moved, if possible. If they can be gained,
much is gained. . . .

Form Auxiliary Societies, both male and female, in every
place where it is practicable. Even if such societies are very small
at the outset, they may do much good as centres of light, and
means of future access to the people. Encourage them to raise
funds and apply them in purchasing and circulating anti-slavery
publications gratuitously. . . .

You are not to take up collections in your public meetings, as
the practice often prevents persons from attending, whom it
might be desirable to reach.

The Attorney General
of Illinois Defends a Mob

---

*In Alton, Illinois, in 1837 a mob destroyed Elijah P. Lovejoy's printing
press while a group of armed men attempted to defend it. During the
confrontation, Lovejoy was shot and killed. Some mob members were
brought to trial and defended by Usher Linder, the state's attorney
general. This portion of Linder's remarks to the jury is abridged from
William S.* Lincoln, Alton Trials: of Winthrop S. Gilman, Who Was
Indicted . . . For the Crime of Riot . . . *(New York, 1838), 72-77.*

I ask you to travel along with me as I relate to you the facts in
this case. Last August [1837], the first press was destroyed: the
"boys" broke it to pieces and threw it into the river. Another was
brought here, and after repeated failures to establish a press by
which they [abolitionists] could disseminate their fiendish doctrines, another course was adopted. A convention [to form a state
antislavery society] was called at Upper Alton. Alton was chosen
as the scene of their operations. Alton was to be made the theatre
of their preachings—and all their presses, and all their preachings,

and all their conventions were to be held in the poor, devoted city of Alton. . . . [T]hese people thought they were going to have it all their own way. But it happened that these Western boys knew a thing or two: knew a trick worth two of that; and so they got together and out-voted them, and the convention blew up in smoke. It was a farce. Not satisfied with this; not satisfied with the blowing up of this farce; not satisfied with the result of this convention, headed by interlopers from other states, headed by an alien to our laws and our country, they issued their handbills, they made proclamation in the streets, of their intention to preach their doctrines in the Church. They posted up placards, notifying the world that Dr. [Edward] Beecher would preach upon this damning doctrine of abolition. . . . [Linder then criticizes the abolitionists' decision to protect themselves with arms.]

. . . So that you see, gentlemen, when all other sources fail . . . the doctrines of abolition are to be forced down our throats. . . . And was not all this calculated to disturb the peace? was not this calculated to excite terror? to stir up the feelings? to rouse the passions, and to provoke an attack? . . .

But the press came at last: the press which was intended to preach insurrection, and to disseminate the doctrines which must tend to disorganization and disunion. With what delight they caught the first glimpse of their new-born child; with what joy they hugged it to their hearts! . . .

. . . Suppose this press had not been guarded; suppose that, taking advantage of the absence of those who had assembled for its protection, the mob had destroyed it. Had these people [the abolitionists] no remedy? Is there no law which would have given them redress? They talk of being friends to good order; lovers of law!! Have they not taken the law into their own hands, and violated the laws of man and of God in depriving man of life? And for what? For a press! a printing press! A press brought here to teach rebellion and insurrection to the slave; to excite servile war; to preach murder in the name of religion; to strike dismay to the hearts of the people, and spread desolation over the face of this land. Society esteems good order more than such a press: sets higher value upon the lives of its citizens than upon a thousand such presses. I might depict to you the African, his passions excited by the doctrines intended to have been propagated by that press. As well might you find yourself in the fangs of a wild beast. I might portray to you the scenes which would exist in our neighbor states from the influence of that press: the father aroused to see the last gasp of his dying child, as it lays in its cradle, weltering in its blood; and the husband awakened from his last sleep by the shrieks of his wife as she is brained to the earth. I might paint to you a picture which would cause a demon to start back with affright, and still fall short of the awful reality which would be caused by the promulgation of the doctrines which this press was intended to disseminate.

[The jury found the defendants not guilty.]

Questions

---

1. *What might account for the anti-abolitionist sentiment of rural and small-town people in northern Ohio, who owned no slaves and who did not live among African Americans? The remarks of Usher Linder provide an explicit explanation for opposition in Alton, Illinois. What is it? Did it have any validity?*

2. *In what ways may abolitionism have especially appealed to women? Why did some oppose their participation?*

3. *Describe the tactics adopted by the abolitionists. Why did they select these? Might different tactics have been more effective?*

4. *Why did abolitionists focus so much of their attention on ministers and church members? Would present-day advocates of fundamental change adopt the same mode of operation? Why or why not?*

FURTHER READING

James Brewer Stewart, *Holy Warriors: The Abolitionists and American Slavery* (New York, 1976), is a concise account of abolitionism. Benjamin Quarles, *Black Abolitionists* (New York, 1969), traces the antislavery activities of African Americans. Merton L. Dillon, *Slavery Attacked: Southern Slaves and Their Allies, 1619-1865* (Baton Rouge, 1990), shows how African Americans, both slave and free, influenced abolitionism. Biographies especially pertinent to these readings are James Brewer Stewart, *William Lloyd Garrison and the Challenge of Emancipation* (Arlington Heights, 1992); Merton L. Dillon, *Elijah P. Lovejoy, Abolitionist Editor* (Urbana, 1961); and Robert H. Abzug, *Passionate Liberator: Theodore Dwight Weld and the Dilemma of Reform* (New York, 1980).

Jefferson Davis' First Inaugural Address

Alabama Capitol, Montgomery, February 18, 1861

Gentlemen of the Congress of the Confederate States of America, Friends and Fellow-Citizens:

Called to the difficult and responsible station of Chief Executive of the Provisional Government which you have instituted, I approach the discharge of the duties assigned to me with an humble distrust of my abilities, but with a sustaining confidence in the wisdom of those who are to guide and to aid me in the administration of public affairs, and an abiding faith in the virtue and patriotism of the people.

Looking forward to the speedy establishment of a permanent government to take the place of this, and which by its greater moral and physical power will be better able to combat with the many difficulties which arise from the conflicting interests of separate nations, I enter upon the duties of the office to which I have been chosen with the hope that the beginning of our career as a Confederacy may not be obstructed by hostile opposition to our enjoyment of the separate existence and independence which we have asserted, and, with the blessing of Providence, intend to maintain. Our present condition, achieved in a manner unprecedented in the history of nations, illustrates the American idea that governments rest upon the consent of the governed, and that it is the right of the people to alter or abolish governments whenever they become destructive of the ends for which they were established.

The declared purpose of the compact of Union from which we have withdrawn was "to establish justice, insure domestic tranquillity, provide for the common defense, promote the general welfare, and secure the blessing of liberty to ourselves and our posterity;" and when, in the judgment of the sovereign States now composing this Confederacy, it had been perverted from the purposes for which it was ordained, and had ceased to answer the ends for which it was established, a peaceful appeal to the ballot-box declared that so far as they were concerned, the government created by that compact should cease to exist. In this they merely asserted a right which the Declaration of Independence of 1776 had defined to be inalienable; of the time and occasion for its exercise, they, as sovereigns, were the final judges, each for itself. The impartial and enlightened verdict of mankind will vindicate the rectitude of our conduct, and He who knows the hearts of men will judge of the sincerity with which we labored to preserve the Government of our fathers in its spirit. The right solemnly proclaimed at the birth of the States, and which has been affirmed and reaffirmed in the bills of rights of States subsequently admitted into the Union of 1789, undeniably recognize in the people the power to resume the authority delegated for the purposes of government. Thus the sovereign States here represented proceeded to form this Confederacy, and it is by abuse of language that their act has been denominated a revolution. They formed a new alliance, but within each State its government has remained, the rights of person and property have not been disturbed. The agent through whom they communicated with foreign nations is changed, but this does not necessarily interrupt their international relations.

Sustained by the consciousness that the transition from the former Union to the present Confederacy has not proceeded from a disregard on our part of just obligations, or any failure to perform every constitutional duty, moved by no interest or passion to invade the rights of others, anxious to cultivate peace and commerce with all nations, if we may not hope to avoid war, we may at least expect that posterity will acquit us of having needlessly engaged in it. Doubly justified by the absence of wrong on our part, and by wanton aggression on the part of others, there can be no cause to doubt that the courage and patriotism of the people of the Confederate States will be found equal to any measures of defense which honor and security may require.

An agricultural people, whose chief interest is the export of a commodity required in every manufacturing country, our true policy is peace, and the freest trade which our necessities will permit. It is alike our interest, and that of all those to whom we would sell and from whom we would buy, that there should be the fewest practicable restrictions upon the interchange of commodities. There can be but little rivalry between ours and any manufacturing or navigating community, such as the Northeastern States of the American Union. It must follow, therefore, that a mutual interest would invite good will and kind offices. If, however, passion or the lust of dominion should cloud the judgment or inflame the ambition of those States, we must prepare to meet the emergency and to maintain, by the final arbitrament of the sword, the position which we have assumed among the nations of the earth. We have entered upon the career of independence, and it must be inflexibly pursued. Through many years of controversy with our late associates, the Northern States, we have vainly endeavored to secure tranquillity, and to obtain respect for the rights to which we were entitled. As a necessity, not a choice, we have resorted to the remedy of separation; and henceforth our energies must be directed to the conduct of our own affairs, and the perpetuity of the Confederacy which we have formed. If a just perception of mutual interest shall permit us peaceably to pursue our separate political career, my most earnest desire will have been fulfilled. But, if this be denied to us, and the integrity of our territory and jurisdiction be assailed, it will but remain for us, with firm resolve, to appeal to arms and invoke the blessings of Providence on a just cause.

As a consequence of our new condition and with a view to meet anticipated wants, it will be necessary to provide for the speedy and efficient organization of branches of the executive department, having special charge of foreign intercourse, finance, military affairs, and the postal service.

For purposes of defense, the Confederate States may, under ordinary circumstances, rely mainly upon their militia, but it is deemed advisable, in the present condition of affairs, that there should be a well-instructed and disciplined army, more numerous than would usually be required on a peace establishment. I also suggest that for the protection of our harbors and commerce on the high seas a navy adapted to those objects will be required. These necessities have doubtless engaged the attention of Congress.

With a Constitution differing only from that of our fathers in so far as it is explanatory of their well-known intent, freed from the sectional conflicts which have interfered with the pursuit of the general welfare, it is not unreasonable to expect that States from which we have recently parted may seek to unite their fortunes with ours under the government which we have instituted. For this your Constitution makes adequate provision; but beyond this, if I mistake not the judgment and will of the people, a reunion with the States from which we have separated is neither practicable nor desirable. To increase the power, develop the resources, and promote the happiness of a confederacy, it is requisite that there should be so much of homogeneity that the welfare of every portion shall be the aim of the whole. Where this does not exist, antagonisms are engendered which must and should result in separation.

Actuated solely by the desire to preserve our own rights and promote our own welfare, the separation of the Confederate States has been marked by no aggression upon others and followed by no domestic convulsion. Our industrial pursuits have received no check. The cultivation of our fields has progressed as heretofore, and even should we be involved in war there would be no considerable diminution in the production of the staples which have constituted our exports and in which the commercial world has an interest scarcely less than our own. This common interest of the producer and consumer can only be interrupted by an exterior force which should obstruct its transmission to foreign markets--a course of conduct which would be as unjust toward us as it would be detrimental to manufacturing and commercial interests abroad. Should reason guide the action of the Government from which we have separated, a policy so detrimental to the civilized world, the Northern States included, could not be dictated by even the strongest desire to inflict injury upon us; but otherwise a terrible responsibility will rest upon it, and the suffering of millions will bear testimony to the folly and wickedness of our aggressors. In the meantime there will remain to us, besides the ordinary means before suggested, the well-known resources for retaliation upon the commerce of an enemy.

Experience in public stations, of subordinate grade to this which your kindness has conferred, has taught me that care and toil and disappointment are the price of official elevation. You will see many errors to forgive, many deficiencies to tolerate, but you shall not find in me either a want of zeal or fidelity to the cause that is to me highest in hope and of most enduring affection. Your generosity has bestowed upon me an undeserved distinction, one which I neither sought nor desired. Upon the continuance of that sentiment and upon your wisdom and patriotism I rely to direct and support me in the performance of the duty required at my hands.

We have changed the constituent parts, but not the system of our Government. The Constitution formed by our fathers is that of these Confederate States, in their exposition of it, and in the judicial construction it has received, we have a light which reveals its true meaning.

Thus instructed as to the just interpretation of the instrument, and ever remembering that all offices are but trusts held for the people, and that delegated powers are to be strictly construed, I will hope, by due diligence in the performance of my duties, though I may disappoint your expectations, yet to retain, when retiring, something of the good will and confidence which welcome my entrance into office.

It is joyous, in the midst of perilous times, to look around upon a people united in heart, where one purpose of high resolve animates and actuates the whole--where the sacrifices to be made are not weighed in the balance against honor and right and liberty and equality. Obstacles may retard, they cannot long prevent the progress of a movement sanctified by its justice, and sustained by a virtuous people. Reverently let us invoke the God of our fathers to guide and protect us in our efforts to perpetuate the principles which, by his blessing, they were able to vindicate, establish and transmit to their posterity, and with a continuance of His favor, ever gratefully acknowledged, we may hopefully look forward to success, to peace, and to prosperity.

From *The Papers of Jefferson Davis*, Volume 7, pp. 45-51. Transcribed from the *Congressional Journal*, Volume 1, pp. 64-66.

Proclamation of Amnesty and Reconstruction

BY THE PRESIDENT OF THE UNITED STATES OF AMERICA:

A PROCLAMATION.

Whereas, in and by the Constitution of the United States, it is provided that the President "shall have power to grant reprieves and pardons for offences against the United States, except in cases of impeachment;" and

Whereas a rebellion now exists whereby the loyal State governments of several States have for a long time been subverted, and many persons have committed and are now guilty of treason against the United States; and

Whereas, with reference to said rebellion and treason, laws have been enacted by Congress declaring forfeitures and confiscation of property and liberation of slaves, all upon terms and conditions therein stated, and also declaring that the President was thereby authorized at any time thereafter, by proclamation, to extend to persons who may have participated in the existing rebellion, in any State or part thereof, pardon and amnesty, with such exceptions and at such times and on such conditions as he may deem expedient for the public welfare; and

Whereas the congressional declaration for limited and conditional pardon accords with well-established judicial exposition of the pardoning power; and

Whereas, with reference to said rebellion, the President of the United States has issued several proclamations, with provisions in regard to the liberation of slaves; and

Whereas it is now desired by some persons heretofore engaged in said rebellion to resume their allegiance to the United States, and to reinaugurate loyal State governments within and for their respective States; therefore,

I, Abraham Lincoln, President of the United States, do proclaim, declare, and make known to all persons who have, directly or by implication, participated in the existing rebellion, except as hereinafter excepted, that a full pardon is hereby granted to them and each of them, with restoration of all rights of property, except as to slaves, and in property cases where rights of third parties shall have intervened, and upon the condition that every such person shall take and subscribe an oath, and thenceforward keep and maintain said oath inviolate; and which oath shall be registered for permanent preservation, and shall be of the tenor and effect following, to wit:

"I, -------, do solemnly swear, in presence of Almighty God, that I will henceforth faithfully support, protect and defend the Constitution of the United States, and the union of the States thereunder; and that I will, in like manner, abide by and faithfully support all acts of Congress passed during the existing rebellion with reference to slaves, so long and so far as not repealed, modified or held void by Congress, or by decision of the Supreme

Court; and that I will, in like manner, abide by and faithfully support all proclamations of the President made during the existing rebellion having reference to slaves, so long and so far as not modified or declared void by decision of the Supreme Court. So help me God."

The persons excepted from the benefits of the foregoing provisions are all who are, or shall have been, civil or diplomatic officers or agents of the so-called confederate government; all who have left judicial stations under the United States to aid the rebellion; all who are, or shall have been, military or naval officers of said so-called confederate government above the rank of colonel in the army, or of lieutenant in the navy; all who left seats in the United States Congress to aid the rebellion; all who resigned commissions in the army or navy of the United States, and afterwards aided the rebellion; and all who have engaged in any way in treating colored persons or white persons, in charge of such, otherwise than lawfully as prisoners of war, and which persons may have been found in the United States service, as soldiers, seamen, or in any other capacity.

And I do further proclaim, declare, and make known, that whenever, in any of the States of Arkansas, Texas, Louisiana, Mississippi, Tennessee, Alabama, Georgia, Florida, South Carolina, and North Carolina, a number of persons, not less than one-tenth in number of the votes cast in such State at the Presidential election of the year of our Lord one thousand eight hundred and sixty, each having taken the oath aforesaid and not having since violated it, and being a qualified voter by the election law of the State existing immediately before the so-called act of secession, and excluding all others, shall re-establish a State government which shall be republican, and in no wise contravening said oath, such shall be recognized as the true government of the State, and the State shall receive thereunder the benefits of the constitutional provision which declares that "The United States shall guaranty to every State in this union a republican form of government, and shall protect each of them against invasion; and, on application of the legislature, or the executive, (when the legislature cannot be convened,) against domestic violence."

And I do further proclaim, declare, and make known that any provision which may be adopted by such State government in relation to the freed people of such State, which shall recognize and declare their permanent freedom, provide for their education, and which may yet be consistent, as a temporary arrangement, with their present condition as a laboring, landless, and homeless class, will not be objected to by the national Executive. And it is suggested as not improper, that, in constructing a loyal State government in any State, the name of the State, the boundary, the subdivisions, the constitution, and the general code of laws, as before the rebellion, be maintained, subject only to the modifications made necessary by the conditions hereinbefore stated, and such others, if any, not contravening said conditions, and which may be deemed expedient by those framing the new State government.

To avoid misunderstanding, it may be proper to say that this proclamation, so far as it relates to State governments, has no reference to States wherein loyal State governments have all the while been maintained. And for the same reason, it may be proper to further say that whether members sent to Congress from any State shall be admitted to seats, constitutionally rests exclusively with the respective Houses, and not to any extent with the Executive. And still further, that this proclamation is intended to present the people of the States wherein the national authority has been suspended, and loyal State governments have been subverted, a mode in and by which the national authority and loyal State governments may be re-established within said States, or in any of them; and, while the mode presented is the best the Executive can suggest with his present impressions, it must not be understood that no other possible mode would be acceptable.

Given under my hand at the city, of Washington, the 8th. day of December, **A.D.** one thousand eight hundred and sixty-three, and of the independence of the United States of America the eighty-eighth.

ABRAHAM LINCOLN

By the President:

WILLIAM H. SEWARD, Secretary of State

The Struggle for
Black Rights
during Reconstruction

Michael Les Benedict

INTRODUCTION

The Civil War and Reconstruction era witnessed a desperate fight for equal civil and political rights for African Americans. The legal position of black Americans had deteriorated in the first part of the nineteenth century, with racism actually growing in the North and South as slavery was rejuvenated by the development of cotton agriculture. The growth of the antislavery movement in the 1840s and 1850s, however, led some Northerners to argue that African Americans were entitled to the rights of citizenship. The Supreme Court's Dred Scott decision was a watershed that dashed black Americans' claims to citizenship. Black hopes and expectations brightened with the passage of the Thirteenth Amendment, but they were dimmed once more by the adoption of restrictive southern Black Codes. Seeing the codes as an attempt to salvage key aspects of slavery, Republicans urged the passage of the Civil Rights Act of 1866 to ensure that all Americans, regardless of color, received the basic rights of citizenship. Congress passed the bill, only to be rebuffed by President Andrew Johnson's veto. Overriding the president's veto, Republicans then passed the Fourteenth Amendment in an effort to secure African-American citizenship and rights beyond constitutional doubt.

While blacks embraced their new citizenship, they continued to demand suffrage. Among the most eloquent was Frederick Douglass, one of the greatest orators of his day. The clamor for black enfranchisement aroused apprehension among southern whites that black voters might overturn the traditional social order. The white people of Alabama were among those who voiced their fears of black dominance in a petition to Congress. Nonethe-

less, Congress imposed black suffrage on the South in the Recon-struction Act of 1867, and in 1870 the requisite number of states ratified the Fifteenth Amendment, which extended the change throughout the nation and made it permanent.

But Republicans proved unable to secure equal civil and po-litical rights for African Americans over bitter southern white resistance. A series of Supreme Court decisions narrowed the definition of federal citizenship and limited Congress's power to protect these rights. The court proclaimed that the postwar consti-tutional amendments authorized the federal government to pro-tect rights only against violations by state authorities, leaving African Americans to rely on unsympathetic state and local offi-cials to protect them against all other invasions of their rights.

SECURING EQUAL RIGHTS: THE DOCUMENTARY RECORD

As slaves, most African Americans had been denied nearly all fundamental rights. But for much of the time before the Civil War, the civil status of free African Americans was uncertain. Many Northern states considered them citizens entitled to basic rights; most of the New England states conceded them political rights as well. Other states denied or limited the basic rights of free blacks to travel, to associate with others, and to sue and testify in court, without making clear whether they were citizens or not. It was uncertain how state citizenship related to United States citizenship. Not until the case of Dred Scott v. Sandford did the Supreme Court answer that question. In this case, the Supreme Court distinguished United States citizenship from state citizenship and held that African Americans were not citizens of the United States, whether they were citizens of individual states or not.

White southerners refused to accept the legitimacy of state governments elected by black voters, and they engaged in systematic violence to resubordinate African Americans and to paralyze the Republican state officials in the South. From 1868 to 1871 much of the violence was instigated by the Ku Klux Klan, loosely organized gangs of white terrorists that sprang up in various southern localities. From 1874 to 1876 the Democratic party organized "White Leagues," "Red Shirts," and less formal armed auxiliaries to break up the Republican party. Both white and black Republicans were victimized.

Most of the southern states passed vagrancy laws that prohibited freedpeople from buying or leasing land or homes, except in towns, and then authorized towns to make their own regulations. The following documents will introduce you to the legislation and arguments associated with the effort to secure equal rights after the Civil War, as well as to the practical effect on the lives of ordinary people. Read them in light of the questions that follow this section, particularly considering how far Republicans intended to change the American system of government in order to protect citizens' rights.

The Thirteenth Amendment

Congress passed the Thirteenth Amendment in January 1865 and it was ratified by December of that same year. The amendment abolished slavery throughout the United States.

Section 1 - Neither slavery nor involuntary servitude, except as a punishment for crime whereof the party shall have been duly convicted, shall exist within the United States, or any place subject to their jurisdiction.

Section 2 - Congress shall have power to enforce this article by appropriate legislation.

The Black Codes

Under President Andrew Johnson's plan of reconstruction, southern state governments, elected by white men who had taken an oath pledging loyalty to the United States, passed laws specifying the rights of the freedpeople. Some were more restrictive than others. All gave freedpeople the right to make contracts and to buy, own, and sell property. Some subjected them to the same criminal laws and punishments that covered white people; others subjected them to the harsher criminal laws that had covered free black people before the war. None of the codes extended political rights or the right to serve on juries. Local communities also passed regulations that limited freedpeople's rights. The following are examples of restrictive state and local provisions that convinced Republicans to intervene.

Selections from the Mississippi Black Code conferring civil rights on freedmen and defining vagrancy are from Laws of the State of Mississippi . . . (1866), 82-84, 91 92.

Mississippi Black Code

An Act to confer Civil Rights on Freedmen . . .

Section 1. . . . [A]ll freedmen, free negroes and mulattoes may sue and be sued . . . in all the courts of law and equity of this State, and may acquire personal property . . . by descent or purchase, and may dispose of the same, in the same manner, and to the same extent that white persons may: Provided that the provisions of this section shall not be so construed as to allow any freedman, free negro or mulatto to rent or lease any lands or tenements, except in incorporated towns or cities in which places the corporate authorities shall control the same. . . .

Sec. 5. . . . [E]very freedman, free negro and mulatto, shall . . . have a lawful home or employment, and shall have written evidence thereof. . . .

Sec. 7. . . . [E]very civil officer shall, and every person may arrest and carry back to his or her legal employer any freedman, free negro or mulatto, who shall have quit the service of his or her employer before the expiration of his or her term of service without good cause. . . .

Mississippi Vagrancy Law

Sec. 2. . . . [A]ll freedmen, free negroes and mulattoes in this State, over the age of eighteen years, found on the second Monday in January, 1866, or thereafter, with no lawful employment or business, or found unlawfully assembling themselves together either in the day or night time, and all white persons so assembling with freedmen, free negroes or mulattoes, or usually associating with freedmen, free negroes or mulattoes on terms of equality, or living in adultery or fornication with a freedwoman, free negro, or mulatto, shall be deemed vagrants, and on conviction thereof, shall be fined in the sum of not exceeding, in the case of a freedman, free negro, or mulatto, fifty dollars, and a white man two hundred dollars, and imprisoned at the discretion of the court, the free negro not exceeding ten days, and the white man not exceeding six months. . . .

Sec. 5. . . . [I]n case any freedman, free negro or mulatto, shall fail . . . after the imposition of any fine . . . to pay the same, . . . it shall be, and is hereby made the duty of the sheriff of the proper county to hire out said freedman, free negro or mulatto, to any person who will, for the shortest period of service, pay said fine . . . .

Debate over African American Rights: The Civil Rights Act

Republicans insisted that all Americans, regardless of color, were entitled to the basic rights of citizenship. In response to the black codes and other deprivations of rights in many states, North and South, they proposed a civil rights act.

Congress passed the Civil Rights bill on 15 March 1866, with southern congressmen still not permitted to take their seats. The bill made it a crime for anyone acting "under the color of law" or "custom" to deny the rights specified in Section 1. It also allowed those denied their rights in the states to transfer civil and criminal cases to the federal courts.

President Johnson vetoed the Civil Rights bill, giving his reasons in the message excerpted below from The Congressional Globe, 39th Congress, 1st Session, 1679-81 (27 March 1866).

To the Senate of the United States:

I regret that the bill which has passed both Houses of Congress . . . contains provisions which I cannot approve, consistently with my sense of duty to the whole people and my obligations to the Constitution of the United States. . . .

By the first section of the bill, all persons born in the United States, and not subject to any foreign Power, excluding Indians not taxed, are declared to be citizens of the United States. This provision comprends the Chinese of the Pacific States, Indians subject to taxation, the people called Gypsies, as well as the entire race designated as blacks, people of color, negroes, mulattoes, and persons of African blood. . . .

The right of Federal citizenship thus to be conferred on the several excepted races before mentioned, is now, for the first time, proposed to be given by law. If, as is claimed by many, all persons who are native-born already are, by virtue of the Constitution, citizens of the United States, the passage of the pending bill cannot be necessary to make them such. If, on the other hand, such persons are not citizens, as may be assumed from the proposed legislation to make them such, the grave question presents itself, whether when eleven of the thirty-six States are unrepresented in Congress, at this time it is sound policy to make our entire colored population and all other excepted classes citizens of the United States? Four millions of them have just emerged from slavery into freedom. Can it be reasonably supposed that they possess the requisite qualifications to entitle them to all the privileges and immunities of citizens of the United States? . . .

Thus a perfect equality of the white and black races is attempted to be fixed by Federal law in every State of the Union, over the vast field of State jurisdiction covered by these enumerated rights. . . . In the exercise of State policy over matters exclusively affecting the people of each State, it has frequently been thought expedient to discriminate between the two races. By the statutes of some of the States, northern as well as southern, it is enacted, for instance, that no white person shall intermarry with a negro or mulatto. . . .

Hitherto every subject embraced in the enumeration of rights contained in this bill has been considered as exclusively belonging to the States. They all relate to the internal policy and economy of the respective States. . . .

In all our history, in all our experience as a people living under Federal and State law, no such system as that contemplated by the details of this bill has ever before been proposed or adopted. They establish, for the security of the colored race, safeguards which go infinitely beyond any that the General Government has ever provided for the white race. In fact, the distinction of race and color is, by the bill, made to operate in favor of the colored and against the white race. They interfere with the municipal legislation of the States, with the relations existing exclusively between a State and its citizens, or between inhabitants of the same State_an absorption and assumption of power by the General Government which, if acquiesced in, must sap and destroy our federative system of limited powers, and break down the barriers which preserve the rights of the States. It is another step, or rather stride, towards centralization and the concentration of all legislative powers in the national Government. The tendency of the bill must be to resuscitate the spirit of rebellion, and to arrest the progress of those influences which are more closely drawing around the States the bonds of union and peace.

Senator Trumbull's Response

Republican senator from Illinois Lyman Trumbull, managing the bill in the Senate, successfully argued for passage of the Civil Rights Act of 1866 over the president's veto. Taken from The Congressional Globe, *39th Congress, 1st Session (4 April 1866), 1756-58, 1760-61.*

What is the bill? It declares that there shall be no distinction in civil rights between any other race or color and the white race. It declares that there shall be no different punishment inflicted on a colored man in consequence of his color than that which is inflicted on a white man for the same offense. Is that a discrimination in favor of the negro and against the foreigner—a bill the only effect of which is to preserve equality of rights?

. . . Why, sir, the very object . . . is to prevent discrimination, and language, it seems to me, could not more plainly express that object and effect. It may be said that it is for the benefit of the black man because he is now in some instances discriminated against by State laws; but that is the case with all remedial statutes. They are for the relief of the persons who need the relief, not for the relief of those who have the right already; and when those needing the relief obtain it, they stand upon the precise footing of those who do not need the benefit of the law.

. . . The bill neither confers nor abridges the rights of any one, but simply declares that in civil rights there shall be an equality among all classes of citizens. . . . Each State, so that it does not abridge the great fundamental rights belonging, under the Constitution, to all citizens, may grant or withhold such civil rights as it pleases; all that is required is that, in this respect, its laws shall be impartial.

. . . This bill in no manner interferes with the municipal regulations of any State which protects all alike in their rights of person and property. . . . How preposterous, then, to charge that unless some State can have and exercise the right to punish somebody, or to deny somebody a civil right on account of his color, its rights as a State will be destroyed.

The Fourteenth Amendment

To secure African-American citizenship and rights beyond constitutional doubt, Congress passed the Fourteenth Amendment later in 1866.

Section 1. All persons born or naturalized in the United States, and subject to the jurisdiction thereof, are citizens of the United States and of the State wherein they reside. No State shall make or enforce any law which shall abridge the privileges or immunities of citizens of the United States; nor shall any State deprive any person of life, liberty, or property, without due process of law; nor deny to any person within its jurisdiction the equal protection of the laws. . . .

Section 5. The Congress shall have power to enforce, by appropriate legislation, the provisions of this article.

Frederick Douglass Argues in Favor of Black Suffrage

Even before the Civil War ended, African-American leaders and radical Republicans were insisting that the national government secure the freedmen the right to vote. By 1867 most Republicans agreed, and by 1869 they were considering a constitutional amendment to bar racial tests for voting. Frederick Douglass, the great African-American orator and newspaper editor, explained "What the Black Man Wants" to a Boston audience in 1865. Note Douglass's allusion to the fact that women did not have the right to vote at this time. Note also his brief appeal to the anti-Irish prejudices of his Republican audience.

Excerpted from The Frederick Douglass Papers—Series One: Speeches, Debates, and Interviews, Volume 4: 1864-80, *ed. John W. Blassingame and John R. McKivigan (New Haven, 1991), 62-63, 66-68.*

I have had but one idea for the last three years to present to the American people. . . . I am for the "immediate, unconditional and universal" enfranchisement of the black man, in every State of the Union. (Loud applause.) Without this, his liberty is a mockery; without this, you might as well almost retain the old name of slavery for his condition; for, in fact, if he is not the slave of the individual master, he is the slave of society, and holds his liberty as a privilege, not as a right. . . .

It may be asked, "Why do you want it? Some men have got along very well without it. Women have not this right." Shall we justify one wrong by another? That is a sufficient answer. Shall we at this moment justify the deprivation of the negro of the right to

A photograph of Frederick Douglass, ex-slave and prominent African-American political activist. (Courtesy the Library of Congress)

vote because some one else is deprived of that privilege? I hold that women as well as men have the right to vote (applause), and my heart and my voice go with the movement to extend suffrage to woman. But that question rests upon another basis than that on which our right rests. We may be asked, I say, why we want it. I will tell you why we want it. We want it because it is our right, first of all. (Applause.) No class of men can, without insulting their own nature, be content with any deprivation of their rights. We want it, again, as a means for educating our race. Men are so constituted that they derive their conviction of their own possibilities largely from the estimate formed of them by others. If nothing is expected of a people, that people will find it difficult to contradict that expectation. By depriving us of suffrage, you affirm our incapacity to form an intelligent judgment respecting public men and public measures; you declare before the world that we are unfit to exercise the elective franchise, and by this means lead us to undervalue ourselves, to put a low estimate upon ourselves, and to feel that we have no possibilities like other men. . . . [H]ere, where universal suffrage is the rule, where that is the fundamental idea of the government, to rule us out is to make us an exception, to brand us with the stigma of inferiority, and to invite to our heads the missiles of those about us. Therefore I want the franchise for the black man.

. . . It is said that we are ignorant; I admit it. But if we know enough to be hung, we know enough to vote. If the negro knows enough to pay taxes to support the Government, he knows enough to vote—taxation and representation should go together. If he knows enough to shoulder a musket and fight for the flag, fight for the Government, he knows enough to vote. If he knows as much when he is sober as an Irishman knows when drunk, he knows enough to vote, on good American principles. (Laughter and applause.)

. . . What have you asked the black men of the South, the black men of the whole country to do? Why, you have asked them to incur the deadly enmity of their masters, in order to befriend you and to befriend this government. You have asked us to call down, not only upon ourselves, but upon our children's children, the deadly hate of the entire Southern people. You have called upon us to turn our backs upon our masters, to abandon their cause and espouse yours; to turn against the South and in favor of the North; to shoot down the Confederacy and uphold the flag—the American flag. . . . And now, what do you propose to do when you come to make peace? To reward your enemies, and trample in the dust your friends? . . . Do you mean to give your enemies the right to vote, and take it away from your friends? . . . In time of trouble we are citizens. Shall we be citizens in war, and aliens in peace? Would that be just?

. . . What I ask for the negro is not benevolence, not pity, not sympathy, but simply justice.

The Nation Supports Black Suffrage

The weekly journal The Nation *was founded in 1865 to support radical solutions to the problem of restoring the Union. The journal endorsed black suffrage.*

284

Excerpted from "Universal Suffrage And Universal Amnesty," The
Nation *(29 November 1866), 430.*

[T]he Federal Government is bound by every consideration of
justice, honor, and decency either to see that the freedmen enjoy
complete security or to furnish them with the means of protecting
themselves. In other words, we are bound either to give the freedmen a police—to see that every man of whom we claim allegiance
can eat or sleep in peace—or we are bound to see that he enjoys a
fair share in the making of the laws and the selection of the officers
who are to execute them. . . . The former of these courses is not
strictly in accordance with the spirit of our institutions; the latter
is. . . .

[T]he ballot will do for the negro what it does for the poor
ignorant Irishman, or German, or Englishman, but no more. It will
secure him against flagrant class legislation, or cruel or unusual
punishments, and against all oppression which is on its face oppressive. It will do more than this; it will cause politicians and
public men—sheriffs, policemen, and the whole race of function-
aries, actual and expectant—to treat him with civility, even with
deference. It will put a stop to outrages and assaults of various
kinds on negroes, and to all open expressions of contempt for
them or dislike of them. . . .

But more than this the ballot will not do for the negro. It will
not make him a good judge of the value or importance of measures not bearing directly and patently on his personal comfort or
convenience; it will not enable him to tell the difference between
statesmen and demagogues; between honest public men and
knavish public men; between his own real friends and his real
enemies; to distinguish laws contrived by scoundrels for his spo-
liation, under a show of immediate benefit, and schemes contrived by statesmen for his permanent advantage.

Opposition to Black Suffrage

*The Reconstruction Act of 1867 enfranchised both black and white
southerners, with the exception of those whites who as officeholders had sworn to
uphold the Constitution of the United States and then joined the rebellion. It*

put the southern states back under military control temporarily. In exchange for restoration to normal relations in the Union, the Reconstruction Act required each southern state to frame a new constitution that would secure equal civil and political rights regardless of race. In the following document, a number of white Alabamans protested against the process.

Excerpted from the Petition and Memorial File, Records of the House of Representatives, 40th Cong., Record Group 233, National Archives, Washington, D.C.

The White people of Alabama send this their humble petition.

We beseech your Honorable Bodies to withdraw yourselves from the influence of the passions and contests of the hour, and contemplate for a brief period, our miserable condition . . . .

. . . [I]t is well known by all who have knowledge on the subject,—that while the negroes of the South may be more intelligent and of better morals than those of the same race in any other part of the world . . . —yet they are in the main, ignorant generally, wholly unacquainted with the principles of free Governments, improvident, disinclined to work, credulous yet suspicious, dishonest, untruthful, incapable of self-restraint, and easily impelled by want or incited by false and specious counsels, into folly and crime. . . .

Are these the people in whom should be vested the high governmental functions of establishing institutions and enacting and enforcing laws, to prevent crime, protect property, preserve peace and order in society, and promote industry, enterprise and civilization in Alabama, and the power and honor of the United States? Without property, without industry, without any regard for reputation, without controul over their own caprices and strong passions, and without fear of punishment under laws, by courts and through juries which are . . . created by and composed of . . . themselves, or of those whom they elect,—how can it be otherwise than that they will bring, to the great injury of themselves as well as of us and our children,—blight, crime, ruin and barbarism on this fair land? . . .

Will you, nearly three years after the war has ended, . . . suffer a whole State full of your kindred civilized white inhabitants, not only those who had opposed the Government, but women, children, and loyal men who had adhered to it,—to be thus consigned over to the horrid rule of barbarian negroes! . . .

. . . [D]o not, we implore you, abdicate your own rule over us, by transferring us to the blighting, brutalizing and unnatural dominion of an alien and inferior race: A race which has never shown sufficient administrative capacity for the good government of even the tribes, into which it has always been broken up in its native seats; and which in all ages, has itself furnished slaves for all the other races of the earth.

The Fifteenth Amendment

To make black enfranchisement permanent and to extend it to the north, Congress passed the Fifteenth Amendment in 1869 and sent it to the states for ratification. The required number of states ratified it in 1870.

Section 1. The right of citizens of the United States to vote shall not be denied or abridged by the United States or by any

The Fifteenth Amendment gave African Americans the right to vote for the first time; however, the end of Reconstruction, followed by the rise of Jim Crow laws in the South, largely marked the end of black suffrage until the Civil Rights movement almost a century later. (Courtesy of HarpWeek.)

State on account of race, color, or previous condition of servitude.

Section 2. The Congress shall have power to enforce this article by appropriate legislation.

Violent Resistance to Equal Rights in the South

The following documents describe Klan activities from several perspectives. Amzi Rainey, a black South Carolina sharecropper, described how the Klan terrorized his family in testimony excerpted from Proceedings in the Ku Klux Trials, at Columbia, S. C. in the United States Circuit Court, November Term, 1871 *(Columbia, S.C., 1872) 279-80.*

Former Senator James Chesnut of South Carolina testified before a congressional committee investigating the Klan. Simpson Bobo, a white lawyer and jack-of-all-trades, testified before the same committee. Their testimony is excerpted from Testimony Taken by the Joint Select Committee to Inquire into the Condition of Affairs in the Late Insurrectionary States, *vol. 1 and 2, South Carolina (Washington, D.C., 1872) 1:446, 449, 2:796-97.*

[Amzi Rainey's Testimony]

I looked out of the window, and I see some four or five disguised men coming up, and I ran up in the loft, and they came on; come to the door; and when they come to the door, they commenced beating and knocking. "God damn you, open the door! open the door! open the door!" . . . and my wife run to one of the doors and they knocked the top hinges off of the first, and she run across the house to the other, and agin that time they got the two hinges knocked off the other door, and the bolt held the door from falling, and she got it open . . . and when they come in, they struck her four or five licks before they said a word . . . .

They asked her who lived here. She said, "Rainey—Amzi Rainey." "What Amzi Rainey? What Amzi Rainey?" And she said, "Amzi Rainey," and he struck her another lick, and says: "Where is he? God damn him, where is he?" And she says: "I don't know."

The chief organization violently opposed to equal rights for African Americans was the Ku Klux Klan, which began in 1866 and relied on intimidation, terror, and murder to enforce white supremacy. (Courtesy the Library of Congress.)

And one said: "O, I smell him, God damn him; he has gone up in the loft." He says: "We'll kill him, too," and they come up then. . . .

I was in a box, and they said: "Oh, he is in this box, God damn him, I smell him; we'll kill him!" and the other says: "Don't kill him yet;" and they took me down. This man that struck my wife first, ran back to her and says: "God damn her, I will kill her now; I will kill her out;" and the one that went after me, he says: "Don't kill her;" and he commenced beating her then; struck her some four or five more licks, and then run back and struck me; he run back to her then, and drawed his pistol, and says: "Now, I am going to blow your damn brains out;" and the one by me threw the pistol up, and says: "Don't kill her." He aimed to strike me over the head, and struck me over the back and sunk me right down. Then, after he had done that, my little daughter—she was back in the room with the other little children—he says: "I am going to kill him;" and she runs out of the room, and says: "Don't kill my pappy; please don't kill my pappy!" He shoved her back, and says; "You go back in the room, you God damned little bitch; I will blow your brains out!" and fired and shot her . . . .

. . . [A]nd then they took me . . . [o]ff up the road, about a hundred and fifty yards; and they wanted to kill me up there, and one said, "No, don't kill him, let's talk a little to him first." Then, he asked me which way did I vote. I told him I voted the Radical [Republican] ticket. "Well," he says, "now you raise your hand and swear that you will never vote another Radical ticket, and I will not let them kill you." And he made me stand and raise my hand before him and my God, that I never would vote another Radical ticket . . . .

[Ex-Senator Chesnut's Testimony]

There is a deep dissatisfaction . . . in the hearts of the people of this State. . . . Three hundred thousand white people here around us, who had been accustomed to self-government, who had had an orderly government and had participated in that government, whose property had been taxed only by those who paid the taxes, beheld the whole thing suddenly subverted and themselves placed at the mercy of ignorance and of corruption . . . . These people are under an absolute despotism, and you will find that the countries where governments are most despotic are precisely those in which secret associations appear; small associations of parties ardent and seeking redress for real or fancied wrongs which they think cannot be avenged through the government. That is the true secret of this thing.

[Simpson Bobo's Testimony]

We have gone through one of the most remarkable changes in our relations to each other that has been known, perhaps, in the history of the world. The negro that was our slave has become our master suddenly . . . ; the bottom rail has got on top . . .—any one living here and knowing all about it, will be surprised that there has been as little disturbance as there has been. If the Government had give us a good government; if it had let us remain under a military government, none of these troubles would have been in this country. . . . There have been a great many . . . cases of the whipping of negroes in this county and some of the adjoining counties, some for one purpose and some for another. I think some of them have been political, and some of them have been with a view of answering special ends. . . . [T]he lower class of white people have a great prejudice against the negro, because he is a competitor for common labor, and wherever they come into collision, these fellows form themselves into a Klan, and take up negroes that come in their way, and punish them. . . . [F]or instance, a white man rents a tract of land to a negro. Some white man wants to get the land. The owner prefers giving it to the negro. For the purpose of punishing the negro, he will then get up a parcel of neighbors, and in disguise they will go and whip the negro half to death.

The Supreme Court Limits the Ability of the Federal Government to Protect Rights

---

In a series of cases interpreting the Fourteenth Amendment, the justices of the Supreme Court made it difficult for the federal government to protect the rights of American citizens in the south. In the Slaughter-House Cases, the Court distinguished between the rights people held as citizens of the United States and those they held as citizens of their states. The rights Americans thought of as basic to citizenship were those they held as state citizens, not as citizens of the United States. The Fourteenth Amendment, the justices said, only authorized the federal government to protect the latter.

Abridged from the Slaughter-House Cases, 83 U.S. 36, at 72-78 *(1873).*

The Slaughter-House Cases

The first section of the fourteenth article . . . opens with a definition of citizenship—not only citizenship of the United States, but citizenship of the States. . . . It declares that persons may be citizens of the United States without regard to their citizenship of a particular State, and it overturns the Dred Scott decision by making all persons born within the United States and subject to its jurisdiction citizens of the United States. . . .

It is quite clear, then, that there is a citizenship of the United States, and a citizenship of a State, which are distinct from each other, and which depend upon different characteristics or circumstances in the individual.

We think this distinction and its explicit recognition in this amendment of great weight in this argument, because the next paragraph of this same section . . . speaks only of privileges and immunities of citizens of the United States, and does not speak of those of citizens of the several States. . . .

The language is, "No State shall make or enforce any law which shall abridge the privileges or immunities of citizens of the United States." It is a little remarkable, if this clause was intended as a protection to the citizen of a State against the legislative power of his own State, that the word citizen of the State should be left out when it is so carefully used, and used in contradistinction to citizens of the United States, in the very sentence which precedes it. It is too clear for argument that the change in phraseology was adopted understandingly and with a purpose.

Of the privileges and immunities of the citizen of the United States, and of the privileges and immunities of the citizen of the State, . . . it is only the former which are placed by this clause under the protection of the Federal Constitution . . . .

The latter must rest for their security and protection where they have heretofore rested . . . .

[The Court then quoted an earlier lower court decision that defined the privileges and immunities of state citizenship:]

"What are the privileges and immunities of citizens of the several states? We feel no hesitation in confining these expressions to those privileges and immunities which are fundamental; which belong of right to the citizens of all free governments, and which have at all times been enjoyed by citizens of the several states which compose this Union. . . . They may all . . . be comprehended under the following general heads: protection by the government, with the right to acquire and possess property of every kind, and to pursue and obtain happiness and safety, subject, nevertheless, to such restraints as the government may prescribe for the general good of the whole."

. . . Was it the purpose of the 14th Amendment, by the simple declaration that no state should make or enforce any law which shall abridge the privileges and immunities of citizens of the United States, to transfer the security and protection of all the civil rights which we have mentioned, from the states to the Federal government? And where it is declared that Congress shall have the power to enforce that article, was it intended to bring within the power of Congress the entire domain of civil rights heretofore belonging exclusively to the states?

. . . We are convinced that no such results were intended by the Congress which proposed these amendments, nor by the legislatures of the states, which ratified them.

Civil Rights Cases

In the Civil Rights Cases, the Court ruled that the Fourteenth Amendment only authorized the federal government to protect people against deprivations of their rights by state officials or people acting under color of state authority.

Abridged from Civil Rights Cases, *109 U.S. 3, at 10-11 (1883).*

The first section of the Fourteenth Amendment . . . is prohibitory in its character, and prohibitory upon the States. It declares that:

"No State shall make or enforce any law which shall abridge the privileges or immunities of citizens of the United States; nor shall any State deprive any person of life, liberty, or property without due process of law; nor deny to any person within its jurisdiction the equal protection of the laws."

It is State action of a particular character that is prohibited. Individual invasion of individual rights is not the subject-matter of the amendment. . . . [T]he last section of the amendment invests Congress with power to enforce it by appropriate legislation. To enforce what? To enforce the prohibition. . . . This is the legislative power conferred upon Congress, and this is the whole of it. It does not invest Congress with power to legislate upon subjects which are within the domain of State legislation; but to provide modes of relief against State legislation, or State action, of the kind referred to. It does not authorize Congress to create a code of municipal law for the regulation of private rights. . . .

The Effect of "Redemption" on Black Southerners

The Supreme Court's narrow interpretation of the Fourteenth Amendment made it difficult to prosecute southern violence. Between 1873 and 1875, the resolve of the federal government to protect the rights of citizens in the south waned. By 1877, southern white Democrats regained control of southern state governments. Southern whites referred to their success as "redemption," and they used fraud in many states to prevent Republicans from regaining power. The following plea from

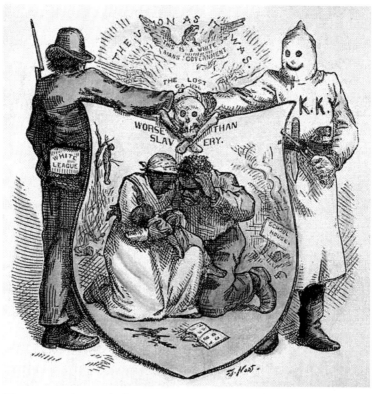

The return of control of state government to southern white Democrats resulted in conditions that, according to this Thomas Nast cartoon, were worse than slavery for American blacks. (Courtesy of the Library of Congress.)

Wilson H. Williams for help from the national government suggests how the change affected African Americans in the South. It had been illegal to teach slaves to read or write, so Williams's literacy, with all its spelling errors, was quite an accomplishment.

From Wilson H. Williams to Senator John Sherman, care of Rev. John D. Haynes, 15 January 1879, John Sherman papers, Manuscript Division, Library of Congress, Washington, D.C.

We poor coul[ored] men have got no more show then a good Dog. The White people is tareing all over the land picking up the poor coul men acreing [forcing] them back to thar old Homes giving them no triel but butchering them up for things that [got] don in 20 and 30 years a go. God hoe [who] made the wourld knows that it is not rite and we know you all ought to do sum thing for ous for we are healpletts cant do eney thing nor say eney thing [P]lease you all stop that thing for it has been going on long anuffe. . . .

Questions

1. *Describe the issues of social justice that affected the lives of free African Americans at the time the Civil War broke out.*
2. *Why did President Andrew Johnson oppose the Civil Rights Act? Did it discriminate in favor of African Americans, as he charged?*
3. *What reasons did proponents of African-American suffrage give for supporting it? Aside from the racism of the petition, did the petitioners have a point about enfranchising former slaves so soon after emancipation? How would Frederick Douglass have answered? Given the hostility of white southerners toward equal civil rights for African Americans, what would you have done to secure their rights?*
4. *To what degree were the Supreme Court decisions interpreting the Fourteenth Amendment consistent with the spirit in which they were passed?*
5. *Over all, to what degree did the civil status of African Americans change during the era of Reconstruction? How much did their status improve? What were the limitations of the change?*

FURTHER READING

The standard, prize-winning work on Reconstruction in general, providing a wealth of information about the effort to restore the Union on the basis of equality of rights, is Eric Foner's *Reconstruction: America's Unfinished Revolution, 1863-1877* (New York, 1988). A briefer and more focused work is Foner's "Rights and the Constitution in Black Life during the Civil War and Reconstruction," *Journal of American History* 74 (December 1987): 863-83. Herman Belz addresses constitutional questions more directly than Foner in *Emancipation and Equal Rights: Politics and Constitutionalism in the Civil War Era* (New York, 1978). Peyton McCrary offers another argument for the radicalism of Republican Reconstruction policy in "Republican Ideas about Politics and Social Change," *Civil War History* 30 (December 1984): 330-50. Robert J. Kaczorowski criticizes the Supreme Court for retreating from the Republican commitment to rights in *The Politics of Judicial Interpretation: The Federal Courts, Department of Justice, and Civil Rights, 1866-1876* (New York, 1985).